Hon Samuel P. Cummings

With the respects of

the author.

E. Anthony

Gen. Geo. L. Brown—
Atty Genl Neb—
Compliments of
C. J. Dilworth.

A

TREATISE

ON THE LAW OF

CONSOLIDATION OF RAILROAD COMPANIES;

BEING AN ARGUMENT IN THE CASE OF

JULIUS WADSWORTH, OF NEW YORK, ET AL.

versus

CHICAGO & NORTHWESTERN RAILWAY COMPANY,
WILLIAM B. OGDEN, ET AL.

— IN THE —

UNITED STATES CIRCUIT COURT

FOR THE NORTHERN DISTRICT OF ILLINOIS,

HON. DAVID DAVIS, OF THE U. S. SUPREME COURT, PRESIDING.

BY ELLIOTT ANTHONY, ESQ.

OF THE CHICAGO BAR.

CHICAGO:
BEACH & BARNARD, PRINTERS, 14 SOUTH CLARK STREET.
1865.

PREFACE.

Aside from their bearing on the present controversy, the questions, which are here discussed, are of the greatest practical importance. They are as applicable to one species of corporation as another. " A vast amount of the business of this country has come to be carried on under corporate forms of organization. Besides innumerable special charters, we have general laws which impart corporate attributes to associations formed according to articles of agreement, for a great variety of purposes ; and these corporations are no longer confined to the exercise of public or political franchises." They are brought into relation with almost every member of the community, and may, in the exercise of their franchises, prove of the greatest benefit, or the greatest injury, according as they are well or illy managed.

To reap their full benefit, requires a combination of qualities and the concurrence of circumstances as favorable as any commercial adventure. To insure their success, honesty is indispensable. The directors and managers are trustees for the stockholders, and should be held to the sternest and most rigid accountability. The greater the amount of capital invested, the greater care and vigilance should be exercised and required. If scheming and designing men obtain control of them, they may be rendered the greatest scourges, and instruments of oppression, of anything in modern times. The position of a director is one of great responsibility. It places in the power of *him* in whom you confide, your property, and, it may be, your reputation. " His virtues and his skill may raise you to the pinnacle of prosperity. His folly or his crimes may strip you of every flourishing branch and leaf, and leave you a naked, withered and dishonored trunk."

The capital stock of corporations is a trust fund—the directors and managers are, we repeat, nothing but trustees for the stockholders, and the whole theory of the management of corporations is nothing but *a succession* of trusts.

" The stockholders confide in the integrity, the faithfulness and watchfulness of directors, the *protection* of all of their interests. This duty they assume when they are elected; this the *law imposes* on them, and this, those for whom they act, have a right to expect. The principals are not present to watch over their interests—they cannot speak in their own behalf—they *must trust to the fidelity* of their agents. If they discharge these important duties faithfully, the law interposes its shield for their protection and defence; if they depart from the line of their duty, and waste or take themselves, *instead of protecting* the property and interests confided to them, the law, on the application of those thus wronged or despoiled, promptly steps in to apply the corrective, and restores to the injured what has been lost by the unfaithfulness of the agent."

The amount of capital which is invested in railroads in this country, has been estimated to be over *One Thousand Millions of Dollars.*

The pecuniary interests at stake cannot, however, outweigh the principles involved; and if it be the law of this country, that the *majority in interest* in corporations can *transfer the minority from one corporation to another, and can, in defiance of their wishes and against their will, make them liable for all of the debts and liabilities of such corporations, however great and however incurred, then every vestige of security in corporate property is at an end, and every inducement for the aggregation of capital ceases.*

The term " consolidation " is of recent origin, and implies aggrandizement much more than it does legitimate enterprise, or the public good. To merge the capital stock of two distinct corporations into one, and to blend together all the rights, privileges and franchises of each, can only be done except by the consent of the legislature and *all* of the stockholders who represent that capital stock, and who are invested with the rights, privileges and franchises of the respective corporations. A charter of a corporation is a contract of a two-fold character; it is, 1st, a contract between the State and the corporation; and, 2lly, between the corporation and the stockholders. The State cannot pass a law impairing the obligations of that contract, neither can a majority of the stockholders, however powerful or however numerous, do anything which materially affects *the contract existing between the corporation and the stockholders.* One stockholder can arrest their action as well as a thousand.

Judge DAVIS, in the case ot *Clearwater* v. *Meredith*, 1 Wallace 40, in illustrating this subject, says: " When any person takes stock in a railroad corporation, he has *entered into a contract with the company*, that his interests shall be subject to the direction and control of the proper authorities of the corporation, to accomplish *the* object for which the company was organized. *He does not agree* that the improvements to which he subscribed *should be changed* in its purposes and character, at the will and pleasure ot a majority of the stockholders, so that *new responsibilities*, and, it may be, *new hazards are added to the orginal undertaking.* He may be very willing to embark in one enterprise, and unwilling to engage in another—*to assist in building a short line railway, and averse to risking his money in one having a longer line of transit.*"

There cannot be a more wholesome exercise of power on the part of courts than to keep these corporations within the limits which the legislature has seen fit to prescribe for them. One of the greatest dangers to which this country is exposed, is the growing *Spirit of monopolies.* It stops at nothing in order to accomplish its purposes. It uses money to corrupt individuals, to corrupt legislatures, and to open a pathway to the polls. To contend against any railroad company requires immense resources and great fortitude and courage. Said the late Lord Chancellor of England, in deciding the case of *Coleman* v. *the Eastern Counties R. Co.*: " There is no project, however wild, which the shareholders, or the persons liable in respect of these companies, have not acquiesced in, from one cause or another, either from cupidity and

the hope of gaining extraordinary profits beyond their first anticipations, or *from terror of entering into* a contest with persons so
powerful."

The contest between an individual and a great corporation is,
indeed, most unequal. But, powerful as they are, the *law* is more
powerful. Our only hope is in the judiciary. Without a firm administration of justice, all will be lost, and this government will
crumble to pieces by the corroding and corrupting influences of
money, without the aid of a traitor or the assault of a single en-
emy. The object of this discussion is to establish, by the settled
principles of law, the *illegality* of one corporation seizing upon
the revenues, rights, privileges and franchises of another, by a
coup d' etat, and *appropriating* them to their own use without the
consent of all who are interested in them. If it can be done,
then the powers of eminent domain are no longer restricted to the
State, but society becomes subject to the will of the strongest.

Said Judge SELDEN, of New York, in the case of *Bissell* v.
Mich. South. R. R. Co., 22 N. Y. 258, in one of the ablest opinions ever rendered, in this or any other country, upon the *public
policy* of confining corporations to their charter powers:

"This question has not, until lately, attracted much attention.
But the recent rapid multiplication of these artificial bodies, and
the extensive powers and privileges conferred upon them, have
made it a question of importance. It has, within a few years
past, been repeatedly presented to the courts, both in this country
and in England, and with one unvarying result. I can not, my-
self, regard it, therefore, in any just sense, open to discussion. If
questions, which have been over and over again considered, and
over and over again decided, are to be treated as still unsettled,
then are we without any stable foundation of law or justice. The
evils attendant upon setting legal principles afloat upon a sea of
uncertainty and doubt, and causing them to depend upon the fluc-
tuations of individual opinion are too obvious to need enumera-
tion. Confidence in courts is only to be retained by their *exhibiting stability* in their *own* decisions, and a *becoming respect for*

those of other tribunals. It has been so often and so uniformly decided, that corporations are not bound by contracts which are clearly *ultra vires*, that, to hold the contrary now, would take the legal profession by surprise, and introduce more or less confusion into this important branch of the law."

The action of corporate authorities has sometimes been likened to that of *sovereignties*, where the governing classes are *everything*, and the *individual nothing ;* but, in this country, an *individual* has just as much right to establish rules for the government of his conduct, under the law, as corporations have for theirs; consequently, courts do not base their decisions on the equality or inequality of interests, but *on the law* of the case. If corporations or their managers see fit to *depart from the law*, and undertake to deal with the interests of stockholders as if they had no rights whatever, they must not complain if they should be held to the strictest accountability.

Immutable as the principles are, which govern and control this subject, there has not, heretofore, been any attempt to collect the cases, or systematize the principles by which it is governed, or to determine the powers of directors over the stockholders. The utility of their application was never more fitly illustrated than by the case here presented ; and with a view to aid in re-establishing those principles, this brief is submitted.

Chicago, May 15, 1865.

TABLE OF CONTENTS.

VI.

Rights of Shareholders.

The shares of stock owned by the complainants in this case, represent—1st, Property, 2d, Rights and Privileges—of which he cannot be divested, except by his own consent, and in the exercise of which rights the law will protect him. Page 84–96.

VII.

When the majority of stockholders in a corporation can bind the minority. Page 97–103.

VIII.

Rights of the minority stockholders in corporations. Page 103–122.

IX.

The jurisdiction of a court of equity, in cases arising between the members of a corporation and the corporation itself. Any individual shareholder can enjoin a corporation of which he is a member, from misapplying its funds, or from exceeding its powers. Page 123–143.

X.

The rights, privileges and franchises of a corporation are created by the sovereign power of a state, and are in fact, a part and parcel of it; and, on grounds of public policy, therefore, they cannot be bought and sold, or bartered away like goods and chattels. Page 143–149.

XI.

Acts which are *ultra vires.* Page 149–158.

XII.

Directors of corporations are trustees for ALL the stockholders, and are subject to all the duties, obligations and liabilities of trustees. Page 158–165.

XIII.

The " consolidation " in question was a sale—the vendor being the G. & C. U. R. R. Co., and the vendee being the C. & N. W.

R. Co.; and as the directors of the G. & C. U. R. R. Co., who made the sale, were also the directors of the C. & N. W. R. Co., or a large number of them were, it became a sale by THEMSELVES TO THEMSELVES; or, if the directors of the G. & C. U. R. R. Co. were merely AGENTS of the stockholders, it presents a case of where the agents acted AS AGENTS for BOTH PARTIES, and is, therefore, if not absolutely void, voidable by a dissenting stockholder, WHO IS THE PRINCIPAL. Page 166–184.

XIV.

The doctrine of trusts, further illustrated in cases of directors of railroad corporations dealing with the property of the company, and how their acts affect stockholders, and under what circumstances they are binding upon them, and when not. Page 184–190.

XV.

By the Charter of the G & C. U. R. R. Co., none but Stockholders can be elected Directors.

We allege that several of the persons who were directors, were not *bona fide* stockholders, but had stock transferred to them for the mere purpose of making them directors. This, we say, was a fraud, both upon the charter and upon the stockholders. Page 191.

XVI.

Proxies.

We show in this case, and the records of the stockholders' meetings of the G. & C. U. R. R. Co. show, that out of all the vast number of stockholders of that company, there were not, at the time of the sale and consolidation, more than fifteen or sixteen persons present, and that, of over 60,284 shares, only 900 shares were owned by those persons who were present; and that the rest of the votes which they pretended to cast, for the sale and consolidation, were cast by names of PROXIES, which were obtained, from most of the shareholders, under the pretense that they were to be used merely for the election of directors. Page 191–198.

XVII.

It is a General Rule of Law, that Delegated Authority cannot be delegated.

Hence, the directors of one railroad company can never transfer THEIR AUTHORITY to the directors of another railroad company, and authorize them to manage it for them; if they do, they will be responsible to the stockholders for all the damage that can possibly arise in consequence thereof.   Page 198–201.

XVIII.

Galena and Chicago Union Railroad Charter—Its History and Powers.

No authority for either a sale, or consolidation, or confiscation of the corporation, and its property and franchises, whatever. Page 201–217.

XIX.

Unauthorized contracts are illegal contracts, and upon the grounds of PUBLIC POLICY, they should not be sanctioned.   Page 217–221.

XX.

History of Chicago and North Western Railway Company.   Page 221–222.

XXI.

History of the Peninsula R. R. Co. of Michigan.   Page 223–230.

XXII.

Expediency has nothing to do with the legal questions at issue—but, was the trade a good trade—for the G. & C. U. R. R. Co.

1. The Expediency.
2. The Trade.   Page 230–238.

XXIII.

The change of the name of the G. & C. U. R. R. Co. was unauthorized and void.   Page 238.

TABLE OF CASES.

STATEMENT.

First. This is a bill in chancery, brought by the complainant as a share and bondholder, in behalf of himself and all others, who may be similarly situated with himself, who choose to come in and contribute to the expense of the suit, against the Chicago and North Western Railway Company and its directors, and the Galena and Chicago Union Railroad Company and its directors, charging them with conspiring together to get control of the Galena and Chicago Union Railroad Company, and then taking and appropriating it to the use of the Chicago and North Western Railway Company.

Second. The bill shows that the Galena and Chicago Union Railroad Company was organized in 1836—to *exist for sixty years*—with " the right to construct, and during its continuance, to main-" tain and continue a railroad, with a single or double track," from the town of Galena, in Joe Daviess county, to Chicago. That by a subsequent act, it had a right to terminate its road at any point this side of Galena, and intersect and connect with the Illinois Central Railroad; that deeming it impracticable to build its road through to the Mississippi river, it did terminate its road at Freeport, and connect with the Illinois Central; that it had also built some branch roads, etc., to Fulton City and Beloit, which are particularly mentioned in the bill.

Third. That said road was one of the very first roads built in the State of Illinois, and was one of the most prosperous and remunerative in the United States, and had always been so managed as to earn large amounts of money for its stockholders, and that it owed no floating debt; that it had provided a sinking fund, which would have paid the entire amount of the bonded indebtedness long before it became due; and that its stock and bonds were at a great premium in the market, and were held as a permanent investment by a large number of persons, in Europe and this country.

FOURTH. That the annual meeting for directors took place at Chicago, on the first of June, 1864, and that at that time, owing to the civil war, and the distracted state of the country, and owing to the fact, that no one suspected any revolution in the affairs of the company, and owing to the further fact, that *no notice whatever, of any character or kind,* was given that the Galena and Chicago Union Railroad Company was to be sold out; that over two millions of stock were in no way represented, but that a number of persons in the interest of the Chicago and North Western Railway Company, in accordance with a previous understanding, attended, and by fraud and conspiracy, got control of the stockholders' meeting, and elected a board of directors in the interest of the Chicago and North Western Railway Company.

FIFTH. The bill further shows, that the persons who were thus elected directors of the Galena and Chicago Union Railroad Company, were elected by persons in the *immediate* interest of the Chicago and North Western Railway Company, and by means of proxies, which had been obtained principally from brokers in New York city, and from others who were unacquainted with the designs and intentions of said persons; that the directors were elected at about 12 o'clock at noon on said first day of June, and consisted of the following persons, to wit:

1. John B. Turner; 2. William H. Ferry; 3. James D. Fish; 4. Thomas D. Robertson; 5. William B. Scott; 6. William R. Sands; 7. James W. Elwell, Alexander C. Coventry, Mahlon D. Ogden, Edwin H. Sheldon, Francis B. Peabody, Ira Y. Munn.

That all of these persons were connected with the Chicago and North Western Railway Company—and several, near relatives of William B. Ogden, the President of the Chicago and North Western Railway Company.

Sixth. It further appears, that as soon as these persons had been elected directors, that the stock and proxy holders took a recess from 12 until 6 o'clock on the evening of that day, and that the persons who had been elected directors, met at *three* o'clock, and organized by electing John B. Turner, President, and A. C. Coventry, Vice-President; that as soon as this had been accomplished — that said Coventry presented to the board, articles of agreement and consolidation of the Galena and Chicago Union Railroad Company with the Chicago and North Western Railway Company, but which articles were nothing more or less than a bill of sale of the Galena and Chicago Union Railroad Company, and moved that *they*, the directors, sell out the entire railroad and all of its property, real and personal, and mixed, together with its rights, privileges and franchises, to the Chicago and North Western Railway Company, which was without any delay whatever immediately *adopted*; and John B. Turner directed to present said bill of sale to the stock and proxy holders who should be present at 6 o'clock, and ask their concurrence therein. That, in accordance with this request, the said Turner did meet with said stock and proxy holders at 6 o'clock, and request them to concur in what the directors had done.

Seventh. That the number of stock and proxy holders who were thus assembled, were about sixteen in number; that in order to preserve the record of so important a transaction, tellers were appointed, which tellers were James R. Young, the Secretary of the Chicago and North Western Railway Company; James Redfield, auditor, or chief examiner of accounts, of said Chicago and North Western Railway Company, and Thomas D. Robertson, who was immediately after elected a director of the Chicago and North Western Railway Company.

Eighth. That after these preliminaries had taken place, that a *viva voce* vote was ordered, on authorizing the directors to execute the bill of sale, which was carried, and the proceedings, together with the bill of sale, duly certified to in the following words and figures, to-wit:

" We, the undersigned, do hereby certify that at the annual
" meeting of the stockholders of the Galena & Chicago Union
" Railroad Company, held at the office of said company in the city
" of Chicago on the 1st day of June, A. D. 1864, we were ap-
" pointed tellers, and that articles of agreement and consolidation
" between the Chicago & Northwestern Railway Company and
" the said Galena & Chicago Union Railroad Company, of which
" a copy is hereto annexed, *were submitted by the President of the*
" *said latter company,* with certain by-laws, resolutions, and pro-
" ceedings of the directors of the said company adopting the said
" articles, subject to the approval of the stockholders; and that a
" resolution in respect to a consolidation with the Beloit & Madi-
" son Railroad Company was also submitted to the said meeting,
" and that the following resolutions, to wit. :

" ' *Resolved,* That the stockholders of the Galena & Chicago
" ' Union Railroad Company, acting *by a majority in interest,* do
" ' hereby approve and consent to the terms of the consolidation
" ' of this company with the Chicago & Northwestern Railway
" ' Company expressed in the articles of agreement and consolida-
" ' tion submitted, and do hereby approve and consent to the action
" ' of the board of directors upon the said articles as reported to
" ' this meeting; and do hereby authorize and request the board
" ' of directors and its officers, as empowered, by the resolutions of
" ' the said board, to cause the said articles to be duly executed in
" ' behalf of this company; and to be carried into full execution.

" ' *Resolved,* That the stockholders of this company hereby au-
" ' thorize the directors of this company to enter into a consolida-
" ' tion with the Beloit & Madison Railroad Company, on such
" ' terms as may be agreed upon by the said board of directors,
" ' and the stockholders of this company do hereby consent to and
" ' approve of such consolidation when made,'
" being moved and seconded and a vote thereon by *viva voce* of
" the stockholders present *or represented by proxy,* being ordered,
" we, the undersigned, did canvas the said votes—that votes on

" 33,847 shares were cast, being a majority of the whole number
" of shares outstanding, all of the votes so cast were in favor of
" each and all of the resolutions aforesaid ; and that thereupon the
" said resolutions and each of them were then and there declared
" to be adopted by a majority in interest of the stockholders of the
" said Galena and Chicago Union Railroad Company.

" In witness whereof, we have hereunto set our hands on this
" 1st day of June, 1864.

" (Signed)   THOMAS D. ROBERTSON,
" (Signed)   JAMES R. YOUNG,
" (Signed)   J. B. REDFIELD."

The Bill of Sale—(called).

" *Articles of Agreement and Consolidation between the Chicago and*
" *North Western Railway Company and the Galena and Chi-*
" *cago Union Railroad Company.*

" Articles of agreement and consolidation made this second day
" of June, in the year of our Lord one thousand eight hundred
" and sixty-four (A. D. 1864), by and between the Chicago and
" North Western Railway Company, duly formed and organized
" under franchises to be a corporation, granted by the States of
" Wisconsin and Illinois, party of the first part, and the Galena
" and Chicago Union Railroad Company, duly formed and organ-
" ized under a franchise to be a corporation, granted by the State
" of Illinois, party of the second part : Witnesseth :

" WHEREAS, The said parties of the first and second parts *are*
" *desirous* of consolidating with each other, and are duly author-
" ized by law to effect such consolidation, as hereinafter provided.

" AND, WHEREAS, The said parties of the first and second parts
" *have agreed* upon the terms and conditions hereinafter set forth
" as the terms and conditions of such consolidation, and have fixed
" upon and *regulated* the proceedings for the purpose of such con-
" solidation, by by-laws duly established by them respectively and
" these articles are framed and executed in pursuance of such by-
" laws :

" And, Whereas, The terms of such consolidation have been
" approved of by a majority of the stockholders of the respective
" parties hereto in interest, in person or *by proxy*, at annual meet-
" ings duly held by them respectively.

" And, Whereas, The said party of the first part has become
" vested with all the railroad property, franchises, privileges and
" rights formerly held by the Dixon, Rockford and Kenosha Rail-
" road Company, by consolidation duly made with the said com-
" pany :

" *Now, therefore, this Agreement Witnesseth :* That in considera-
" tion of the mutual agreements, covenants, provisions and grants
" herein contained, the said parties of the first and second parts
" do, by these presents, merge, combine,and consolidate their respect-
" ive capital stocks, *franchises, grants, immunities, privileges, capac-*
" *ities, properties and rights of way, of every name and nature,* into
" *one* company, to be called and known by the corporate name
" and style of the Chicago and North Western Railway Company,
" which said consolidated company shall from henceforth have and
" possess all and singular the rights, franchises, powers, immuni-
" ties, privileges and capacities which are or have been granted to
" or conferred upon, or possessed, or enjoyed by either of the said
" parties hereto, by or under the laws or enactments of the said
" States of Illinois or Wisconsin, or either of the said States.

" *And this agreement further Witnesseth,* That the said parties
" of the first and second parts have agreed upon and by these
" presents, do agree upon and *prescribe* the following as *the terms*

" *and conditions* of such consolidation ; which terms and condi-
" tions the said parties of the first and second parts mutually cov-
" enant, promise and agree to observe, keep and perform, viz. :

" ARTICLE 1.   The persons who shall be *directors of the Chicago*
" *and North Western Railway Company,* at the time of such con-
" solidation, shall be the first *directors of the said consolidated*
" *company,* and shall act as such until the next annual election of
" directors as is herein prescribed, and until their successors are
" duly elected.

" ART. 2.   The number of the directors of the said consolidated
" company shall be not less than thirteen nor more than seventeen.
" The board, as constituted by the preceding article, may, in their
" discretion, fill up their number to seventeen.   The number for
" any year within such limits as are established by law, may be
" fixed at the annual meeting of the stockholders by a by-law
" adopted at such meeting.

" ART. 3.   The first regular annual meeting of the stockholders,
" or the stock and bond holders of the said consolidated company,
" shall be held on the first Thursday in June, 1865.   Special meet-
" ings may be called at any time by a majority of the board of
" directors.

" The board of directors of the said consolidated company shall,
" at their first meeting, appoint all necessary officers, and adopt
" such by-laws as they see fit, and may alter the same as they shall
" from time to time think proper.

" ART. 4.   The corporate seal of the consolidated company *shall*
" *be* that of the *present Chicago and North Western Railway*
" *Company* until otherwise ordered.

" ART. 5.   The common stock of the present Chicago and North
" Western Railway Company shall be and continue common stock
" of the said consolidated company.

" Art. 6.   The said consolidated company shall issue a preferred
" stock, which shall be entitled to preferences to the extent of ten
" (10) per cent. in the dividends which may be declared in any
" year out of the net earnings of such year, in the manner follow-
" ing: First, to a preference of seven (7) per cent. and after divi-
" dends of seven (7) per cent. on the common stock, then, secondly,
" to a further preference of three (3) per cent., after a further div-
" idend of three (3) per cent. on the common stock, both classes
" of stock shall be entitled to equal rates per share in any further
" dividends.

" Art. 7.   The *certificates* for the *preferred* stock of the *present*
" Chicago and North Western Railway Company, issued or au-
" thorized to be issued by said company, shall be *exchanged* for
" *certificates* for the same number of shares in the aforesaid *pre-*
" *ferred stock of the consolidated company.*

" Art. 8.   The stock of the said Galena and Chicago Union
" Railroad Company *shall be convertible* into the *preferred* and
" *common* stocks of the consolidated company, at the rate of one
" share of the preferred stock of the consolidated company, and
" one share of the common stock of the consolidated company, for
" one share of the stock of the Galena and Chicago Union Rail-
" road Company, and the said stock of the Galena and Chicago
" Union Railroad Company shall also on such conversion be enti-
" tled to the payment of three ($3) dollars in money for each
" share of the said stock.

" Art. 9.   The *capital stock* of the said consolidated company
" *is hereby declared to be the aggregates of the stocks—preferred, com-*
" *mon and special*—which the respective companies *were authorized*
" *to create by virtue of the laws or enactments applicable thereto, or*
" *which the consolidated company is authorized to create by vir-*
" *tue of the act of consolidation, or the laws authorizing the same,*
" *all of which powers are hereby expressly preserved to the con-*
" *solidated company.*   But the *actual amount of the preferred*
" stock, when the consolidation shall take effect, *shall be deemed*

" *to be the aggregate of the amount of the preferred stock which*
" the party of the first part, *had issued, or agreed to issue,* and of
" the amount of the stock which the party of the second part had
" issued, *or agreed to issue ;* and the actual amount of the common
" stock shall be deemed to be the aggregate of the common stock,
" which the party of the first part had issued, *or agreed to issue,*
" and of the amount of stock which the party of the second part
" had issued, *or agreed to issue.*

" Art. 10. Each and every existing bond, lease, contract,
" agreement, obligation or liability heretofore entered into, as-
" sumed or agreed to, either *by the present* Chicago and North
" Western Railway Company, *or* by the Galena and Chicago
" Union Railroad Company, shall be sacredly discharged, fulfilled
" and observed by the consolidated company hereby created ; and
" each and every of the acts, assumptions, proceedings, resolutions
" and doings of the respective boards of directors of the said com-
" panies and of their authorized agents, officers and committees
" shall be and the same are *hereby ratified, confirmed and made
" valid,* and shall be observed by the consolidated company hereby
" created.

" Art. 11. The holders of the bonds in the said Galena and
" Chicago Union Railroad Company shall have the right and
" power to vote at all regular and called meetings of the stock
" and bond holders in the said consolidated company to the same
" extent and with the same rights and power as is now held and
" enjoyed by the bond holders of the present Chicago and North
" Western Railway Company, if the power exists in the parties
" entering into this consolidation to confer and grant such right
" and power, and all needful legislation shall be applied for to
" more effectually confirm such rights and privileges in said bond
" holders.

" Art. 12. Consent and approval is hereby given to a consoli-
" dation between the company formed by these presents and the
" Peninsular Railroad Company, of Michigan, on the terms of an

" issue of a special stock under chapter 256 of the laws of Wiscon-
" sin for 1864, in place of the stock of the said company, which
" special stock entitles the holder to the net earnings of the said
" railway, and the other privileges authorized by said act; and the
" directors may agree to make such special stock convertible into
" the stocks of this company in such proportions as they shall
" deem for the interests of this company, and may make by-laws
" and do all acts and things necessary or proper to carry such con-
" solidation into effect.

" And these presents further witness, that the said party of the
" first part, in consideration of the premises and of the sum of one
" dollar, duly paid by the said party of the second part, the receipt
" whereof is hereby acknowledged, doth hereby grant, convey,
" assign, set over and out in said consolidated company, for the
" purposes of such consolidation, all the railroads of the said party
" of the first part, and all the equipments, implements, and mate-
" rials used or acquired therefor, and the rights, privileges, fran-
" chises, powers and all the lands and rights to lands, and property,
" money and effects, real and personal and mixed, and all rights
" of action, and things of every name and nature, now held or
" owned by the said party of the first part, or in or to which the
" said party of the first part hath any right, title, interest or claim,
" either in law or equity ; and also all the lands and rights to lands
" to which the said party is entitled by, through or under any and
" all laws and enactments which have been or may hereafter be
" passed by the Congress of the United States, or the legislatures
" of the States of Wisconsin or Illinois.

" And the said party of the second part in consideration of the
" premises and of the sum of one dollar to it paid by the party of
" the first part, the receipt whereof is hereby acknowledged, doth
" hereby grant, convey, assign, set over to and vest said consoli-
" dated company for the purposes of such consolidation, all the
" railroads of the said party of the second part, and all the equip-
" ments, implements and materials used or acquired therefor, and

"the rights, privileges, immunities, franchises, powers, and all the
" lands and property, money and effects, real and personal and
" mixed, and all rights of action and things of every name or na-
" ture, now held or owned by the said party of the second part, or
" in or to which the said party of the second part hath any right,
" title, interest or claim either in law or equity.

" And the said parties of the first and second parts, for the con-
" solidation aforesaid, do mutually agree and declare that the said
" consolidation shall take effect and the said consolidated company
" shall *go into operation immediately* upon the due execution of
" the present articles.

" And the board of directors of the said consolidated company
" shall have full powers to carry the said consolidation into effect
" by all necessary or proper acts and things for that purpose.

" In testimony whereof, the said parties of the first and second
" parts have caused their respective common and corporate seals
" to be hereunto affixed and the same to be attested by their re·
" spective presidents and secretaries, in the day and year first
" above written.

" [SEAL]   (Signed) The Chicago and North Western Railway
" Company,
" By WILLIAM B. OGDEN, President.

" (Signed) JAMES R. YOUNG, *Secretary.*

" [SEAL]   (Signed) Galena and Chicago Union Railroad Com-
" pany,
" JOHN B. TURNER, President.

" Attest, W. M. LARRABEE, *Secretary.*"

Viva Voce—Poll Book.

" Statement of the vote of the stockholders of the Galena and
" Chicago Union Railroad Company, cast at their annual meeting,
" held January 1st, 1864, in favor of the resolutions of consolida-
" tion with the Chicago and North Western Railway Company,
" and with the Beloit and Madison Railway Company.

Names of Stockholders.	Names of Proxies.	No. Votes.
H. T. Morgan, Ex'r,	John B. Turner,	452
James D. Fish,		500
Fritz Brose,	James D. Fish,	800
James De Lamator,	"	1600
Filer & Wood,	"	650
Ebenezer Thayer,	William B. Ogden,	157
C. B. Farwell,	"	5
Abner H. Davis,	"	3000
Robert Bayard,	"	· 600
John M. Barker,	",	2900
E. Mott Robinson,	"	5000
C. H. Shafford,	"	5
Israel Sheldon,	"	230
C. A. Meigs & Son,	"	2800
Merriam & Bell,	"	300
John M. Hartshorn & Bro.	James W. Elwell,	100
L. Holbrook,	"	350
John Wollott,	"	200
Lathrop & Mott,	"	100
Lockwood & Co.	"	100
A. M. Ferris & Bro.	"	250
David Groesbeck & Co.	"	1100
Robinson, Cox & Co.	William R. Sands,	50
Ira Y. Munn,	"	5
James R. Young,	"	10
Elijah Purdy,	"	200
R. F. Romaine,	"	100
Polhamius & Jackson,	"	50
John Tenbroek,	"	25
George Manley & Co.	"	300
J. H. Underwood & Son,	"	100
Penvert & Co.	"	500
N. Y. Life Ins. & Trust Co.	"	291
John Warre _ & Son,	"	1000
L. L. White,	"	2300

Names of Stockholders.	Names of Proxies.	No. Votes.
Jacob Little,	William R. Sands,	25
L. W. Jerome & Co.	"	100
S. S. Sands & Co.	"	3194
W. T. Coleman & Co.	"	3000
Chas. M. Callin,	"	150
Mahlon D. Ogden,		43
S. J. Tilden,		20
William Edgar,	William B. Scott,	50
Geo. M. Bartholomew,	"	100
Cammann & Co.	"	50
Clark, Dodge & Co.	"	50
A. B. Marks,	"	18
M. K. Jessup & Co.	"	100
S. P. Merrill,	"	10
E. H. Sheldon,		10
A. C. Coventry,		20
John Yourt,		37
Wm. H. Gilman,		20
Ralph Emerson, Jr.		6
Elizabeth Emerson,	Ralph Emerson,	2
Charlotte Emerson,	"	2
Est. of R. Emerson,	"	8
Thomas D. Robertson,		20
E. A. Robertson,		5
Wm. T. Robertson,		1
Jane M. Robertson,		1
Mary P. Robertson,		1
Wm. H. Ferry,		150
Wm. H. Ferry, Guardian,		212
M. A. W. Ferry,		30
M. A. H. Ferry,		250
M. G. Leonard,		1
Mark Ramsey,		31
Total, - - -		33,847

(Signed)   " THOS. D. ROBERTSON, ⎫
(Signed)   " JAMES R. YOUNG,   ⎬ Tellers."
(Signed)   " J. B. REDFIELD,   ⎭

NINTH. It further appears that on the next day or day after, the Chicago and North Western Railway Company, held *their* annual meeting at Chicago, and elected the following persons directors of said company, to-wit:

1. John B. Turner; 2. William H. Ferry; 3. James D. Fish; 7. Thomas D. Robertson; 5. William B. Scott; 6. William R. Sands; 7. James H. Elwell, William B. Ogden, Perry H. Smith, J. J. R. Pease, A. L. Pritchard, M. C. Darling, George M. Bartholomew, Samuel J. Tilden, William A. Booth, H. H. Boody, and Sewell Holbrook.

TENTH. That *these persons*, by the *fraud* and connivance of the Galena and Ohicago Union Railroad Company directors, of which they formed a large part, immediately took possession of the Galena and Chicago Union Railroad, and all of its branches, and all of its money, and all of its property, and have .been in full and complete possession of the same, and receiving all of the tolls and revenues up to the present time.

ELEVENTH. It further appears, that no notice whatever of any character or kind was ever given of any intention on the part of the directors or anybody else; that the road was to be sold out, and that the complainant knew nothing whatever about it until long after the sale had been made.

TWELFTH. The bill charges, that at the time of the sale and consolidation, there were many thousand dollars in the treasury of the Galena and Chicago Union Railroad Company, which the Chicago and North Western Railway Company took and appropriated to their own use, besides a great deal of other property; and that since that time, the funds of the road have been, and *are, constantly* being *diverted* and appropriated to other purposes than what is provided in the charter of the Galena and Chicago Union Railroad Company.

THIRTEENTH. That the Peninsular Railroad Company of Michigan, which is referred to in the bill of sale and articles of agreement, is more than four hundred miles distant from the nearest point of the Galena and Chicago Union Railroad Company—is 120 miles north of the northern terminus of the Chicago and North Western Railway Company, and can only be reached by a journey overland or a sea voyage; that the Chicago and North Western Railway Company immediately after taking possession of the Galena and Chicago Union Railroad Company, issued several millions of dollars worth of stock; that they have taken up about eight miles of the track of the Galena and Chicago Union Railroad; that they have taken and carried away a great number of the cars and locomotives, and threaten to take up a number of miles more of track of the Galena and Chicago Union Railroad, and to put a mortgage on the entire property.

FOURTEENTH. The complainant further shows, that he is the owner of a number of bonds of the Galena and Chicago Union Railroad Company, in and by which it is *expressly provided*, that the revenues of the road shall be faithfully applied to the payment of the interest as principal.

FIFTEENTH. That he is the trustee for the first mortgage bond-holders, and is bound by said trust deed, and by law, to see that the property shall suffer no waste or diminution; that the railroad is rapidly going to decay, and is being constantly despoiled, and its property taken and carried away, and its revenues appropriated for the benefit of the Chicago and North Western Railway Company.

SIXTEENTH. That the bill further shows the complainant is a shareholder of the Galena and Chicago Union Railroad Company, and has been for many years; that he has been identified with it from the first organization, and that as such shareholder, he has rights which he claims have been trampled upon and entirely ignored; that by the charter he is entitled to his proportionate share of all the earnings and all of the property of said railroad, and that by the sale and consolidation he has been and is entirely deprived of all his rights as a stockholder in the Galena and Chicago Union Railroad Company. That the Chicago and North Western Railway Company is in debt many millions of dollars, and that if the stockholders of the Galena and Chicago Union Railroad Company are to be saddled with all the debts and liabilities of the Chicago and North Western Railway Company, and all of its consolidated railroads, that his stock will be utterly worthless.

SEVENTEENTH. That the directors were trustees for all the stockholders, and when they accepted the trust, they were bound to fulfill their duties as such trustees in good faith, and that neither they or the stockholders acting separately or together, had any *right, power or authority*, to sell out the entire property, for which they had become trustees. That the sale was in law a fraud, and was made *by themselves to themselves*, and was an act utterly inconsistent with their duties as trustees.

EIGHTEENTH. That any such sale is a violation of the implied contract, which, as a stockholder, he entered into with the corporation when he became a member, and is void both by the constitution of the State of Illinois, and of the United States.

These are the main and substantial points in the case.

NINETEENTH. The details of the transaction are set forth at length in the bill of complaint, and in the evidence, and will be referred to in other parts of this brief. The complainant claims that as he has never acquiesced in any way in the pretended sale and consolidation, that the consolidation changed the entire character of the original enterprise, and that it is, so far as he is concerned, *utterly void*, and was *unauthorized by the charter* or by any law of the State of Illinois, or of the United States, and the whole thing should be set aside, and that the companies should not be allowed to fight him by using his money and others similarly situated to him, but that an injunction should be granted and a receiver appointed.

PRELIMINARY.

The sudden and complete extinction of one of the oldest and most successful railroad corporations in this country without a word of warning, has no precedent.

A bare statement of the case stamps it as a *coup d'etat.* Its very success contributed to its destruction. It never assumed a position that it could not sustain, and its generous rivalry caused it to be unsuspecting, and made it an easy victim. It seemed at first like a trick. It lacks the sanction of law, and if permitted to stand, may become a most dangerous monopoly. The way and manner in which it was accomplished, does not excite our highest admiration. It was done without notice to any body of any character or kind. It was hurried through with most indecent haste, and involves in it principles and practices which we do not believe are adapted to the simple habits of a wide-spread prairie country.

To say nothing of the disregard of private rights, we do not think that it can be successfully defended, on grounds of public policy, or the good of the State. Until the legality of this transaction is settled by an authoritative adjudication, it puts an end to all investments in railroad corporations in this State.

To insure confidence in any enterprise of a financial character, everything like fraud or deceit must be excluded. The man who contributes his money to aid in building a railroad from Chicago to Galena, would not *ordinarily suppose* that he was liable to be transported to enterprises " beyond seas " or across distant States. The case at bar takes a wide range ; it is not confined to any territorial limits. He who drew the charter of the Galena and Chicago Union Railroad Company, and fixed its termini " from the town of " Galena in the county of Jo. Daviess, to such point at the town " of Chicago as shall be determined after a survey shall be made " of the route, to be *the most* eligible, proper and *direct* and con- " venient therefor," would now require something besides a chart and compass to guide him to its " consolidated " end.

Rufus Choate's definition of the boundary line between Rhode. Island and Massachusetts, which " started at a bush and extended " from thence to a blue jay, from thence to a hive of bees in " swarming time, and from thence to three hundred foxes with " fire brands on their tails," *is the soberest description* which can " possibly be given of the present " consolidated" condition of the Chicago and North Western Railway Company and the Galena and Chicago Union Railroad Company in their collected ramifications over the country from the Mississippi River to the Upper Peninsula of Michigan.

To call such a scatteration " consolidation" would seem at first to be an entire misnomer, and we should so regard it, if we were not *gravely* informed that this arrangement betokens the highest evidence of genius, and that this gigantic project comes clearly within the purview of our venerable magna charta. We do not intend to state this case any stronger than the facts themselves will allow, but as our rights are to be determined by the law itself, we are willing to give to human ingenuity every possible advantage that the circumstances of the case may require, and when it has exhausted itself in endeavors to convince the mind that this transaction is reconcilable with the provisions of the charter itself, we may still be inclined to exercise our credulity as to the legality of embracing within its grasp matters so foreign to the original undertaking.

By law a corporation is not self-adjusting. It has no expansive qualities whatever. It is a mere *creature* of the statute, and in order to determine whether we are bound by the acts of those who have chosen to embark the Galena and Chicago Union Railroad Company in most of the railroad enterprises in *esse* and in *posse* between Chicago and the shores of Lake Superior, we propose to examine briefly,

1. The character of this corporation.

2. What powers are granted and what implied in the charter or act of incorporation.

3. The duty of courts to hold corporations to the strictest letter of their grants.

4. The character of the contract which a share-holder enters into when he becomes a member of the corporation.

5. The rights of a share-holder to the corporate property and to have the funds of the company applied to the *objects* expressed in the charter.

6. What acts are and what are not ultra *vires*.

7. The rights of the majority of share-holders.

8. The rights of the minority.

9. Proxies.

10. The power of a corporation to sell its franchises.

11. The effect of amalgamations on the property of bond-holders.

12. Can corporations, when they have the right to consolidate, *prescribe* that the stockholders shall take common or preferred stock, or both, in payment.

13. Can railroad corporations issue preferred and common stock, without *special authority* from the legislature for that purpose.

14. Can the name of a corporation be changed without an act of the legislature.

15. Extra territorial acts.

16. The jurisdiction of courts of equity over corporations.

17. The rights, duties, and liabilities of directors.

18. The public policy of the matter.

19. The doctrine of trusts as applied to directors.

20. When a ratification or confirmation by share-holders of the illegal and unauthorized acts of directors is binding and when not.

I.

POINTS AND AUTHORITIES.

It is an aphorism in law that a corporation is the mere *creature of the statute*, and has *no* powers whatever except those that are *expressly given it.*

In Perrine v. *Chesapeake & Delaware C. Co.*, 9 How. 184, TANEY, C. J., said :

" It is the well-settled doctrine of this court, that a corporation created by statute, is a mere creature of the law, and can exercise no powers except those which the law confers upon it, or which are incident to its existence."

See, also—

Head & Amory v. *Providence Insurance Co.*, 2 Cranch, 127.

Dartmouth College v. *Woodward*, 4 Wheaton, 127.

Bank of U. S. v. *Dandridge*, 12 Wheat. 64.

Charles River Bridge v. *Warren Bridge*, 11 Pet. 544.

Bank of Augusta v. *Earle*, 13 Pet. 587.

Straus et al. v. *Eagle Ins. Co. of Cincinnati*, 5 Ohio, 61.

See—

The Mayor of Norwich v. *The Norfolk Railway Co.*, 30 E. L. & Eq., 137.

In this case, the court say, that " the principle of the limited power of corporations is founded on the soundest principles, and established by several cases."

In the case of *White's Bank of Buffalo* v. *Toledo Insurance Company*, 12 Ohio State Rep. 605—

It is too well settled to be disputed at this time, that the *powers and capacities* of a corporation are derived solely from its charter, which, like every other statute, is to be construed as an entirety, and with a view to ascertain the intention of the legislature, and, if practicable, to harmonize its various provisions; and if, upon a fair construction of its charter, the contract under consideration is not *expressly given*, nor clearly implied from the granted powers, the powers cannot be said to exist.

A corporation, which is a mere *creature* of the law, can only exercise such powers as are conferred upon it by the act of incorporation.

> 21 Ill. 205.
> *Trustees, etc.*, v. *McConnell*, 12 Ill. 140.
> *Perrine* v. *Chesepeake & Del. Canal Co.*, 9 How. 184.
> 2 Cranch, 127.
> *Dartmouth Coll.* v. *Woodward*, 5 Wheat., 636; 12 id., 64.
> *Charles River Bridge* v. *Warren*, 11 Peters, 544; 13 id., 587.

A corporation is the mere creature of law, and cannot act at all without law. A contract made by it, without authority, is void, even in the hands of a bona fide holder for value. Its legal capacity to contract cannot be enlarged by estoppel.

> *Conn. Medical Life Ins. Co.* v. *Cleveland, &c.,*
> *R. R. Co.*, 41 Barb., 25.
> 1 American Law Register, 282.
> 1 R. I., 165.

A corporation is not only incapable of making contracts which are forbidden by its charter but in general it can make *none* which are not necessary, either directly or indirectly, to effect *the objects* of its *creation*.

> *Rock River Bank* v. *Sherwood*, 10 Wis., 231.
> *Head et al.* v. *the Providence Insurance Co.*, 2 Cranch 154.

Chief Justice MARSHALL said that a " corporation is the mere creature of the act to which it owes its existence, all the qualities and disabilities annexed by the common law to ancient institutions of this sort it may correctly be said to be precisely what the *incorporating* act has made it, to derive all its powers from that act and to be capable of exerting its faculties only in the manner which that act authorizes."

> *Charles River Bridge* v. *Warren Bridge*, 11 Peters 420.
>
> *Bank of Augusta* v. *Earle*, 13 Peters, 587.
>
> *Debolt* v. *Ohio Life Ins. & Trust Co.*, Ohio, 574.
>
> *Pearce* v. *Madison & Indianapolis R. R. Co.*, 21 How 443.
>
> *Head et al.* v. *the Providence Insurance Co.*, 2 Cranch, 154.
>
> *Rock River Bank* v. *Sherwood*, 10 Wis., 235–6–7.
>
> *The Penn., Del., & Md. Steam Navigation Co.* v. *Dundridge*, 8 Gill. & J. 248.

Angel & Ames, in their work upon corporations, Sec. 256, say : " And here we would observe that a corporation and individual stand upon very different footing. The latter existing for the general good of society may do all acts and make all contracts which are not, in the eye of the law, inconsistent with this great purpose of his creation ; whereas, the former haing been created for a specific purpose, not only can make no contract forbidden by its charter, which, as it were, the *law of its nature*, but in general can make *no* contract which is not necessary, either directly or indirectly to enable it to answer that purpose."

> *Rock River Bank* v. *Sherwood*, 10 Wis. 236.
>
> *Madison, &c., Plank Road Co.* v. *Watertown, &c., Plank Road Co.*, 7 Wis., 59.

In *Bartholomew* v. *Bentley*, 1 Ohio State Repts. (N. S.), 41, the court said : " No principle of law is, at this day, better established or supported by stronger reason than that 'a corporation is strictly limited to the exercise of those powers which are specifically conferred upon it. The exercise of the corporate franchise being restrictive of individual rights cannot be extended beyond the letter and spirit of the act of incorporation.' "

> 4 Peter, 152.
> *Bank of Chilicothe* v. *Swayne*, 8 Ohio, 286.

The books literally swarm with cases which establish this doctrine, and could be multiplied almost indefinitely.

II.

RULES OF CONSTRUCTION OF CORPORATE CHARTERS.

1. *No Corporate Power is ever Created by Implication or Extended by Construction.*

In the case of *Charles River Bridge* v. *Waaren Bridge*, 11 Peters, 543, TANEY, C. J., said:

" Much has been said, in the argument, of the principles of con-
" struction by which this law is to be expounded, and what under-
" takings, on the part of the State, may be *implied*. The court
" think there can be no serious difficulty on that head. It is the
" grant of certain franchises by the public to a private corporation,
" and in a matter where the public interest is concerned. The *rule*
" *of construction* in such cases, is well settled, both in England and
" by the decisions of our own tribunals. In 2 Barn. & Adol., 793,
" in the case of the proprietors of the Stourbridge Canal, against
" Wheely and others, the court say, ' the canal having been made,
" ' under an act of parliament, the rights of the plaintiffs are de-
" ' rived *entirely from that act*. This, like many other cases, is a
" ' bargain between a company of adventurers and the public. The
" ' *terms* of which *are* expressed in the statute, and the rule of

" ' construction in all such cases, is now fully established to be
" ' this : That any ambiguity in the terms of the contract, must
" ' operate against the adventurers, and in favor of the public and
" ' the plaintiffs, *can claim nothing that is not clearly given them
" ' by the act."* '

* * * * * * * *

Borrowing, as we have done, our system of jurisprudence from the English law, and having adopted in every other case, civil and criminal, its rules for the construction of statutes, is there anything in our local situation, or in the nature of our political institutions, which should lead us to depart from the principle where corporations are concerned ?

Can any good reason be assigned for excepting this particular class of cases from the operation of the general principle; and for introducing a new and adverse rule of construction in favor of corporations, while we adopt and adhere to the rules of construction known to the English common law, in every other case without exception ? We think not—and it *would present a singular spectacle, if, while the courts in England are restraining within the strictest limits, the spirit of monopoly and exclusive privileges in the nature of monopolies, and confining corporations to the privileges plainly given to them in their charter, the courts of this country should be found enlarging these privileges by implication,* and construing a statute more unfavorably to the public, and to the rights of community, than would be done in a like case in an English court of justice.

In the case of *Winter* v. *The Muscagee R. Co.*, 11 Georgia, 438, the court said that, " corporations can exercise *no* power over the " corporators, beyond those conferred by the charter to which they " have subscribed, except by obtaining their agreement and con- " sent."

The powers and provisions of a charter of corporations, are, as Judge SELDEN said once in regard to penalties :

" *Strictissimi juris* to be enforced when they clearly exist, but
" never to be sought after or arrived at by an interpretation which
" is either strained or unnecessarily rigid."

      See— *Newhall* v. *Gal. & C. U. R. R. Co*, 14 Ill. 275.

Said Judge Breese, in the case of *Petersburgh* v. *Metzker*, 21
Ill., 205 : " The powers of all corporations are limited by the
" grants in their charters, and *cannot* be extended beyond them."

Corporations possess only *jura minorum*. They *have not* the
power of contracting on all subjects, like persons of full age, *sui
juris*. They have only just such powers as are conferred on them
by the charter, and no more.

      Seibrecht v. *New Orleans*, 12 La. Ann. 496.
   See, also— *Smith* v. *Morse*, 2 Cal. 524.

In the case of the *Pennsylvania Railroad Company* v. *Canal
Commissioners*, 21 Penn. State Rep. 9, Black, C. J., said :

" It may be, that the privileges which the relator claims, might
" arise by implication out of their charter, or some other of the
" acts cited by their counsel, if we were at liberty to give to them
" the broad construction which we sometimes apply to other laws
" of a different character. *But corporative powers* can *never be
" created by implication, nor extended by construction.* No privi-
" lege is granted, unless it be expressed in plain and *unequivocal
" words*, testifying the intention of the legislature in a manner too
" plain to be misunderstood. When the State means to clothe
" a corporate body with a portion of her own sovereignty, and to
" disarm herself to that extent of the powers which belong to her,
" it is so easy to say so, that we will *never* believe it to be meant
" *when it is not* said ; and words of equivocal import are so easily
" inserted by mistake or fraud, that every consideration of justice
" and policy requires that they should be treated as nugatory when
" they do find their way into the enactments of the legislature.
" *In the construction of a charter, to be in doubt, is to be resolved,*

"*and every resolution which springs from doubt, is against the cor-*
"*poration.   This is the rule sustained by all the courts in this coun-*
"*try and in England.* • No other has received the sanction of any
" authority to which we owe much deference.   This court has as-
" serted it times without number.   We have ruled five or six im-
" portant cases upon it within the last year.   We seem not to have
" made much impression on the professional mind, and we are
" probably making as little now.   But when *respectable counsel*
" *call on us hereafter,* (as they doubtless will,) to *enlarge corporate*
" *powers by construction,* we can only repeat, again and again,
" that our duty imperatively forbids.   The privileges of the Penn-
" sylvania Railroad Company may be too rigidly restricted.   If
" the usefulness of the company would be increased by extending
" them, let the legislature see to it.   But let it be remembered that
" nothing but plain English words will do it."

See, also— *The President of Jacksonville College* v. *Mc-*
Connell, 12 Ill. 138.

To show how strictly corporations are held to the very letter of
their charter, it is only necessary to refer by way of a novel illustration to the case of the *Auburn & Cato Plank Road Company*
v. *Douglass,* 5 Selden, 451, which was a suit brought by the
plank road company against the defendant, praying for an injunction and for damages, because he, the defendant, had thrown open
his premises on *each* side of the plank road, near the toll-gate, so
that persons could pass around it if they saw fit.   The court, in
deciding this case say, " If the extent of the plaintiff's franchise
is to be· determined by the terms of their charter, then all the
rights they have is, to acquire the right of way for their road,
lay down their plank and set up a toll gate and receive tolls.   There
is not a word in the plank road law giving them an exclusive privilege whatever, or any right as against the adjoining proprietors.
Do they take such rights *by implication ?* "   The court then say:
" It involves the great question, whether acts of the legislative
power, conferring special privileges and parceling out the sovereign rights of the people, are to be construed strictly according to

their terms, or liberally with a view to make the grant as beneficial as possible to the grantee; whether corporations are to be con-
tent with what is expressly conceded to them by their charters, or
are to encroach beyond the terms of those charters upon the legislative power, and upon the rights of individuals, and to take by
implication whatever may be necessary or convenient for the exercise, or essential to the value of, their corporate rights "—and they
decide that nothing is given by implication.

2. *Effect of clause in a charter of a corporation declaring the act
public.*

Shelford on R. vol. 1, p. 88.

If an act of parliament be of a private nature it does not derive
any additional weight or authority from having a clause declaring
it to be a public act. The usual clause for effecting this is, "that
" this shall be a public act and shall be judicially taken notice of
" as such." It must still be construed as a private act, the only
object of the proviso making it a public act, is that it may be judicially taken notice of, and to save the expense of proving an attested
copy. Such acts, passed on the petition of individuals, are to be
construed as private agreements between parties. (3 Bos. & P.
565 : 8 T. R. 468, 2 T. R. 705, 2 Bl. Com. 346.

A local act with a clause declaring it to be a public act, and that
it shall be taken notice of as such by all judges, &c., without being specially pleaded, need not be proved either to have been
examined with the parliament roll, or to have been printed by the
king's printer. (Woodward *v.* Cotton, 1 C. M. & R. 44; Beau-
mont & Mountain 10 Bing. 105, 4 M. & Scott 177; see Brett *v.*
Beales, Moo. & M. 421.) A local act of parliament, though con-
taining a clause making it a public act, is not public notice of its
powers over land therein mentioned. (Ballard *v.* Way, 1 Mees. &
W. 520; 2 Gale 61.)

Whether an act of parliament is to be deemed a public act,
binding on all the queen's subjects, or merely a private act, de-

pends upon the nature and substance of the case, and not upon the technical consideration whether the act does or does not contain a clause that it shall be deemed a public act. (Dawson *v.* Paver, 5 Hare 415.)

On the effect of an act conferring private rights, although declared to be a public act, see Prince's Case 8 Rep. 1; Perchard *v.* Haywood 8 T. R. 468; Hesse *v.* Stevenson 3 Bos. & P. 565; Perry *v.* Skinner, 2 Mees. & W. 471; 19 Vin. Abr. Tit. Statute (D) pl. 5 p. 500.)

Statutes relating to subjects in which the public at large are interested are to be expounded largely and beneficially for the purposes for which they are enacted; while statutes which are applicable to *private grants to individuals,* of powers and privileges conferred and to be exercised with a special reference to their own advantages, although involving in their exercise incidentally benefits to the community, generally are to be construed strictly as against the grantees. (Bradley *v.* New York and New Haven Company 21 Conn. 194.

3. *Ambiguous words.*

In the case of Morgan *v.* Commissioners of Miami Co., 2 Black (U. S.) 723, Judge Wayne said that " neither privileges, powers " nor authorities can pass, unless they are given *in unambiguous* " *words,* and that an act *giving special privileges must be construed* " *strictly.*"

Shelford, in his work on Railways, vol. 1, p. 82, says:

" Ambiguous words in a private act of parliament incorporating " a public company are to be construed *against the company* and " in favor of private property. (Scales *v.* Pickering 4 Bing. 448, " 1 M. & P. 495.) Where by a statute a special authority is delegated to particular persons affecting the property of individuals, it must be strictly pursued, and appear to be so upon the face of their proceedings. (Rex *v.* Croke, Cowp. 26.)

" Ambiguous words in an act of parliament authorizing a public company to take land by compulsory process, are to be construed against the company in favor of private property. (Webb *v.* Manchester and Leeds Railw. Co., 1 Railw. C. 576; 4 My. & Cr. 116.)

Where a bargain is made between a company of adventurers and the public, the terms of the bargain are contained in the act. The company can derive nothing which is not *clearly given*. (Kingston upon Hull Dock Co. *v.* La Marche, 8 B. & C. 42.)

Where the language of an act of parliament obtained by a company imposing a tale or toll upon the public *is ambiguous,* that construction is to be adopted which would be most favorable to the interests of the public, and *most against that of the company,* because the company in bargaining with the public ought to take care to express distinctly what payments they receive, and because the public ought not to be charged, unless it be clear that it was so intended.

Ambiguous words in a charter are to be construed most strongly *against* the *corporation*. (Perrine *v.* Chesapeake & Delaware Canal Company, 9 Howard 172.) And a corporation created by statute can exercise no powers but those which are expressed or necessarily implied. (Ib.)

This arises from a principle of staid construction. See also Stormfeltz *v.* Manor Turnpike Company, 13 Penn. (1 Harris) 555.
Nota Bene.—See *Morden* v. *Commissioners of Miami Co.,* 2 Black, 723.
Commonwealth v. *Erie & North East R. Co.,* 27 Penn. 351.

III.

It is the duty of Courts of Equity to keep all Corporations within the powers which their charters give them.

In the case of the *River Dee Navigation Co.* v. *North Midland Railway Co.*, 1 English Railway Cases, 114, the Lord Chancellor said, " I am not at liberty (even if I were in the least disposed, *which I am not,*) to withhold the jurisdiction of this court as exercised in the first case in which it was exercised, that of *Agar* v. *the Regents' Canal Company*, Coopers' Rept., 77, where Lord Eldon proceeds simply on this, that he exercised the jurisdiction of this court for the purpose of keeping these companies *within* the powers which the acts give them, and *a most wholesome exercise of the jurisdiction it is*, because, great as the powers necessarily are to enable the companies to carry into effect works of this magnitude, it would be most prejudicial to the interests of all persons with whose property they interfere, if there were not a jurisdiction continually open and ready to exercise its powers *for the purpose of keeping them within that limit which the legislature* has thought proper to *prescribe* for the *exercise* of *their powers*. On that ground I should never be reluctant to entertain any such application. I think it *most essential to the interest* of *the public,* that such jurisdiction should exist, and should be exercised whenever a proper case for it is brought before the court, otherwise the result may be that after your property has been taken and destroyed, after your house has been pulled down and a railway substituted in its place, you may have the satisfaction at a future period of discovering that the railway company were wrong. It would be a very tardy recompense, and one totally inadequate to the injury of which the party has to complain, and individuals would be made to contend with companies who often have vast sums of money at their disposal, and that too not the money of the persons who are contending. It is a most material point to consider when you enter into a contest with an individual, whether he is spending his *own money* or *money over which he has a control,* or in which he has comparatively a small interest."—(NOTE.—This suggestion of the Lord Chancellor of the unequal contest which a minority wages against the illegal and high-handed acts of a majority is, we are aware, most aptly illustrated in the case at bar, because the defendants here are using our own money, which belongs to us as share-holders, to carry on the litigation against us, and we might perhaps hesitate if the same appreciative judge did not immediately add, but)—"if these companies go beyond the powers which the legislature has given them, and in mistaken exercise of those powers interfere with the property of individuals, *this court is bound to interfere*, that was Lord Eldon's ground in *Agar* v. *the Regents' Canal Co.*, Cooper's Rept., 77, and *I see no reason whatever to depart from the rule there laid down and acted upon.*"

In the case of *Kemp* v. *the London & Brighton Railway Co.*, 1 English Railway Cases, 371, the court says : "Now I consider that there cannot be a more *useful exercise* of the jurisdiction of the court than in interfering to ascertian the rights between parties circumstanced as in this case. I look at the great powers which are necessarily given to these companies ; the variety of interests with which those powers may interfere, if not strictly exercised, according to the provisions of the acts; the necessity of immediate interposition ; the injury to both parties if there be not a jurisdiction constantly open, by which their respective rights may be ascertained ; and then it appears to me *that this* is of all others a situation of things in which this court ought to exercise that jurisdiction.

" My predecessors have established the authority of this court to interfere in these cases, and I certainly feel it my duty not to repudiate a jurisdiction, the exercise of which I believe to be most essential to the interests of the numberless persons who are, in some way or other, affected by these great works which are now so universally being carried on throughout the country."

The inconvenience to the company who were assuming to exercise doubtful powers having been urged, the Lord Chancellor,

p. 374, said : "I have no power, and if I had *I should not* exercise it, to deprive *one party* of what *he is entitled to because* it is *inconvenient* to another party.

"The *company* may or may not have taken proper measures to secure to themselves those powers which are necessary for the sake of convenience in carrying their works into effect; if they have not, it is *their* misfortune. These companies procure ample powers, to be bestowed upon them ; but it not unfrequently happens, that, in the course of their works, they find that they have *not* powers sufficient for *perfecting all they* contemplated. * * * * * I do *not sit in this court* to *enlarge* those powers *but to keep* both parties *within the limits which the legislature has prescribed.*"

In the case of *Webb* v. *Manchester & Leeds R. Co.*, 4 Mylne & Craig, 119, the court said : "It is extremely important to watch over the interests of those whose property is affected by these companies to take care that the company shall not, in any misrepresentation they may make, if they have made any, be permitted to exercise *powers beyond* those which the act of parliament gives them, and to keep them most strictly within the powers of the act of parliament. The powers are so large, it may be necessary for the benefit of the public, but they are so large and so injurious to the interests of individuals, that I think it is the duty of every court to keep them most strictly within those powers, and if there be any reasonable doubt as to the extent of their powers they must go elsewhere and get enlarged powers; but they will get none from me, by way of construction of their act of parliament."

Natusch v. *Irving*, Gow on Partnership, p. 398.

Commonwealth v. *the Pittsburg & Connellsville R. R. Co.*, 24 Penn. State Rep., 159.

Bill of equity in the Supreme Court and motion for a preliminary injunction. The bill charged that the defendants were partially filling up one of the locks at the outlet of the state canal at Pittsburgh, and casting an arch over it in such a manner as to obstruct the use of it, and prayed for injunction to prevent them. The defendants admitted that they were doing so in the construction of their road, and urged as an excuse that that portion of the canal had never been of any valuable use to the state, and that for many years it had lain in a condition of utter abandonment and desolation ; and such seemed to be the fact, and in his opinion, Lowrie, Judge, says:

" And when railway companies or individuals *exceed their statutory* powers in *dealing with other people's property*, no question of damage is raised when an injunction is applied for ; but simply one of the invasion of right, 1 Railway C., 135; 4 My. & Cr., 254. And railway companies will not be allowed to exercise their discretion capriciously, 1 Rail. C., 238, but the court will supervise their discretion, &c. Railway companies must stand upon a strict construction of their chartered privileges: 21 State R., 22 ; 9 Beavan, 391; 2 Man. & Gr., 134; 7 *id.*, 252 ; 1 Railway C., 576 ; 3 *id.*, 563 ; 21 Eng. L. & E. R. 620. With the immense powers that are freely and loosely given to them, this much restraint is essential to the protection of private rights: S. Railway C., 154, 504, 636 ; 4 Myl. & Cr., 120.

If they step one inch beyond their chartered privileges to the prejudice of others, or 'of the stockholders, or offer to do any act without the prescribed preliminary steps, they are liable to be enjoined irrespective of the amount of damage.

Damage or no damage to others, *they must obey their charter*, and that was our decision in the late case of *Manderson* v. *Commercial Bank*. This will be the order, even if the plaintiff's title is doubtful, if the duty be plain. 6 Ves. 703, 2 Mer. 29. And they may be enjoined from commencing their road without sufficient capital. 1 My. & K. 154 ; 2 M. & W. 824. Such, at least, is the practice elsewhere, and it may be well for us to learn by the experience of others.

A corporation has only the powers vested in it by law. 1 Kyd. on Corp. 65 ; 2 Cranch. 127 ; 7 *Id.* 290 ; 8 Wheaton, 388. It is limited to the powers granted to it. 2 Kent, 298 ; 4 Pet. 152 ; 5 Id. 641 ; 1 Sumner, 47 ; 13 Peters, 521 3 Kelly, 31 ; 25 Minn. 493 ; 6 W. & S. 101 ; 9 *Id.* 97 ; Manning & Granger, 870 ; 6 Paige, 234 ; 20 Vermont, *Whitcomb* v. *Rood.* The franchises of a corporation cannot be granted away by its own act. 9 W. & S. 17 ; 22 Pick. 122."

Louisiana State Bank v. *Orleans Nav. Co.,*
3 Louisiana Annual Reports, 314.

The court in this case said, " that a corporation being the creature of the law, possesses only those powers which the charter of its creation confers upon it, either expressly or as incidental to its *very* existence. And it is our duty to follow it and to impress on all those intrusted with municipal authority, the necessity of conferring this action within the just, lawful, and well defined limits."

Everhart v. *Philadelphia and West Chester R. R. Co.,* 28 Penn. 352.

The court in this case say :

" Nothing is plainer than that an alteration of a charter by the legislature may be so extensive and radical as to work an entire dissolution of the contracts entered into by the subscriber to the stock, as by procuring an amendment which *superadds to the original undertaking an entirely new enterprise.* Every individual owner of shares expects, and indeed stipulates with the other owners as a body corporate, to pay them his proportion of the expense which a majority may please to incur in the promotion of the particular objects of the corporation. By *acquiring an interest in the corporation, therefore, he enters into an obligation with it in the nature of a special contract, the terms of which are limited by the specific provisions, rights and liabilities, detailed in the act of incorporation.* To make a valid change in this private contract as in any other, the assent of both parties is indispensable. The corporation on one part can assent by a vote of the majority—the individual on the other part by his own personal act. Consequently where an assessment is sued for, to advance objects essentially different from those originally contemplated, they cannot be recovered, because they are not made in conformity to the defendant's special contract with the corporation. Angell & Ames on Cor. 538; *Union Lock of Canal Co.* v. *Towne,* 1 N. H. R. 44; 8 Mass R. 268; 10 Mass. 384; 7 Barbour R. 157; 1 Harris; *Hester* v. *Charleston R. R. Co.*"

Commonwealth v. *Erie and North East R. R. Co.,* 27 Penn. 351.

In deciding this case, Chief Justice BLACK said:

" This case requires us to give a construction to the charter of a private corporation. The frequency of such cases excites some surprise, when we reflect than an act of incorporation is, and always must be, interpreted by a rule so simple, that no man, whether lawyer or layman, can misunderstand or misapply it. That which a company is authorized to do by its act of incorporation, it may do; beyond that all its acts are illegal. And the power must be given in plain words or by necessary implication. All powers not given in this direct and unmistakable way, are withheld. It is strange that the Attorney-General, or anybody else, should complain against a company that keeps itself within bounds, which are always thus clearly marked, and equally strange that a company that has happened to transgress them, should come before us *with the faintest hope* of being sustained. In such cases, ingenuity has nothing to work with, since nothing can be either proved or disproved by logic or inferential reasoning. If you assert that a corporation has certain privileges, *show us the words* of the legislature conferring them. Failing in this, you must give up your claim, for nothing else can possibly avail you. A doubtful charter does not exist; because whatever is doubtful, is decisively certain against the corporation.

" If loss or injury comes to anybody in consequence of an ignorant disregard of this principle, it is not our fault. We have done all that in us lay to impress it on the public mind, and to warn corporations of the danger they might incur by disobedience. We enforced it to the utmost on the *Bank of Pennsylvania* v. *The Commonwealth; Susquehannah R. R. Co.* v. *Sanbury & Erie R. R. Co.; The Pennsylvania R. R. Co.* v. *Canal Commissioners; The Commonwealth* v. *The Franklin Canal Co.*, and in many other cases. All of our predecessors on this bench occupied the same ground. The doctrine is maintained by the Supreme Court of the United States, and in many States of the Union. Even in England, the justice and necessity of it are universally acknowledged and acted upon. But we do not mean to discuss the subject over again. The lawyer who is not already familiar with the numerous authorities upon it, to be found in every book of reports, will probably never become so ; and the citizen who does not believe it to be a most salutary feature in our jurisprudence, *would hardly be convinced, though one rose from the dead.* See *Moran* v. *Commissioners of Miami Co.*, 2 Black. 723."

In the case of *Reg.* v. *Eastern Counties of Railway Co.*, 2 Railway Cases, 736—p. 752–754, Lord Cheatham said :

" It is extremely important, to watch over the interests of those whose property is affected by these companies, to take care care that the company shall not in any misrepresentation they may make, if they have made any, be permitted to exercise powers beyond those which the act of parliament gives them, and to keep them most strictly within the powers of the act of parliament. The powers are so large and so injurious to the interests of individuals, that I think it is the duty of every court, to keep them most strictly within those powers ; and *if* there be reasonable doubt as to the extent of their powers, they must go elsewhere and get enlarged powers; but they will get none from me by way of construction of their act of parliament. *Webb* v. *Manchester & Leeds Railway Co.*, 4 My. & Cr. 120 ; 1 Railway Co. 599 ; see *Scales* v. *Pickering*, 1 M. & P., 195 ; 4 Bink. 448. These companies procure ample powers to be bestowed upon them; but it not unfrequently happens, that, in the course of their works, they find that they have not powers sufficient for perfecting *all* they contemplate ; when *that is* the case, they *must* either *make* what bargain they can with the persons whose rights are adverse to them, or they must again apply to parliament to have their powers enlarged. The Court of Chancery does *not sit* to *enlarge* such powers, but to *keep* both parties *within the limits* which the legislature has prescribed· *Kemp* v. *London & Brighton Railway Co.*, 1 Railw. C. 508. See 8 and 9 Vict. c. 18, s. 16, n. post."

See—   1 Shelford on Railways, 71–72.

Private acts of incorporation, which confer power to subject private property to public use, should be strictly construed.

> *Moorhead* v. *Little Miami R. R. Co.*, 17 Ohio, 340.

In all questions of power, arising under the act *of* a legislature, granting a franchise like that of a railroad company, the test of the existence of the power is to be found in the inquiry whether the same is *expressly granted*, or whether it is incidental to any express grant or power, and necessary to its accomplishment.

> *State of Maryland* v. *Baltimore & Ohio R. R. Co.*, 6 Gill., 363.
> Shelford on R., vol. 1, p. 98.

IV.

A CHARTER OF A CORPORATION IS A CONTRACT.

1st, Between the State and the corporation ; and, 2d, between the corporation and the shareholders, and every act which impairs these contracts, whether by the State towards the corporation or by the corporation towards the shareholders, is unconstitutional and void.

1. In the case of *The Northern R. R. Co.* v. *Miller*, 10 Barbour, 28, the court said :   It is proper then to inquire who are the

parties to the contract created by the granting and acceptance of a charter of incorporation. These are, primarily, the State which makes the grant, and the trustees, directors or other persons, by whatsoever name they are called, by whom the affairs ot the corporation are managed. The corporators, or stockholders, by whom the funds are advanced and who expect to be reimbursed by the profits on the business of the company, are also parties. The corporation itself, which is the offspring of the charter, and is an artificial being, invisible, intangible and existing only in contemplation of law, is also, in a certain sense, a party. But as the latter can only act through the medium of its trustees, directors, or other managers, it is more proper to say that the State, the trustees, &c., and the corporators are the parties to the contract, [4 Wheat., 636, 643, 657, 700.] It is not denied that an act of the legislature altering a charter in a material respect, without the consent of the corporation, is an act impairing the obligation of the contract, and is therefore unconstitutional and void, [*Dartmouth Coll.* v. *Woodward*, 4 Wheat., 518.]

Miss., O. & Red R. R. Co. v. *Cross*, 20 Ark., 449.

The court said "that the charter is the law of the contract between the corporation and a *subscriber to its capital* stock. That the *corporation* has *no right to* depart from the *law* or violate the contract of the subscriber," and on page 452, the court said, " that if directors undertake to make an unwarrantable departure from the provisions of the charter, in the location or construction of the road, *or in the appropriation of the funds of the company, the stockholder has his remedy by injunction.*"

Young v. *Harrison*, 6 Geo., 130.

The law which must control in this case is laid down by J. Davis in the case of

Clearwater v. *Meredith*, 1 Wallace, 39, 40, 41, 1 C.

See also— *New Orleans R. R. Co.* v. *Harris*, 27 Miss., 509.

In *Mann* v. *Pentz*, 2 Sandford Ch., 258, it was decided that a shareholder holding one hundred shares of stock, on which more than half- of the nominal amount had been paid, by an agreement with the directors, received full scrip for sixty shares, and soon after relinquished the remainder to the corporation. On the corporation subsequently passing into the hands of a receiver, it was held, that the creditors and *other* stockholders who did *not assent*, were not affected by that arrangement, and that *such* shareholder must make the whole hundred shares full stock, if it were necessary to discharge the corporate liabilities ; and this was on the ground that, the shareholder had, by subscribing, contracted with all the other shareholders that he would furnish so much as he subscribed to the capital stock, and this shows the interest which each shareholder has in the funds of a corporation.

In the case of *Mann* v. *Currel*, 2 Barbour's Rept., 299, the court decided that a certificate of stock is a contract between the stockholder and the corporation, and that a person remains a stockholder until he surrenders up his stock to the company and a transfer is made on the books of the company ; and then the court adds that, an agreement to consolidote the stock could not affect the rights of creditors of the company or of the other stockholders who were not parties to the arrangement.

Charters of corporations are contracts made by the legislature in behalf of every person interested in anything to be done under them.

> 1 Shelford on Railways, p. 71.
> *Blakemore* v. *Glamorganshire Canal Naviga-tion Co.*, 1 My. & K., 162–3.
> *Rex* v. *Cumberworth*, 3 B. & Ad., 108; 1 Nev. & P., 197.
> *Rex* v. *Greenwich R. Co.*, 4 Nev. & M., 458.
> *Lee* v. *Milnre*, Mees. & W., 839.
> *Shand* v. *Henderson*, 2 Dow P. C., 521.
> *Lee* v. *Milner*, 4 Y. & Coll., 618.

Hence, every substantial alteration of a charter, without the consent of the corporation, is void.

The Commonwealth v. *Cullen*, 13 Penn., 133.

In *Blakemore* v. *the Glamorganshire Canal Co.*, 1 Myl. & Keen, 162, Lord ELDON says: "When I look upon these acts of Parliament, I regard them all in the light of *contracts* made by the legislature on *behalf* of *every person interested in anything to be done under them;* and *I have no hesitation in asserting* that, *unless that principle is applied* in construing statutes of this description, they *will* become *instruments of greater oppression than anything in the whole system of administration under our constitution.* Such acts of parliament have now become extremely numerous, and from their number and operation they so much affect individuals, that I apprehend those who come for them to parliament, do, in effect, undertake that they shall do and submit to whatever the legislature empowers and compels them to do; and that they shall do and shall forbear all that they are required to do and to forbear, as well with reference to the interests of the *public* as *with reference* to the *interests* of *individuals.*

See also to the same effect,

Lee v. *Milner*, 2 You. & Coll., 618.

2.   The contract of a shareholder in a corporation cannot be altered or varied by the corporation without the assent of the individual shareholder; and every substantial alteration, without his consent, is void.

Hartford & New Haven R. R. Co. v. *Croswell*, 5 Hill, 386. This was a case where the legislature of Connecticut in May, 1833, passed an act incorporating the Hartford and New Haven R. R. Co., with power to construct a railroad from the town of Hartford to the city of New Haven. In May, 1839, the legislature of Connecticut amended the act of incorporation authorizing the company to procure, charter, or purchase and hold such number of steamboats to be used in connection with their road, as they might deem expedient, to an amount not exceeding $200,000. On the 2d of July, the board of directors resolved to accept the amendment, and in September, 1839, the stockholders formally accepted the amendment; but the defendant, who was a subscriber to the original stock, was not present and it did not appear that *he* had ever signified his acceptance. The defendant was called upon to pay an installment, but refused. Suit was brought against him. The defence was, that the plaintiffs were seeking to enforce a different contract from that into which the defendant entered when he subscribed for the stock. The opinion was rendered by C. J. NELSON, who said:

"The contract thus entered into was as specific and definite as the charter of the company could make it; and the meaning and intent of the parties cannot therefore be mistaken. It was a contract to take stock in an association incorporated for a particular object, having such limited and well defined powers as were necessary to the accomplishment of that object. The defendant assented to the object by his subscription, and thereby agreed that his interest should be subject to the direction and control of the powers thus expressly conferred, but nothing more.

"Since entering into this contract, the plaintiffs have procured an amendment of their charter, by which they *have superadded to* their original undertakings a new and very different enterprise, and for aught that can be known, a very hazardous one, with the necessary additional powers to carry it into effect. Instead of confining their operations to the construction and management of their railroad between Hartford and New Haven, they have undertaken to establish and maintain a line of water communication by means of steamboats, at an expense not to exceed $200,000; to all which, it is insisted, the contract of the defendant has become subject without his approbation or assent.

"It is most obvious, if incorporated companies can succeed in establishing this sort of absolute control over the original contract entered into with them by the several corporators, there is no limit to which it may not be carried, short of that which defines the boundary of legislative authority. The proposition is too monstrous to be entertained for a moment. Corporations possess *no such power*. Indeed, they can exercise no powers over the corporators beyond those conferred by the charter to which they have subscribed, except on the condition of their agreement to consent. This is so in the case of private associations, where the articles entered into and subscribed by the members are regarded as the fundamental law or constitution of the society, which can only be changed by the unanimous voice of the stockholders. (*Livingston* v. *Lynch*, 4 John Ch., Rept. 573; Coll. on Part., 641.) So here, the original charter is the fundamental law of the association—the constitution which prescribes limits to the directors, officers and agents of company not only, but to the action of the corporate body itself, and no radical change or alteration can be made or allowed, by which *new and additional objects* are to be accomplished *or responsibilities incurred by the company*, so as to bind the individuals composing it, without their assent.

" The question has been the object of consideration in Massachusetts and Pennsylvania; and in each, the courts have not hesitated to maintain the inviolability of the contract as originally entered into, denying to the company the power of altering it essentially, and of binding the subscribers who have not given their assent."

Macedon & Bristol Plank R. Co. v. *Lapham*,
18 Barb. 318.

Chapman et al. v. *M. R. & L. E. R. R. Co.*,
5 Ohio State, 136.

Hester v. *Memp. & C. R. R.*, 32 Miss. 373.

Champion v. *Memp. R. R. Co.*, 35 Miss. 692.

The number of cases which could and can be adduced in support of the above doctrine, is almost innumerable, and can be found in the reports of almost every State in the Union—and the great principle which they establish is, that *no legislature* can alter or change the fundamental contract of the shareholders ; and if this is so, how can a set of stockholders, who happen temporarily to be in the majority, alter and change that contract *without the consent of all the parties to that contract?* Are not the *minority of stock-holders as much parties* to the contract *as the majority ?* Is it in the power of human ingenuity to disprove this position ?

" An *assent* of stockholders to amendments changing or extending the objects, or increasing the powers, or enlarging the liabilities of the corporation, in any matter fundamental, is *not to be* presumed, but must be proved.

" There is no proof in this case, that these plaintiffs or their grantors *have ever consented* to any change in the contract as originally made between the corporations, of which they are members, whatever the directors or *a majority of the corporation* may have done on their own account."

March v R. R. Co., 43 N. H. 525-6.

If the sale, consolidation and extermination of the Galena and Chicago Union Railroad Company, as a distinct and independent corporation, and its amalgamation with the Chicago and North Western Railway Company, and all of the railroads it has ever built, bought, or absorbed—together with the assumption of millions of debts and liabilities—is not something of an alteration and change of the *fundamental contract* of the shareholders of that company, and of the objects with which it was formed, then the human understanding is incapable of comprehending what constitutes a change or alteration in the affairs of man.

In the case of *Wetter* v *Mississippi Railroad Company*, 20 Ark. 463, the court held that, where the charter, under which a railroad corporation was formed, having definitely fixed the *termini* and route of the road before the appellant became a subscriber to its capital stock, this was held to give the law of his contract.

Where a company was incorporated to build a railway across the State, as a continuous project under one management with a common interest, and the charter was afterwards amended so as to divide the project into three parts, to be under separate control : *Held*, that it was such a change in the contract as would release the subscribers.

Supervisors v. *Miss. R. R. Co.*, 21 Ill. 338.

Amendments proposed to a charter, are *not* to be regarded *as* the acts of the corporation, *merely because* they are offered *under* the corporate seal. The court may inquire into the authority by which the seal was affixed.

St. Mary's Church, 7 S. & R. 517.

In corporations, where there are different classes, if there be no provision in the charter concerning alterations, the majority of each class must consent, before the charter can be altered. *Ib.*

Therefore, where the trustees of a corporation consisted of three clerical and eight lay members, and one of the former was excluded from the board, without authority, by a resolution of the latter, it was decided that resolutions, passed in the absence of the excluded clerical members, for altering the fundamental articles of the charter, were illegal. *Ib.*

The directors of an incorporated company, to whom the management of the concern is given generally, *have no authority to apply* to the legislature to *increase their powers ;* and a resolve of the legislature, passed on such application *without authority from the company, giving power to the company* to raise an additional assessment on the stockholders, *is void.*

Marlborough Manf. So. v. *Smith,* 2 Conn. 679.

Illinois Cases.

The defendants in this case, in order to substantiate their claims and justify their action, have placed before the court and the public, certain decisions of the Supreme Court of the State of Illinois, relating to amendments of charters by the legislature, and have cited several instances where consolidations of railroads have been made *without any question*, and they seek to draw the inference therefrom, that *they* were perfectly justified in pursuing the course which they did; in overwhelming and drowning the Galena and Chicago Union Railroad Company.

But we remark, in the first place, that there is *no* case in the State of Illinois, which has ever come before *any* court which we have ever heard of, where a *shareholder* sought to test the legality of any consolidation, such as the present, by a direct proceeding like that of the complainant in this case.

2. That all of the reported cases, but three, which are in any way analogous, or which involve the principles that enter into the general subject of consolidations, are actions at law, brought to collect the amount of subscriptions to the stock of the companies; and do not involve any such questions as are here presented, of compelling a stockholder in one corporation to become liable for millions of dollars of the debts of another corporation.

3. That most every case in Illinois, where subscribers to the stock of corporations have questioned the propriety of amendments, have been cases where the changes were *not* fundamental at all, but mere deflections from *a crooked* to a straight line—a change from one town to another, on the general course, to a given point— and were not considered a *radical* change at all.

4. That there is no reported case whatever in Illinois where any shareholder ever contested the *terms* of any consolidation at all, or where the facts and circumstances correspond to the case at bar.

5. The cases which have been decided, in regard to amending charters, have not been characterized by any particular uniformity, and in several of the most important ones which are relied upon, the judges themselves did not agree, and in two instances, at least, dissenting opinions were delivered ; and it may be remarked, that the Supreme Court of Illinois is composed of three judges, and that Judge CATON, judging from his opinions, does not seem to believe in the vested rights of corporations or corporators at all, and *seems* to hold to the opinion, that it is an implied understanding always, that the contract of a shareholder in a corporation, is liable to be changed to any extent at any time. Judge BREESE and Judge WALKER do not seem to entertain any such views whatever.

But however this may be, this case is to be determined by the United States Court—and " although it is the practice of the Supreme Court of the United States to follow the latest *settled* adjudications of the State courts giving construction to the laws and constitutions of their own States, it will not necessarily follow decisions which may prove but oscillations in the course of such judicial settlement.

Nor will it follow any adjudication to such an extent as to make a sacrifice of *truth, justice and law*."
Gelpcke v. *City of Dubuque*, 1 Wallace, 175.

Moreover, " where private rights are to be determined by common law rules, this court does not feel bound by the decision of State courts."
Chicago City v. *Robbins*, 2 Black. 418.

Neither are the decisions of State courts binding on this court, *in a question of constitutional law.*
Jefferson Branch Bank v. *Skelly*, 1 Black. 436.

And in order that there may be no misunderstanding as to what the Illinois cases actually do decide, we propose to refer to the most important cases which have been decided, in order that the court may see how they compare with the cases in other States and especially with the decisions of the United States Supreme Court.

1. *Sprague* v. *Illinois River Railroad Company*, 19 Ill. 175.

This was a bill in equity, filed by Charles Sprague, a simple tax payer of Cass county, to prevent the county of Cass from issuing bonds to aid in the construction of the Illinois River Railroad, to which enterprise that county had become a subscriber by a vote of the people. It appeared from the bill—

1. That the railroad was incorporated February 11, 1853, for the purpose of building a railroad from Jacksonville, Morgan county, to LaSalle, LaSalle county, Illinois. 2nd. That on March 1, 1854, the legislature passed an act amending the charter of the Illinois Railroad Company, by which amendments, it first repealed the original corporators out, and appointed new ones.

2. It provided that the Illinois Railroad Company might consolidate with any road, built, or to be built, and to make connections with such road at any point on the route of the Illinois Railroad, and that the company should not be required to build north of such connection. 3rd. That the subscription of Cass county, as voted, shall not be affected by the amendment.

3. On the 10*th of May*, 1854, the Cass county court directed the county judge to subscribe $50,000 stock to the company, which he did.

4. At the session of the legislature, in 1857, two acts were passed, amending the charter—one section expressly declares that the vote of Cass county, in 1853, to subscribe to the stock of the Illinois Railroad Company, was legal, and that the subscription on the 10th of May, 1854, was legally taken, and requires and directs the County Court of Cass county to issue bonds to the company for $50,000.

5. The bill further alleged, that the Illinois Railroad Company had located their road from Virginia, Cass county, north to Pekin, and from thence across to the Illinois river, to the junction of the Peoria & Hannibal road, and are now building a bridge across the Illinois river at Pekin, with a view to terminate said road at said junction, and that the character of the country is such as to render the building of a road impracticable.

6. The bill then shows that the county court was just about to issue $50,000 county bonds to the Illinois Railroad by virtue of the subscription above referred to, and which had been legalized.

An injunction was granted, *ex parte,* and the county judge admitted all of the facts stated in the bill, and merely stated that when he made the subscription, he did not know of the existence of the amendments of 1854, as the laws had not at that time been published.

The Illinois River Railroad Company answered, admitting all the allegations of the bill, with the following qualifications:

1. That the directors of the Illinois River Railroad Company had never established any northern terminus at any point north of La Salle.

2. That, although the road had been located from Pekin, across the Illinois river, to the line of the Peoria & Hannibal Road, and an arrangement had been made with said road for *running cars* over their road, yet they had *not* terminated their road at the junction, but that the road will be extended further north.

3. The answer then set out the order of the County Court of Cass county, directing the subscription of the $50,000 stock, and the issuing of the bonds, and claimed that the transaction was legal and right.

This statement has been made with some care, and in detail, in order to see what was at issue, and if we were to stop here, it would be impossible to tell what particular right of Charles Sprague had been invaded, or what illegal act the county of Cass had been guilty of, and if the investigation be further diligently pursued, we shall not be much wiser. All that the record shows, is, that when the cause came on to be heard, that the *bill* was dismissed, and that the plaintiff took the case up to the Supreme Court, and assigned for error; *the dissolution* of the injunction—not a point is given ; and what questions were argued at the bar, is nowhere stated ; but as the whole record was before the court, it is inferred from the opinion of the court, that the right of the legislature to amend the charter, was in some way questioned, and the subject of consolidations broached, but as it *nowhere*, from beginning to end, appears that any *consolidation* was *ever* made by the Illinois River Railroad Company, with any other, of any sort or character, or kind, it is impossible to tell how *that* question came before the court—and when it is considered that the subscription which Sprague was fighting was made to the *very* charter that *authorized* consolidations *to be* made, and was expressly legalized by the legislature, it still further excites our wonder. The names of very able counsel are appended to the record, but how this subject of consolidations came up, when none had been made, is not now apparent.

It is possible that the usually very accurate reporter may have entirely omitted something from the case, for we do not understand how so extraordinary an opinion could have been rendered if there was not something in the case to warrant it—more than now appears.

Charles Sprague does not appear to have been a stockholder in the road at all ; but, in the commencement to the statement of the case, it is said that " Charles Sprague filed his bill in the Cass Circuit Court, showing that he is a resident of Cass county, and the owner of real estate situated in Cass county and of personal estate on which taxes are regularly levied for county purposes." It nowhere appears that he had suffered any injury over and above any body else at all, and we do not see what other question was or could come legitimately before the court, than the right, power and authority of Cass county to issue the $50,000 of bonds in payment of the stock which they had, by a vote of the citizens, authorized to be taken, and the bonds issued : and yet, Judge CATON, after having, in the very opening sentence, decided the whole case by stating that the change which had been authorized by the legislature was not an essential and material departure from the purposes and objects specified, then proceeds to give his views at length, upon the propriety, in many instances, of allowing railroads to consolidate with each other, in order to accomplish the end which the projectors had in view, to-wit, " to make the undertaking a success and the investment a profitable one." And he illustrates what he means, by citing the New York Central Railroad, which was at first composed of a number of distinct corporations and which afterwards became consolidated into one *continuous* line, by virtue of some act of the legislature of the State of New York, in which he argues generally, that, in such cases, the majority should rule, and he depicts with considerable earnestness what the consequences might be if one " stupid or obstinate holder of one share should tie up the hands of all the rest. He thinks that there is, under such circumstances, no vested right to be interposed, and as a matter of public policy should be so declared ;" and then significantly adds that, " there must be a *palpable abuse of power by the majority, or governing authority, to the prejudice of the minority or dissenting portion, before the courts would be authorized to declare its exercise illegal.* Bad faith or fraud, says he, would vitiate such acts as well in these as in other cases."

He then proceeds to say, that, in the history of our State, there have been numerous instances of amending charters, and that many charters contain power in them authorizing consolidations, and that no instance can be found where the unanimous consent of all the shareholders of the corporations is made necessary to an acceptance of such amendments, or to effect a proposed consolidation. Just then it appears to have occurred to the judge, that there was something in the point that such things were not quite so regardful of the rights of individuals as they might be, and he says: " But it may be objected (page 180) that this course of legislation and action, however uniform and long continued, *cannot acquire* the force of constitutional law, or rather of constitutional construction, and that this question involves the sacred right of individuals to possess, manage, and enjoy their own as they may think best, as well as the right of contract, expressed or implied, upon entering into these associations." And how was this objection, which suddenly forced itself upon his mind, as it would any reflecting mind, answered ? Will it be believed that all the answer that was given to this objection was that, "long continued and uniform acquiescence in the exercise of this power, by those interested *in the stocks of these* corporations and by the profession, *shows* the undoubted understanding of all, that this is a rightful and *necessary* exercise of power, and he is a bold man indeed who, supposing that he has been favored with some glimmer of constitutional light which has never been vouchsafed to any other, shall hold that this has all been usurpation of power and ruthless trampling upon individual rights. A becoming distrust of our own capacity should induce us to hesitate long before upturning everything which has been so long considered settled, and so uniformly acquiesced in."

And this is a faithful specimen of the reasoning which pervades this entire opinion. It is one of the most extraordinary opinions ever penned by an enlightened jurist. It is the veriest satire upon magna charta and constitutional rights which any man ever composed, and holding aloff this host of reasons he calls upon all to witness that, "those interested in the stocks of those corporations and the *profession* have *acquiesced*" in such things until they have become law. We do not know how those interested in stocks have regarded acts such as these of destroying the property of a minority by the will of a majority, but we protest, in the name of all that is sacred, against committing the profession to any *such constitutional law.*

We do not know, it is true, of the *particular* acts which Judge CATON would commit us to, but if he means to say that there *have* been *many* instances in which the majority in corporations have done most outrageous and high-handed things, and that they have been acquiesced in, we agree with him ; but if he means to say that these things have been so frequent in this State, and have been acquiesced in so often, that stockholders in corporations and some briefless barristers have stood by and seen them done, and *therefore* it has become law, we will not, for one humble disciple of Edward Coke, esq., submit to any such imputation, and we say that the constitution of the United States, of this State, and numerous decisions of the United States Court are against him, and that as distinguished a jurist as he may be, that he should hesitate long before " upturning everything which has been so long considered settled and so uniformly acquiesced in." We do not interpose our feeble powers, but we cite him to the opinions of MARSHALL, STORY, KENT, SHAW, TANEY, WAYNE and DAVIS, and beg leave to refer to numerous adjudications in the courts and of the various States of the Union, so utterly at variance with these views, that we do not feel at all disheartened in our attempt to expose these fallacies, especially when they appear to be almost volunteered, and when the questions did not, and could not, come *legitimately* before the court.

We have now given copious samples of the reasoning made use of in this case ; and we have been constrained to do so, as this case *has been cited* as establishing principles directly the reverse of those for which we contend, but we feel great satisfaction in knowing that Judge BREESE dissented *in toto* from all the positions here assumed by Judge CATON, and we feel more than assured that these views do not, and did not, meet the mind of Judge WALKER, and have since been essentially repudiated by him.

We have one other remark to make, lest this court, and others, may be misled by the reference made by Judge CATON to the way and manner in which the several railroad corporations, composing the N. Y. Central Railroad, were consolidated. One would suppose, from reading the opinion of Judge CATON, that the consolidation was effected, and they were all combined by a simple act of the legislature, without consulting the stockholders at all. Now, such is not, and was not, the fact; and if any one will turn to the session laws of New York for 1853, page 110, they will find *the* law, under which those vast interests were combined. They will there see that the rights of the stockholders were not only *respected*, but *protected*, to the last degree; and that, when the stockholders could not agree, that their rights were settled in a *court* of their own selection—they were not slaughtered by a merciless and unscrupulous majority. The difficulties which surrounded that consolidation do not appear in Judge CATON's opinion; and if any one will inquire of those who know, they will find that the consolidation of the several railroad corporations from Schenectedy to Buffalo, which now compose the New York Central Railroad Company, baffled the very best lawyers and jurists of that State.

And that the legislature only interfered, when the *interruptions* to travel, by the breaks in the line, became so great as to render it, in the estimation of the legislature, a public nuisance; and they ordered it abolished by the exercise of the sovereign powers of the State, and ordered the stockholders to combine their interests into one common fund, and make an *unbroken, continuous* line, or they would do it for them; and they, finally acting upon that principle and upon the principle of *eminent domain*, directed that the stock of any recusant stockholder should be *taken* and *condemned* precisely as an interposing shantie is demolished—by asking for appraisers and then those appraisers fixed the value of the stock, and he was paid and they then passed on.

This was the only way in which *that* consolidation was or could be accomplished, and stands forth as a perfect anamoly in the history of all railroads in this country, and has no more analogy to the one under consideration than the Dead Sea has to the Atlantic Ocean.

2. The case of the *Ill. River R. R. Co.* v. *Zimmer*, 20th Ill., 654, was an action of assumpsit, brought against the defendant upon a subscription to the capital stock of the company.

The defence was that, although the defendant had made a *general and unqualified subscription* to the capital stock of the company, yet that the company had since that time procured certain amendments to be made, one of which allowed the subscriptions to be applied *in* counties *where subscribed*, and in that way the road might never be built through, but would be built in sections ; and another *was*, that the amendment required subscriptions to be paid on a notice of *twenty days* instead of ninety days. Several other minor matters were set out as being irregularities, and the defendant upon those grounds claimed that he ought to be released from his contract.

The court, Judge CATON, in deciding the case said that, "when this subscription was made, the defendant knew that the charter was not unalterable. He knew that it might be amended by the legislature, and that the company might accept such amendment, when that would become the law of the company. If the *ninety* days' notice were deemed essential and designed to be made a condition precedent to a legal liability to pay the money, it should have been inserted in express terms in the agreement of subscription, when the condition precedent would have to be performed before the liability would become complete.

There is in *this* case, the same implied reservation of the right to change the law, and thus vary the precise extent of the liability, that there is in case of official bonds, given by public officers and their sureties, conditioned that they shall faithfully perform the duties of their office according to law. In *that* case, it is well settled that new or additional duties may be imposed upon the officer, so as they are *germain* to the office, and the sureties are bound for his faithful performance of those new duties, although the extent of their liability is thereby increased *beyond* what it was when they executed the bond; and this, too, notwithstanding the great strictness which is usually observed in favor of sureties.

> *Governor* v. *Ridgeway*, 12 Ill., 14.
> *Bartlett* v. *the Gov.*, 2 Bibb., 586."

The court then proceeds to dispose of the case, by saying that, "this is *not* one of those cases where the provisions of the law are by implication incorporated into the contract and constitute a part of it, unless we also introduce into the contract by *implication* that other principle of law, by which the right to the legislature and the company is reserved to change the provisions of the charter, as the public good and the interests of the company at large may require."

Now, the theory which Judge Caton here lays down is utterly at variance with all ideas of vested rights; and he seems to regard railroads as public corporations, and subject to have their charters changed and modified precisely as municipal corporations. He may be correct, and that may be entirely the best policy, but this view is not adopted by any other court in the United States, and is not the view which has been taken of the subject by Judges Breese and Walker, or the Supreme Court of Illinois, as at present constituted, at all.

Judge Caton seems to attach no sort of importance to the rights of an individual stockholder, and places the railroad absolutely under the control of the majority of the stock. He does not stop to consider whether the majority of opinions, or wills, is the correct rule, but he sets up an oligarchy of money, and then says, every shareholder must look for the promotion of his individual interest, to the advancement of every other shareholder; and drops out of sight, every idea of a contract, which may, by such a course, be impaired, and treads over all constitutional questions, as if they were a worn out pathway.

" Whatever advances that general interest," says he, " must necessarily be held to be a promotion of his interest. *Each* shareholder *has a right to expect the cordial co-operation of all his co-shareholders* in everything which tends to promote that general good. No one should be permitted to turn traitor to the cause, and set up an *individual interest as hostile to it.* No one can be known in the concern except by the stock which he represents, and all must be presumed to have a single eye to the enhancement of the value of that stock. These are general considerations which must be ever borne in mind in considering of amendments to charters of incorporations.

" If an amendment is promotive of the general interest of the company, it is not necessarily promotive to the individual interest of each shareholder to the extent of his shares in the company ; and any company has an undoubted right to accept any amendment to its charter, which it believes promotive of the objects and interests of the company. Of this, the company is necessarily the judge, and those who represent and act for the company, so long as they act with an honest purpose and *bona fide* intent, must be held to have acted for the best ; or, at least, their action must be sustained, as obligatory upon the company, the same as in the exercise of any other discretionary power with which they are vested, although it may turn out that they may have erred in their judgment. They are no more likely to err in this than in the exercise of any other important power with which they are invested.'

Here, it will be observed, he takes the ground, that " each shareholder has a right to expect the cordial co-operation of *all* his co-shareholders in everything which tends to promote that general good."

And recognizes the rights of an individual in the broadest manner, but in the very next sentence, he says, that, " *no one* should be permitted to turn traitor to the concern, and set up an individual interest as hostile to it." Now, suppose that all the stockholders, but one, turned traitors, to the concern at once—suppose that they resolved to rebel and overturn the entire corporation—sell it out, and blot it out altogether—and suppose one man stood by the old corporation, and demanded to have it preserved, and insisted that it should not be destroyed, either by " foreign foes or domestic traitors,"—who, then, in such a case, would be the traitor ? Would it be the man who struck for the corporation, or those who sought to destroy it ?

This doctrine, if taken as laid down, cannot be sustained. It proves altogether too much ; and would, if carried out, justify any act of revolution or rebellion against the fundamental law. Knowing the soundness of Judge CATON's views generally, we do not believe that he meant to lay down and establish any such rule whatever. He undoubtedly meant that, within the scope of their authority, and to carry out any enterprise which the stockholders had *a right to* accomplish, the majority of stockholders might rule; but he never meant to say that the majority could do anything and everything they pleased, even to the destruction of the corporation itself. And in proof of this, we refer to his remarks near the close of the opinion, on page 663, where he says, in speaking of amendments to the charter, that, " If the act of acceptance by the board of directors, or other controlling power, is prompted by sinister motives, and not with a single eye to the general good of the company, it becomes fraudulent, and for that reason, void, and might, as such, be repudiated by the corporators or shareholders."

The cases of *Alton and Sangamon Railroad Company* v. *Barret*, 14 Ill. 504; *Sprague* v. *Illinois River Railroad Co.*, 19 Ill. 174; *Price* v. *Rock Island & Alton R. R. Co.*, 21 Ill. 93; and *Terre Haute & Alton R. R. Co.* v. *Earp*, 21 Ill. 293—all decided by Judge CATON, establish the doctrine that *the* charters, which *were* amended, and which were brought in question, were *not* such fundamental changes as to release the subscribers, although Judge BREESE *dissented in the case of Sprague,* and Judge WALKER delivered a long and able dissenting opinion in the case of the *Terre Haute & Alton R. R. Co.* v. *Earp*; and we respectfully submit, that the opinions of Judge BREESE and Judge WALKER are far more in consonance with the opinions of the courts of most other States in the Union than Judge CATON's. Indeed, it will be seen by comparison, that Judge CATON's theory leaves out of sight all rights of individual stockholders, and all ideas of vested rights.

3. The views of Judge BREESE are entirely different from those of Judge CATON—and he held, in the case of *Supervisors of Fulton County* v. *Miss. & Wabash R. R. Co.*, 21 Ill. 510, that where a continuous line of railroad was by an amendment to the original charter, divided up into divisions, and placed under commissioners, who should manage and control *it*, was such a fundamental change in the charter as to work a dissolution of the original contract between the corporation and the subscriber. He further said that, " the *presumption always is*, that such investments are made *with a view to the profits* to be derived from the stock subscribed *as an investment*. The expected *dividends* are to be considered as the moving cause of subscription to the stock."

He then discusses the effects of thus dividing up a continuous line of railroad, and says: " we cannot but think, in this view, that the alteration of the original charter, by dividing this great road, was fundamental, and the stockholders released from their subscriptions."

But it is argued, said the court, that the company *has accepted* the alteration, and such acceptance is binding on the subscribers. *If this is so, the stockholders would not be liable.*

In the cases referred to, *Barnet* v. *The Alton & Sangamon Railroad Company*, 13 Ill. 504; *Sprague* v. *Illinois River Railroad Company*, 19 Ill. 174; and *Illinois River Railroad Company* v. *Zimmerman*, 20 Ill. 654—it is *nowhere* intimated that fundamental changes by the legislature shall not release subscribers to stock, though those changes in the charter be *accepted* by the directors. It is only such alterations as may be fairly regarded as auxiliary to the original design."

4. The case of the *Terre Haute & Alton Railroad Company* v. *Earp*, 21 Ill. 292, was an action of assumpsit, brought against Earp, to recover the amount of ten shares of his subscription to the above named railroad. The defense set up was, that the de-defendant subscribed for the building of the railroad from Terre Haute to Alton; but after said road had been built, that the Terre Haute and Alton Railroad Company had " acquired control of the Belleville and Illinoistown Railroad, and were building the road through from Alton to Illinoistown, opposite St. Louis, which was a deflection of some twenty miles, although it made one continuous line of road, and was operated under the same management."

There is nothing in the case to show when the defendant became a subscriber; but Judge CATON, in deciding the case, said that, " by the second section of the act amending the charter of the plaintiff, passed on the 28th of February, 1854, it was *authorized to take stock in other roads, and in pursuance of that authority, it purchased a majority of the stock* of the road from Alton to Illinoistown, and this is the act set up as releasing the defendant from his subscription. That it was for *the interest* of the plaintiff to obtain control of that road, and thus secure a continuous route to Illinoistown *may be* easily appreciated, and is to be *presumed* from the fact, that it was authorized by the legislature to do so, and that in pursuance of that authority, it purchased the stock, and obtained such control. The judge then cites the cases of the *Alton and Sangamon R. R. Co.* v. *Barrett*, 13 Ill. 504; the case of *Sprague* v. *Illinois R. R. Co.*, 19 Ill. 17; the case of *Zimmer*, 20 Ill. 654; and *Price* v. *Rock Island Railroad Co.*, and thinks those sufficient.

But it is a little remarkable, that it is nowhere suggested by Judge CATON, in this case, that such a use of the funds of the company to buy other railroads, and build beyond the original terminus, might be *ultra vires* or a misapplication of the funds of the stockholders, or that it was an impairing of the obligations of the defendant's contract; but the reasons given by Judge CATON, are: 1. " That it was for the interest of the plaintiff to obtain control of that road;" and—2. " They did it in pursuance of an act of the legislature."

We have the highest respect possible, for the opinions of Judge CATON; but we most respectfully submit, that such reasons are just no reasons at all; they assume precisely what should be proved, and are entirely unsatisfactory in every way.

So unsatisfactory indeed, were they, that Judge WALKER dissented *in toto*, and, as we believe, laid down the doctrine, which is *now universally* recognized, and followed in this country."

" The plea," said Judge WALKER, " alleges that the defendant subscribed ten shares to plaintiff's road, under a charter for its construction from Terre Haute, in Indiana, to Alton, in Illinois; and that after the road was constructed, the plaintiff purchased a controlling interest in the Belleville and Illinoistown Railroad Company, and by virtue of the charter, that company constructed a railroad, from a point four miles east of Alton to Illinoistown, a distance of twenty-five miles from Alton, and that by this suit, the money subscribed by defendant is sought to be applied to this last named road, without his consent. This plea, the truth of which is *admitted* by the demurrer, raises the question of, whether the change of the charter of the company was such, when acted upon by it, as to absolve the defendant from paying his subscription.

" Any fundamental change in the charter of such a company, releases subscribers for shares from payment of the subscription.

" This rule is too familiar and *firmly* established to require a review or reference to adjudged cases.

" But the alteration, either in the charter of the company *or the* line of the road, to exonerate the subscriber for stock, must be one that *removes the* prevailing motive for the subscription, or else materially and fundamentally alters the *responsibilities and duties of the company* in a manner not provided for or contemplated by either the charter or the general laws of the State. These are principles which, it is believed, none will controvert; and if this case falls within their application, the defendant is legally discharged from payment of his subscription. The original charter of this company was for the construction of a road from Terre Haute, in the State of Indiana, to Alton, in this State; and in none of its provisions do we find any authority to purchase the Belleville and Illinoistown road or to construct this branch to Illinoistown.

" *No* such authority is either expressly or impliedly given, and its existence depends upon subsequent enactment. And when this subscription was made, no such powers could have been exercised ; and they were objects not in the contemplation of the legislature, the directors or subscribers, when the charter was granted and the company organized.

" The appropriation of the money to be raised on this subscription, at the time it was made, was not intended to be appropriated to any other purpose than the construction of a road between *the points* designated in the charter; and that was the prevailing motive which entered into and formed a part of the contract between the company and the subscribers for its stock.

" And having entered into the contract and become a part of it, *neither the legislature nor the directors* had any power to change the *terms* or *obligations* of the contract by authorizing the money to be perverted to the *purchase or construction* of other roads.

" By his subscription,this party agreed to pay the money, and the company agreed to apply it in the construction of a road between the points named in the charter; and there is *no* power to apply it to *other purposes* or on other roads, without his consent, and that is denied in the plea.

" If the legislature could authorize a change in the contract, so as to authorize the application of this money to the purchase of the

Belleville and Illinoistown road, no reason is perceived why they might not authorize *its* application to the purchase of any other road, however remote. Or, if they may authorize the construction of a branch to Illinoistown, that they may not authorize the construction of a branch to Galena or Cairo, and apply this money for the purpose.

"It is *no answer* to say that this stock *is more* valuable, since *it is not what* defendant agreed to receive for his money; and *he alone* has a right to determine whether it best promotes his interest.

"*Neither the legislature* or *directors* have a right to determine this for him. This change is *not a mere* change of location, still maintaining its points of terminus according to the original design, but *is superadding* other roads *leading to other points* of *termination*, and I think the alteration of the charter removes the prevailing motive that induced the subscription and changes essentially and materially the terminus of the road."

It may be observed, that it has been repeatedly decided in this country and England, that any misapplication of funds of a corporation is good ground for the interposition of a court of equity.

5. In the case of *Rice* v. *Rock Island and Alton Railroad Company*, 21 Ill., 95, which was a case where the defendant undertook to question the regularity of the organization of the company when sued upon his subscription, and the court decided that that could not be done; but "if it has assumed to exercise corporate functions before it had a right by law to do so—if it has usurped franchises *not* granted by the statute—that should be more properly inquired into by a direct proceeding to seize the franchises to the people and dissolve the corporation."

In the following cases, the Supreme Court decided that acts of incorporation of private corporations are contracts between the

State and the company, and cannot be changed except by the consent of both contracting parties.

> *Neustadt* v. *Ill. Cent. R. R. Co.*, 31 Ill., 484.
> *Ill. Cent. R. R. Co.* v. *The County of McLean*,
> 17 Ill., 291.

6. In the case of *Brueffett* v. *Great Western Railroad Company*, 25 Ill., 357, the court say: "*If* the legislature might release such bodies from liability to perform their engagements, or from paying their debts or damages incurred by a breach of contract, *or of duty*, they *would thereby impair the obligation of contracts existing between individuals and the company*. The exercise of such power is prohibited. As long as the company exists it must remain bound for its debts and liabilities until legally discharged. If the legislature might release the company from the liability to creditors *and stockholders* at the request of a large creditor, by enacting a transfer of the charter franchises and property, they might do the same thing at the request of a small creditor or of any other person. *If the power is admitted* in the one case, it must be in the other."

The court then goes on to show that a corporation may sell and dispose of all of its property, but the rights, privileges and franchises of the corporation remain, and *cannot be sold unless authorized by the legislature*.

7. In the case of the *City of Chicago* v. *Evans*, 24 Ill., 56, the court say, Judge WALKER delivering the opinion, that "railroads could not extend their roads beyond the line of their territorial district to which their charters limit them. And if they were to attempt to continue their roads beyond, or to construct a road outside of, those limits, under the city ordinance alone, they may *undoubtedly be prevented* by an appropriate remedy."

8. The case of *Robertson* v. *City of Rockford*, 21 Ill., 458, was a bill in equity brought by Robertson, as a tax payer, asking to have the city of Rockford enjoined from issuing bonds for $50,000 to the Kenosha, Rockford and Rock Island Railroad Company, on the ground that the city of Rockford was authorized to subscribe to the capital stock of the Kenosha and Rockford Railroad, and that since the city was thus authorized, the Kenosha and Rockford Railroad Company had consolidated with the Rockford and Rock Island Railroad Company, and therefore it was claimed that it was not the same company. The great question, it seems, was to ascertain whether cities had any power to loan their credit to aid and assist in the building of railroads, but as the court had decided that question in the case of *Prettyman* v. *Supervisors of Tazewell County*, 19 Ill., 406, that question was immediately disposed of; and as to the question of consolidation, the court said expressly, that as it appeared (see page 458) that both companies had, by their charters, express powers given them to consolidate their capital stock and use each other's roads, and " as *no objection* was urged against the manner in which the consolidation was accomplished, they therefore should regard it as regular;" and so regarding it, they then said that they must regard the power of the city to subscribe for stock still subsisting, and that, although the particular company had been consolidated with another, it was still the company created by the acts of the legislature, and all the powers of both companies were thus conferred on the company, and that the metempsychosis did not affect the city at all. This was the reasoning of the court and has no analogy to the case at bar at all.

In fine, there is not a reported case in the State of Illinois which, when examined, can be found to affect the case at bar at all; and not a solitary one where a shareholder sought to test the terms of a consolidation in any way, shape or manner.

This case is not dependent on a single adjudicated case of the State of Illinois; for no court in the State was ever called upon to pass upon such case.

How, then, can it be seriously contended that the cases of *Sprague* and *Zimmer* can have any bearing on this case. *They* lack every characteristic which could make them cases of any doubt, and were neither complicated by fraud or by any act of illegality.

The case at bar is suffused with both, and comes within the more recent case of the Grand Trunk Railroad Company, decided by Judge WALKER in the 29th Ill., 242, and of *Banet* v. *the Alton & Sangamon R. R. Company*, 13 Ill., 507.

OHIO CASES.

A subscriber to the capital stock of a railroad company cannot be compelled to pay the same when there has been, after his subscription, a substantial change in the name and powers of the corporation.

> *M. & Cin. R. R. Co.* v. *Elliott*, 10 Ohio State
> Rep., 57.
> *Coe.* v. *Col. Piq. & Ind. R. R. Co.*, 10 Ohio
> (St. Rep.), 372.

U. S. CASES.

Said Chief Justice MARSHALL, in describing the jurisdiction of the court over corporations, it belongs to it " the duty of protecting from legislative violation those *contracts* which the constitution of the country has placed beyond legislative control," and in defining the extent of the prohibition he says : " Before the formation of the constitution, a course of legislation had prevailed in many if not all the States, which weakened the confidence of man in man, and embarassed all transactions between individuals by dispensing with a *faithful* performance of engagements.

" To *correct* this mischief by *restraining* the power which produced it, the State legislatures were *forbidden* to pass any law impairing the obligation of contracts; that is, of contracts respecting property under which some individual could claim a right to something beneficial to himself."

And, acting upon this understanding, and influenced by these considerations, we find that the United States Supreme Court have, over and over again, decided that the grants to c rporations must, in the first p ace, be construed in the strictest manner possible; but when the grants have been established, that they will be prote ted, and that as the rights of a corporation are thus protected, the rights of the *corporators* which arise under the charter, will also be protected.

The first class of cases are illustrated by—

> *Ohio Life Ins. Trust Co.* v. *Debolt,* 16 How. 472.
>
> *Piqua Branch of the State Bank of Ohio* v. *Knoop,* 16 How. 369.
>
> *Dodge* v. *Woolsey,* 18 How. 361.
>
> *Charles River Bridge* v. *Warren,* 11 Peters, 420.
>
> *Providence Bank* v. *Billings,* 4 Peters, 461.
>
> *Dartmouth College* v. *Woodward,* 4 Wheat. 518—553.

And numerous others, which will readily occur to the court.

And the second, by *Clearwater* v. *Meridith,* 1 Wallace, 39, which we insist is perfectly decisive of this entire case.

V.

The Funds and Capital Stock of the Company are Trust Funds, and are held for the benefit of Creditors and Stockholders, and can never legally be diverted to any other purpose whatever than is provided in the Charter.

The sound doctrine of equity is, that the capital or property and debts due to banking, trading and other moneyed corporations, constitute a trust fund, pledged to the payment of the dues of creditors and stockholders, and a court of equity will lay hold of this fund, into whosoever hands it may pass, and collect and apply it to the purposes of the trust.

Angel & Ames on Corporations, sec. 779.

In the case of *MacGregor* v. *The Official Manager of the Deal and Dover, etc., R. Company*, 16 L. Law & Eq. R. 180—

The chairman of the South Eastern Railway Company promised the managing committee of a proposed railway company that, in consideration of their not abandoning their project and intention of applying to parliament for an act to authorize the making of the proposed line, the South Eastern Railway Company would, in case of rejection of the scheme, insure the company of which the plaintiffs were the managing committee, against loss which might be occasioned to such preposed railway company by such rejection and failure, and would defray and pay all expenses incurred by them in endeavoring to obtain the act. The South Eastern Railway Company, by their acts, were authorized to apply their funds for certain purposes only, not including the payment of the costs of the proposed proceeding in parliament:

Held, That the agreement was void, as it was an agreement made by contracting parties (who must be presumed to have full knowledge of the powers conferred on the South Eastern Railway Company by their acts of parliament, which were public acts) that *that* company should do an act which was illegal, contrary to public policy and the provisions of the statutes.

Alderson, B., in rendering the decision, says:

" The question, we think, is determined by the decision of the Court of Common Pleas, in the *East Anglican Railway Company* v. *The Eastern Counties Railway Company*. It is there laid down that a railway company incorporated by act of parliament, is bound to *apply all the funds of the company for the purposes directed and provided for by the act, and for no other purpose whatever;* and that the defendants having *inter alia* covenanted to pay the costs of soliciting bills then pending in parliament, it was held, that the act incorporating the defendants, being a *public act*, must be presumed to be known to the plaintiffs, and that they could not recover, inasmuch as the covenant entered into by the defendants, was beyond the scope of their authority as a corporation, and was, therefore, illegal and void." The court there say, such a contract is illegal, because it is *contrary to the act* of parliament which was passed to give them certain powers as a corporation for public purposes of advantage to the country at large, as well as for the private gain of the individual members of the corporation, and they add that the actual assent of the whole body of shareholders would make no real difference in the matter.

The East Anglican R. Co. v. *The Eastern Counties Railway Company*, 21 L. Rep., (N. S.), and especially referred to in *Mac Gregor* v. *The Official Manager of the Deal & Dover R. Co.*, 16 Eng. L. & Eq., 182.

This case holds that corporations should be held to the strict letter of their powers, *in every respect.*

22 N. Y. 258.

1 Am. Law Reg. (N. S.) 241.

In the case of *Anglican Railway Company* v. *Eastern Counties Railway Company*, 7 Eng. L. & Eq., 508—the court say:

" This act is a public act, accessible to all, and the plaintiffs must therefore be presumed to have dealt with the defendants with a full knowledge of their respective rights, whatever those may be. It is clear that the defeudants have a limited authority only, and a corporation only for the purpose of making and maintaining the railway sanctioned by the act, and that their funds can only be applied for the purposes directed and provided by the statute. Indeed, it is not contended, that a company so constituted can engage in new trades not contemplated by their act; but it is said, that they may embark in other undertakings, however various, provided the object of the directors be to increase the profit of their own railway. This, in truth, is the same proposition in another form ; if the company cannot carry on a new trade, because it is not contemplated by the act, they cannot embark in other undertakings not sanctioned by their act, merely because they hope the speculation may ultimately increase the profit of the shareholders.

" They cannot engage in a new trade, because they are a corporation only for the purpose of making and maintaining the Eastern Counties Railway. What additional power do they acquire from the fact that the undertaking may in some way benefit their line, whatever be their object or the prospect of success ?"

In the case of the *Caledonian R. Co.* v. *the Helensburgh Harbor Trustees*, 39 Eng. L. & Eq., 31, the Lord Chancellor (Lord CRANWORTH) (1856–7) said :

" When a capitalist, believing in the probable success of any particular project sanctioned by the legislature, is satisfied with the terms of incorporation embodied in the act, he reasonably advances his money on the *faith of those terms*, and if the project turns out a failure he has no right to complain. The speculation was one as to the prudence of which he had the means of judging, and no injustice is done to him, if, in the result, he sustains a loss. But surely, the case is very different, if, behind the terms of incorporation expressed in the act, there are others of which the public has no notice, but which are to be held equally binding on the shareholders, as if they formed a part of the charter of incorporation. If such secret or unexpressed terms are to be held binding on those who take shares, the result may be ruinous to those who act on the faith of what appears on the face of the legislative incorporation.

" The principle on which all railway acts, and acts of a similar character proceed, is, to specify the sum to be raised and the shares into which the funds of the company are to be divided, to incorporate the shareholders and to prescribe the objects to which the funds are to be applied.

" It is inconsistent with the policy of such acts to hold that there can be any other terms binding than what appear on the face of the act itself.

" Not only is such a doctrine calculated to occasion injury to shareholders, but it may often be a fraud, or at all events, a surprise on the legislature. The statutory powers are given on the faith of the terms apparent on the act itself.

" It may well be that the additional terms, if communicated to parliament, would have prevented the passing of the act at all.

" Special terms as to particular cases, or particular persons, are often made the subject of special clauses, and then neither the legislature nor any persons taking shares can complain.

" The whole truth is disclosed; the legislature sanctions the special provision and the shareholder purchases with full notice of the exceptional enactment."

Again, as to the misapplication of funds.

The court say, in the same case on page 38, that it is in vain to say that such an application of the funds *might*, if the projected branch line from Dunbarton to Helensburgh had been made, have been beneficial to the railway company. It is sufficient answer to such a suggestion, that it is not the purpose for which the shareholders subscribed their money, and there are numerous authorities, both in England and Scotland, to show that such a diversion of the funds from their statutory destination cannot be permitted.

Any shareholder in a railway company may, by legal proceedings, prevent its directors from applying its funds to a purpose not authorized by the act of incorporation.

It is not necessary to refer to authorities in support of this proposition. They have, in the course of the last twenty years, been very numerous both in England and in Scotland.

Again, on page 39, the court says: It is not enough (for the company) to show that the proposed application of the funds will be beneficial to the company. That can only be matter of opinion. The question is not whether it will be beneficial, but whether it will be beneficial in the mode sanctioned by the act.

If the branch line had been carried to Helensburgh, the construction of a pier and harbor there would probably have been useful to the railway company by increasing the facilities for their traffic; but there is nothing in the railway act which authorizes such a mode of dealing with the money of the shareholders.

See authorities cited at commencement of this case.

12 Conn., 499–530; 16 *id.*, 593.

Chapman et al. v. *M., R. & L. E. R. R. Co. and S. C. & I. R. R. Co.*, 6 Ohio State, 136, decides that a fundamental change in the charter of a railroad company cannot be effected without the consent of *all* the stockholders.

In the case of the *Mayor, &c., of Norwich* v. *the Norfolk Railway Company*, 30 Eng. Law & Eq. Rep., 120, which was an action upon a deed, whereby defendants covenanted that they should forfeit and pay to plaintiffs the sum of £1,000 on failure to erect certain works within a given time.

ERLE J. says: It remains to be considered whether this contract was illegal, as not authorized by the act incorporating the defendants' company, and therefore prohibited by that act. The case of the *East Anglican Railway Company* v. *the Eastern Counties Railway Company*, 16 Jur., 249, 250; S. C., 7 Eng. Rep., 505, is the leading case in support of this objection, where it was held that a contract by the defendants to pay the costs of the plaintiffs, incurred in an application to parliament for a bill, was not authorized; and was, therefore, prohibited by a statute incorporating the defendants for the purpose of *making, maintaining, and working their own railway;* the present defendants contending that, as they were incorporated for the *purposes of making, maintaining and working the railway specified* in their act, *the only contracts authorized* are those for the *work and materials necessary for executing those purposes, and all others are prohibited, and the present* contract, to pay compensation in respect of a deviation, *is not within the authorized class* of contracts, *and is prohibited.*

It may be presumed, probably, without dispute, that *parliament, in granting powers to a company incorporated for certain public purposes, prohibited, by implication,* the intentional use of those powers in order to defeat the purposes of the incorporation ; and I collect from the authorities that it is upon this principle, when applied to contracts, that certain contracts are held *to be prohibited by implication.* If a company is incorporated for the purpose of *making, maintaining and working a railway—and various powers,* among others, powers of raising funds, are granted for executing that purpose, *any diverting of the funds* so raised for that purpose of incorporation, and applying them to a purpose unconnected therewith, would be an intentional use of the powers granted for the purpose of the incorporation, in order to defeat that purpose ; for, if the appropriate funds are lost, the purpose probably will not be effected. So a contract for a purpose unconnected with *the purpose of incorporation, is or may result in an* application of the funds to a purpose unconnected with the purpose of incorporation, and is, therefore, held to be prohibited and void.

In respect, also, of the subject matter of the suit: *the question in equity is, whether the interest of the shareholder is put into hazard to an unreasonable degree beyond what he is presumed to have assented to in subscribing—and, if so, his interest is protected according to equity.*

The *principle of a limited power in corporations* to contract is founded *on the soundest principle*, and established by several cases: it may be enough to refer to two only, cited in the argument, one in equity, and the other in law—*Colman* v. *the Eastern Counties Railway Company*, before Lord LANGDALE, 10 Beav., 1, and the *East Anglican Railway Company* v. *the Eastern Counties Railway Company*, 11 C. B., 755; S. C. 7 Eng. Rep., 505. This latter case was cited with approval, and acted upon, in the Court of Exchequer Chamber, in *MacGregor* v. *the Official Manager of the Deal & Dover Railway Company*, 17 Jur., 21; S. C. 16 Eng. Rep., 180, and it was there considered that a "railway company incorporated by act of parliament was bound to apply *all the funds* of the company for the purposes directed and provided for by the act, and for no other purpose whatever," and that a *contract* to do *something beyond these purposes was a contract to do an illegal act;* the illegality of which, appearing by the provisions of a public act of parliament, must be taken to be known to all the world.

Where a corporation has been created for the purpose of carrying on a particular trade, *or making a railway from one place to another*, and it attempts to substitute another trade, or to make its railway to another place, the objection is to its entire want of power for the new purpose; its life and functions are the creation of the legislature, and they do not exist for any other than the specified purpose; for any other, the members are merely incorporated individuals.

If the directors of a railway company were to enter into a contract, under the seal of the company, for the purchase of a large quantity of iron rails, and to pay for them at a fixed price, as the vendor had reasonable grounds for supposing that the rails were wanted for the purpose of the railroad, it would be no defence to an action for the price, or for not accepting them, that the rails were illegally purchased on speculation, to be resold by the directors for their own profit. But, suppose that the directors of a railway company should purchase a thousand gross of green spectacles as a speculation, and should put the seal of the company to a deed covenanting to pay for the these goods, here would be a clear excess of authority on the part of the directors; this excess of authority would necessarily be known to the covenantee, and he, being *in pari delicto*, I conceive that the maxim would apply, "*potior est conditio possidentis.*" This would be an illegal contract, to misapply the funds of the company, and the illegality might be set up as a defence.

The *Equity Reports abound with cases* in which injunctions have been granted against the application of the funds of such companies *to purposes not authorized by the acts of parliament creating them, although professedly for the benefit of the shareholders;* and I apprehend that a contract, against the performance of which an injunction would be granted in equity, *must be* considered *illegal and void at law*, on proof that, to the knowledge of both parties, it is beyond the power of the directors, and leads to a misappropriation of the funds of the company.

In the case of *Cunliffe* v. *The Manchester and Bolton Canal Company*, 2 Russ. & Mylne, 481, the court said :

" It is a breach of trust towards a shareholder in a joint stock incorporated company, established for certain definite purposes, prescribed by its charter, if the funds or credit of the company are, *without his consent, diverted from such purpose*, though the misapplication be sanctioned by the votes of a majority; and, therefore, he may file a bill in equity against the company in his own behalf, to restrain the company by injunction from any such diversion or misapplication."

In *Ware* v. *Grand Junction Water Company*, 2 Russ. & Mylne, Lord Brougham said :

" Indeed, an investment in the stock of a corporation must, by every one, be considered a wild speculation, if it exposed the owners of the stock to all sorts of risk in support of plausible projects not set forth and authorized by the act of incorporation, and which may possibly lead to extraordinary losses."

Bagshaw v. *The Eastern Counties Railway Co.*, and the celebrated case of *Coleman* v. *Same Co.*, 10 Bevan's Reports, 10, are all quoted with approbation, in *Dodge* v. *Woolsey*, 18 How., by the court.

Capital Stock of Corporations is a Trust Fund.

The capital stock of a corporation, both that which has actually been paid in, and that which remains unpaid, is regarded in law, *as a trust fund*, in which creditors and stockholders are alike ininterested. And *it cannot be diverted to any other purpose, than the purpose for which it was subscribed and paid..*

Adler v. *Mil. Pat. Brick Co.*, 13 Wis. 57.

In *Bagshaw* v. *Eastern Counties Railway Company*, 7 How. Ch. R. 114; and *Colman* v. *Eastern Counties Railway Company*, 16 Beav. Ch. R., the same doctrine is held. In the last case, it was contended, that the corporation might pledge, without limit, the funds of the company, for the encouragement of other transactions, however various and extensive, *provided the object* of that liability was to increase the traffic upon the railway, and thereby to increase the traffic to the shareholders. But the Master of the Rolls, Lord LANGDALE, said: "There was no authority for anything of the kind." It is not only illegal for a corporation to apply its *capital* to objects not contemplated by its charter, but also so to apply its *profits;* and, therefore, a shareholder may maintain a bill in equity against the directors of the company, to *have refunded* to them any of the profits thus improperly applied. It is an improper application for a railway company to invest the profits of the company in the purchase of shares in another company, and it cannot be authorized by legislative sanction. "The *dividend*," says Lord LANGDALE, Master of the Rolls, in *Solomons* v. *Laing*, 14 Jurist for Dec., 1840, "which belongs to the shareholders, and is divisible among them, may be applied by them severally as their *own* property; but the company itself, or the directors, or any number of shareholders, assembled at a meeting or otherwise, have no right to dispose of the shares of the general dividends, which belong to the particular shareholder, in any manner contrary to the will, or without the consent or authority of that particular shareholder."

The funds of the company cannot be applied to any other purpose whatever than for the specific objects pointed out in the charter.

In *Munt* v. *The Shrewsbury and Chester Railway Company*, 3 Eng. L. & Eq., 149, the court say: " This company was established for the construction of a railway. It became important, that the railway should afford an outlet to the minerals produced from the lands near which it passed. It was to come up to the banks of the River Dee, upon which the company was authorized to erect wharves and warehouses. I find no fault with the statement, that the company was not only a railway company, but also a company for the erection of wharves and warehouses, in which they might have a very extensive business, and it could not fail to be known to everybody connected with the railway, that they were materially interested in the navigation of the River Dee ; it might also be supposed, that they knew the state of the navigation, and it must be concluded, that the railway, and the wharves and warehouses, were constructed with reference to the known state of the river; and that it was supposed to be sufficient for the railway company to make the railway, and the wharves and warehouses, profitable, with reference to the then existing state of the navigation. If it had been thought necessary to improve the navigation of the River Dee for the purposes of this railway, there seems to be no reason why powers to contribute towards that improvement should not have been contained in the 12 and 13 Vict., c. 55, as well as powers to construct the wharves and warehouses which must have had reference to the navigation. But it is perfectly clear, that it was not contemplated by any of the acts of Parliament; they contain no words authorizing the employment of the capital in any way relating to the navigation ; but, on the contrary, they seem to exclude any such intention. It is subsequently discovered by the company, that the navigation of the River Dee is not so good as formerly, and that it is deteriorating to such an extent,that there has been a report made, upon a government commission, that it will, in time, be checked, unless effective means are taken to prevent it. This was information important to the railway company, whose prosperity depended probably, materially, on the navigation of the river being kept in a good state, and it was natural they should wish not only to prevent the deterioration of the navigation, but, if possible, to improve it ; and had there been funds applicable, it would, no doubt, have been advantageous to the company, to have employed them in improving the navigation of the river, and it might have been a most useful and profitable application of those funds ; but as the acts of parliament contain no powers which extend to this case, the company, who *have funds applicable only to the particular purposes authorized by the act of Parliament, cannot apply them to any other purpose.* I do not think that this question has ever been before the House of Lords ; but, so far as the power of the Court of Chancery extends, *it has unalterably decided, that companies possessed of funds for objects which are distinctly defined by act of parliament, cannot be allowed to apply them for any other purpose whatever, however beneficial or advantageous it may appear, either to the company, or to individual members of the company.*

NOTA BENA.—*Coleman* v. *Eastern Counties Railway Co.*, 10 Beav. 1.

Bagshaw v. *Eastern Union R. Co.*, 6 Railway Cases, 152.

East Anglican Railway Co. v. *Eastern Counties R. Co.*, 7 Eng. Law & Eq. 505.

McGregor v. *Official Manager of Deal and Dover R. Co.*, 16 Eng. & Eq. 180.

March v. *Eastern R. R Co.*, 43, N. H. 515.

This was a bill in equity, filed by March, and a few others who joined with him; and who together represented about 500 shares out of a capital of some three million dollars—the shares being one hundred dollars each. The circumstances of the case were substantially these : The Eastern Railroad Company of New Hampshire was authorized by statute of 1839, to lease a part or the whole of its road to such person or corporation on *such* terms as *might be deemed proper*. On the 18th of February, 1840, a lease was made to the Eastern Railway of Massachusetts for ninety-nine years, of the entire line of the New Hampshire road, on a rental which was specially reserved to be paid out of the joint earnings of the road.

The vote of the New Hampshire Company, which was supposed to authorize the lease, recites that the two companies had by concurrent votes, " agreed to unite their routes and capitals as a basis of dividends," and empowered the president and directors to carry into effect this vote, and make such stipulations to effect the true meaning and purpose of said union and of said corporations as they should find proper.

After this, additional powers were granted upon the subject of this union, by the legislature of Massachusetts. After the lease had been made, several branch roads were built, by the concurrent action of the two companies, shares taken in other roads—all to increase the business, as it was claimed. The shareholders received their dividends, without any question, up to July, 1854, when the " consolidated " company ceased. The net income of both roads having been applied to reduce the large debt contracted by the Massachusetts company, in building a continuous track into Boston, in building branch roads and in taking stock in continuous roads. The plaintiffs were interested in the stock of the New Hampshire company, at the time of filing their bill, but only one was an owner of shares before June, 1859, when the transfers of stock terminated ; and hence, it was contended, that under no circumstances could any one but Jones, who held no stock prior to that date, obtain any share of the rent. It was held by the court, that as the original charter authorized a lease to be made upon such terms and conditions as might be agreed upon ; and the lease having been made by the assent of *all* the stockholders, that the directors of both roads, and the majority of the stockholders, must conduct and administer said roads accordingly, and that their liability to the stockholders was just the same as if it had been done by the legislature. But that the lease and the terms and conditions, although the earnings of the roads, and the incomes had been all mixed up and blended together, did not provide for a union of interest or of the capitals of the respective roads, or of an equality of dividends between the stockholders of the two corporations.

It was further held, that "such lease or contract between the roads must be construed with reference to the objects proposed by the existing charters of each at the time the lease or contract was made, and its construction or operation can not be effected or changed by any change of the plans, purposes, or objects of the corporation without or beyond the existing scope of their chartered powers at the time of the making of such lease or contract.

Such roads may, as between themselves, vary the terms of their agreement or contract with each other, and may consent to a different appropriation of the funds, profits, or dividends from that provided for in the original contract; but stockholders in either roads, who have not thus assented, may, in equity, hold both corporations to perform their original contract, and apply their funds and profits in the way *provided for in the original contract*, so far as relates to themselves.

Hence, when the fundamental contract between two roads provides that all disputes between the two roads shall be settled by arbitration, and one road has made an illegal misapplication of funds or profits belonging to both, *with the assent of a majority of the other* road, if stockholders in the latter road, not thus assenting, bring their bill to recover their share of such profits, this court *will enjoin both* roads, if necessary, from settling or attempting to settle the claims, made by such stockholders, by arbitration.

The dividends which are divisible among the shareholders of a corporation must be considered *as their own property*, and can not be applied by the directors to any purpose not included in their charter, or fundamental contract, without the consent of such shareholders.

To constitute an illegal application of the funds or money of a corporation, it is *not necessary* that *there should be any intentional wrong or actual fraud ;* and to give this court jurisdiction in equity in such a case, the plaintiff need *not* allege or prove *any* such actual and willful fraud or collusion on the part of the company or companies, or the directors thereof.

But when the money that should have been divided among the stockholders has been applied by a company or companies to a purpose not warranted by, and not within the scope of, the charter, or fundamental articles of agreement, that constitutes a sufficient illegality to give a court of equity jurisdiction, and such proceedings of a majority of such company or companies, and of the governing body or power thereof in such cases, will be treated in equity as a breach of trust toward the minority, and as a fraud upon them, if they have not assented to such misapplication ; and courts of equity will prevent such illegal application of such funds or profits, and such fraud and breach of trust, by injunction, and will relieve against it when committed, at the suit of such stockholders as have not assented thereto.

Cohen v. *Wilkinson et al., the Directors of the Direct London & Portsmouth R. Co., and the Corporation,* 5 R. Cases, 565. Cohen was a shareholder (and it does not appear that he was the owner of more than one share) in the Direct London and Portsmouth Railroad Company, which was chartered to build a railway from London to Portsmouth. After building a portion of the railway the company resolved to abandon the project ; but about one month before their powers for taking land had expired, in consequence of an agreement with another railway company, they determined, with the assent of the majority of the stockholders present at a general meeting convened for that purpose, to complete four miles of the railway, as far as L., and then stop. The court held that such a proceeding was illegal, and contrary to the charter, to use the funds for the purpose of completing the road to L. alone, *because* the funds were obtained for building the *entire* line specified in the charter, and not to L. alone, and an injunction granted accordingly. In deciding this case, Lord Langdale said, (see pages 571–2) that

"The plaintiff is a person who has subscribed and *paid his money*, no doubt *on the faith of an undertaking sanctioned* in parliament on the ground of its being expected and intended to produce public benefits by its completion. His object may be his own particular benefit, *but his advances are made on a scheme, the whole of which must be considered as that which alone has been approved and authorized by parliament*, which is to be *conducted* and *managed* in the way approved by parliament, for the deed proposed by parliament, and for *no other* end, and the governing body of which must be considered to have entered *into the obligation* to complete the work authorized. *It is on these expectations that the shareholders become members;* and I am of opinion that they *are entitled to have these expectations realized, if they can be.* The company is *not like* a partnership for general trading—a partnership in which *one portion of the business may be encouraged* and *another discouraged* or *abandoned*, according to the contingencies of trade, and in which there is a general authority to use the capital to the best advantage; but it is a partnership for a public purpose, for effecting a work which it is a duty to complete, and for *which alone the capital is advanced in shares*, or authorized to be raised. The *obligation* to complete the work appears to me to be *co-extensive with the authority to make it.* Neither this act, nor any of these acts, contains authority to substitute a less work, or part, for the whole; and if the governors or directors of the company take on themselves to determine that they will not perform the whole work, but will apply the *capital collected* on the faith of the whole work being completed, in completing only a part of it, I am of opinion that the determination is without authority, and contrary to the provisions of the act of parliament."

This case is of a novel character, but it shows how strict the English courts are in compelling corporations to carry out the *very object* specified, and that they can neither stop short of it, or go beyond it.

In *Hichens* v. *Congreve*, 4 Russell, 576, the Lord Chancellor said: "The suit is instituted by certain shareholders on behalf of themselves, and all others who may choose to come in and take the benefit of the suit.   *   *   *

" Here is a fund in which all the shareholders are interested; £15,000 has been improperly taken out of it; a fraud has been committed on them all.   Is it necessary that all should come into a court of justice for the purpose of joining in a suit with a view to obtain redress?   It is possible that the number of shareholders may be six thousand, for the capital of the company is fixed by the act of parliament at £300,000 divided into shares of £50 each and justice never could be obtained, if any very great number of plaintiffs were put on the record.   It is said that there is nothing on the face of the bill which shows that the shareholders are so numerous, that they could not all be joined as parties without inconvenience.   I think it does appear sufficiently that if all were joined the number of complainants would be inconveniently great; first, because the shares are 6,000 in number; and, secondly, because it appears, by the act of parliament, that there were then upwards of two hundred shareholders.   It is clear, therefore, that justice would be unattainable, if all the shareholders were required to be parties to this suit.

It having been suggested that each shareholder should bring a suit, the Lord Chancellor said: " In the present case, it appears to me, that justice may be done in one suit.   All the shareholders stand in the same situation; the property has been taken out of their common fund; they are entitled to have that property bought back again for the benefit of the concern.

" When all parties stand in the same situation, and have one common right, and one common interest, in what respect can it be inconvenient that two, or three, or more, should sue, in their own names, for the benefit of all?"

See, also—
Wallworth v. *Holt*, 4 Myl. & Cr., 619.
Burbridge v. *Burton*, 2 Beav., 539, 559.
Story's Eq. Pl., 74, 113, 126; Lube's Eq. Pl. 22 & n. 1.
Foss v. *Harbottle*, 2 Hare, 489.

In this last case the court say, distinctly, that, " if a transaction be void, and not merely voidable, the corporation cannot confirm it so as to bind a dissenting minority of its members." See page 505. See, also, *Preston* v. *Grand Collier Co.*, 11 Simons, 327.

In the case of *Bromley* v. *Smith*, 1 Simons, 11, the court said: " Where a matter is, necessarily, injurious to the common right, the majority of the persons interested can neither excuse the wrong, nor deprive all other parties of their remedy by suit.

"The attorney-general may file an information, in a case like this, in respect of the public nature of the right; and the proceeding must be by the attorney-general where *all persons* are parties to the abuse; but where that is not the case, I am not aware of any."

In *Bagshaw* v. *the Eastern Union Railway Company*, (6 R. Cases, 136,) the Lord Chancellor said:

" I am clearly of the opinion, that those who subscribed for the purposes of the two acts have a right to *have their money applied to the purposes held out to them,* not only by those acts, but by the resolutions of the company, stating the purposes for which their money was to be applied ; and, upon the authority of the case I have before referred to, *I entertain no doubt that the parties have a right which this court will enforce; for I find the positive allegation, that they not only intend to misapply the money, and apply it for other purposes, but that they have actually done so, and intend to persevere in so doing.* On the authority of the case I have referred to, *it is equity* that the *party whose money has been so applied*, and which *is intended* to be *hereafter so applied,* is *entitled to the interposition of this court,* for the *purpose* of *keeping the company,* in the application of his money, to those purposes *for which it was said it was to be advanced."*

VI.

Rights of Shareholders.

The shares of stock owned by the complainant in this case, represent : 1 — property ; 2 — rights and privileges, of which he cannot be divested except by his own consent—and in the exercise of which rights, the law will protect him.

March v. *Eastern Railroad Co.,* 43 N. H. 520.

The court say : " The purchaser of a share of stock in a corporation, takes the share with all its incidents ; and among these is the right to receive *all future dividends—that is, its proportionate share of all profits* not then divided ; and, as we understand the law and the usage of such corporations, it is wholly immaterial at what times or from what sources these profits have been earned ; they are an incident to the share to which a purchaser becomes at once entitled, provided he remains a member of the corporation until a dividend is made. *Harris* v. *Stevens,* 7 N. H. 454 ; *Hagur* v. *Dandesen,* 2 Exch. 741 ; *Rogers* v. *Huntington Bank,* 12 S & R. 77."

The court also particularly refers to the case of *Stevens* v. *Rutland and Burlington R. R. Co.,* 29 Vt. 545 ; and the case of *Cole-*

man v. *Eastern Counties Railway*, 5 Eng. Railw. Cases, 573 — in which he says, it was held that directors have no right to enter into, or to pledge the funds of the company in support of any project not pointed out by their act, although such project may tend to increase the traffic upon the railway, and may be assented to by a majority of the stockholders, and the object of such project may not be against public policy, and that acquiescence by shareholders in such a project, for ever so long time, affords no presumption of its legality.

> *Macedon Plank Road Company* v. *Lapham*,
> 18 Barb. 312.
> Redfield on R., 92.

New York Cases.

Mechanics' Bank v. *New York and New Haven R. R. Co.*,
3 Kern. 617.

In this case, Comstock, J., said : " The thirty thousand shares of original stock subscribed and paid for by the persons to whom the genuine certificates were issued, belonged to them in their individual rights, and were as much their separate and *individual property, as any other possession,* which they could acquire.

" The entire capital was represented in the property and franchises of the corporation, and *the owner of each share was entitled to a fixed and unalterable proportion of that capital.*

" And from this, it follows, that any attempts to create a greater number of shares by the issue of additional certificates, is not only a violation of the organic law of the corporation, but a direct invasion of the contract between it and each holder of the original stock. Now, while it cannot be denied, that the value of every share may be reduced by misfortune or accident in the management of the business of the corporation, or by the neglect and misconduct of its agents, acting within their acknowledged powers, it is equally plain that this result cannot be effected by a change in the fixed proportion which each share bears to the aggregate number. It has been said, that the limitation of the capital, and the number of shares was imposed from considerations of public policy alone. This is not so. *Those who asked for the charter, and proposed to invest their private capital in the enterprise which it contemplated, required such a limitation for their own protection; and every individual who subscribed and paid for shares of stock, must be deemed to have done so, relying upon the charter for the safety of his investment.*" On page 627, the court said : " Certificates of stock are not securities for money in any sense— much less are they negotiable securities. They are simply the *muniments and evidence of the holder's title to a given share in the property and franchises of the corporation of which he is a member.* The *primary use and design, I must be allowed to say, of this species of property, is to afford a steady investment for capital rather than to feed the spirit of speculation.* I am aware that people will speculate in stocks, as they sometimes do in lands, and there is no law which absolutely forbids it ; but such, I am persuaded, is not the use, for which we should hold them, chiefly intended.

" The question is capable of some further elucidation, by attending to the rules which have been settled in regard to the transferability of other instruments, and the effect of transfer. A certificate of stock is, in some respects, like a bill of lading, or a warehouse or wharfinger's receipt. Each is *the representation of property existing under certain conditions,* and the documentary evidence of the title thereto. They are all alike transferable by endorsement and delivery. And the *title to the property thus represented* passes by such transfer. So far, they resemble each other—but there are distinctions to be noted. Bills of lading and wharfinger's receipts, are commercial instruments, and their transferability, or, as it is sometimes termed, their *quasi* negotiability, depends on the custom of merchants, and the conveniences of trade. Certificates of stock are not commercial instruments, and the title to the property they represent, passes in equity only by indorsement and delivery, where, by any law or rule of the corpor- ation, the transfer is required to be made on the books. With these resemblances and these distinctions, if a bill of lading is not negotiable in the sense which must be contended for in the present case, there is much greater difficulty in affirming that such a quali- ty belongs to a stock certificate."

The court further said on page 626–7 : " Stocks are not like bank bills, the immediate representative of money and intended for cir- culation.

" The distinction between a bank bill and a share of bank stock it is not difficult to appreciate. Nor are they, like notes and bills of exchange, less adapted to circulation, but invented to supply the exigencies ot commerce, and governed by the peculiar code of the commercial law. They are not like exchequer bills and gov- ernment securities, which are made negotiable, either for circula- tion, or to find a market. Nor are they like corporation bonds, which are issued in *negotiable form* for sale, and as a means for raising money for corporate uses."

When a subscription is made to the capital stock of an existing corporation, if the corporation accepts the subscription, it no doubt impliedly undertakes, that the subscriber *shall have and enjoy a share of its property* and franchises, corresponding to the *amount* of the subscription.

So, in the present case, the law would raise by implication such a promise on the part of this corporation, the instant it was brought into existence, and as the defendant had suffered his subscription to stand unrevoked up to that time, it was the same in effect as if then for the first time made.

In this way, both mutuality and a sufficient consideration, are shown.

Buffalo & N. Y. City R. R. Co. v. *Dudley,*
4 Kern, 354, (14 N. Y.)

A suit may be maintained against officers of a corporation for the fraudulent over issue of stock by any stockholder, injured thereby, through the depreciation of his stock, and such suit may be against such officers, jointly.

Cazfaux v. *Mali,* 25 Barb. 578.

The term " capital stock," in an act of incorporation, means the *amount* contributed, or *advanced by the stockholders* as members of the company.

The State v. *Morristown Fire Association,* 3 Zabr. 195.

Pennsylvania Cases.

Everhart v. *Philadelphia & Westchester R. R. Co.,* 28 Penn. 352, the court said, in regard to a shareholder's rights : " That by acquiring an interest in the corporation, therefore, he enters into an obligation with it in the nature of a *special contract,* the terms of which are limited by the specific provisions, rights and liabilities, detailed in the act of incorporation."

To make a valid change in this private contract, as in any other, the assent of both parties is indispensable.

Commonwealth v. *Erie and North East Railroad Company,* 27 Penn., 351. This case is *directly in point,* and decides that a corporation can take nothing by *construction,* and will be confined to its exact and plain powers specified in the charter.

Commonwealth v. *Pittsburgh and Connellsville R. R. Co.,* 24 Penn. 160, is excellent.

Lauman v. *The Lebanon Valley R. R. Co.*,
30 Penn, 47, 48, and 49.
Erie & North East. R. R. Co. v. *Casey*, 26
Penn. 201.

Shares of stock in railroad companies, are personal property.
Johns v. *Johns*, 1 Ohio State, 356.
Arnold v. *Ruggles*, 1 R. I. 165.

Fry's Executors v. *Lexington & Big Sandy R. R. Co.*, 2 Metcalf's
Ky., 321, the court say:

Each shareholder, in an incorporated company, has a right to insist on the prosecution of the particular objects of the charter.

He cannot be deprived of his rights or privileges without his assent. Such alterations of the charter as are necessary to carry into effect its main design, may be made without his consent.

But an alteration which materially and fundamentally changes the responsibilities and duties of the company, or which superadds an entirely new enterprise to that which was originally contemplated, may be resisted by the stockholders, unless such alterations are provided for in the charter itself, or in the general laws of the State in force, at the time the act of incorporation was passed. The charter of this road contains no provision authorizing amendments to be made, nor was there any general law in force at the time it was granted, by which they were authorized.

The *subscribers*, therefore, *who do not assent* to the amendment, have the right, if they think proper, to exercise it to prevent the company from proceeding to act under the amended charter, and to compel it to confine its operations solely to the promotion of the objects designed to be accomplished by the original charter. Or, they may waive this right, permit the company to proceed under the amended charter, and dissolve their connection with it upon equitable terms. Being members of the corporation, they are entitled to *all the rights and privileges* conferred by the charter, *of which they cannot be deprived by the act of the company in accepting an amendment to which they are opposed, and which produces a material and radical change in their rights,* and in *the duties and liabilities of the company.*

Redfield on R., p. 422, note 14; Id., 23.

In the case of *Nazro* v. *Merchants Mutual Ins. Co.*, 14 Wis., 301, the court say, that, " the company having set on foot measures by which dissenting members have been deprived of the chartered *rights and privileges,* on the faith of which they invested their money, ought not to object to any fair proceeding by which they seek a return of it.

"Their claims are most equitable, and every principle of natural justice would seem to require that they should be protected. The amendatory acts were, in effect, a grant of authority to the trustees to organize a new company for the same general purposes, but upon entirely different principles, with the privilege to such members of the old company, as wished, to convert their premium certificates into the stock of the new. The new company was to take the place of the old, which was to cease, and such holders of premium certificates, as refused to convert them into stock, were to have no voice in the management of its affairs. The result is, that the new organization has, without their consent, become possessed of so much of the funds of these dissenting certificate holders, which it is against conscience for it to retain.

*   *   *   *   *   *   *   *

" The capital stock of incorporated companies is a trust fund ; the *proper application* of which, courts of equity will enforce by virtue of their inherent jurisdiction over trusts and frauds."

Willard's Eq., 739–40.

Zabriskie v. C. C. C. R. R. Co., 23 How. 394.

The Proprietors of the Union Locks and Canals v. *Joseph Towne,* 1 N. H., 44.

This was an action brought to recover assessments on stock which had been subscribed for by defendant, in a corporation to render the Merrimac River navigable from Reed's Ferry to Amoskeag Falls.

The defence was, that, after the subscription, the purpose and scope of the corporation had been materially changed, and that an amendment had been procured, giving authority to extend the work to Cromwell's Falls.

In deciding this case, Judge WOODBURY said: " This is a dispute between a private corporation and one of its members. A recurrence to the nature of the liabilities of members to their own corporation, will, we apprehend, divest the case of many of its difficulties. Every individual owner of shares, whether a petitioner, an associate, or purchaser, expects, and, indeed, stipulates, with the other owners, as a corporate body, to pay them his proportion of the expense which a majority may please to incur, in the prosecution of the particular object of the corporation. By acquiring an interest in the corporation, therefore, he enters into an obligation with it, in the nature of a *special contract, the terms of which contract* are *limited* by the specific provisions, rights, and liabilities detailed in the act.

" To make a *valid* change in this private contract, as in any other, the *assent of both parties* is *indispensable.*"

The subject is then discussed by him in various ways, and the rights of the majority in interest considered; but he held, that the democratic principle of majorities did not apply in such a case, and he then adds: " It is impossible to state the case without perceiving a variation from the contract originally made, and a variation, too, which reaches the gravamen or essence of the contract. Many cautious men would be willing to hazard assessments which might be made on a share under the restrictions of the first act, who would never risk those which his more wealthy or more adventurous associates might make, under the indulgencies of the second one." The court further held, that, in all cases where it was set up that a party had assented to amendments "extending the objects, or increasing the powers, or enlarging the liabilities of the corporation, it is not to be presumed, but *must be expressly shown.*"

In the case of *Banet* v. *Alton & Sangamon R. R. Co.*, 13 Ill., 511, the court (Justice TREAT) say: "An amendment which essentially changes the nature or objects of a corporation will not be binding on the stockholders. A corporation formed for the purpose of constructing a railroad, cannot be converted into a company to construct an improvement of a different character, without the consent of *all the corporators.* A road intended to secure the advantages of a particular line of travel and transportation, cannot be so changed as to defeat that general object.

"The corporation must remain substantially the same, and be designed to accomplish the same general purposes, and subserve the same general interests.

"But such amendments of the charter as may be considered useful to the public, and beneficial to the corporation, and *which will not divert its property to new and different purposes,* may be made without absolving the subscribers from their engagements.

*   *   *   *   *   *   *   *

"The alteration must be accepted by the managers of the company, before it becomes obligatory on the stockholders; and the latter will not even *then* be bound, *if their interests are materially affected by the alteration;* and, in such case, they may not only avoid the payment of their subscriptions, but recover back such sums as they have advanced."

Madison, &c., Plank Road Co. v. *Watertown, &c., Plank Road Co.*, 7 Wis., 50.

This decides that, " a corporation can exercise no powers except those which are expressly conferred by its charter, or are necessarily incidental to the objects and purposes of its creation, and cannot appropriate its funds to any other purpose than pertains strictly to the corporation."

In *Bissell* v. *Michigan Southern and Northern Indiana Railroad Company*, 22 N. Y. (8 Smith), 258, where two corporations, chartered respectively by the States óf Michigan and Indiana, with power to each to build and operate a railroad within its own State, have united in the business of transporting passengers over a third road in the State of Illinois, beyond the limits authorized by the charter of either. COMSTOCK, C. J., says :

" There has been, I think, some want of reflection, even in judicial minds, upon the reasons and policy which mainly govern in the granting of charters to corporations, with certain specified powers, and no others. A *private* or *trading corporation is essentially a chartered partnership*, with or without immunity from personal liability beyond the capital invested, and with certain other convenient attributes, which ordinary partnerships do not enjoy. It is also something more than a partnership, because the legal or artificial person becomes vested with the title to all the estate and capital contributed, to be held and used, however, *in trust for the shareholders*. Now, in a well regulated unincorporated partnership, the articles entered into by the associates specify the objects of their association."

" It is the undoubted right of stockholders to complain of any diversion of the corporate funds to purposes unauthorized in the charter. This, as a general principle, cannot be too strongly asserted. By this principle, justly applied to particular instances, the question in such cases is to be resolved. The original subscribers contribute the capital invested, and they, and those who succeed to their shares, are always, in equity, the owners of that capital.

" But the equitable rights of shareholders, will enable them, in many circumstances, to claim the affirmative interposition of the courts to *arrest* an unauthorized course of dealing, or to prevent a threatened diversion of the capital to improper uses. Of this character are many of the cases usually cited, to prove that corporations cannot exceed their powers."

> *Dodge* v. *Woolsey*, 18 How. U. S. 331.
> *Bolt* v. *Rodgers*, 3 Paige, 154.
> Ang. & Ames on Corp., 424, 4th ed., and cases cited.

" So, too, it is plain, without citing authority, that a stockholder, who can show that he has sustained a pecuniary loss by such a use ot the capital, may have his redress in damages against the individuals who commit the wrong, unless he has himself acquiesced.

" These are extensive, and it would seem, ample remedies to prevent or redress the abuse of power; and it appears to me a much higher and better policy, that private shareholders should be confined to these remedies, than to sacrifice the interests of the rest of the community by conceding to these bodies absolute immunity whenever power is thus abused. But the principles which belong *to this* question need not present that naked alternative.

" Stockholders in corporations have such an interest in the company as excludes them from being witnesses for the company."

> *Thrasher* v. *Pike County Railroad Company*, 25 Ill. 409.
> *Ryder* v. *Alton and Sangamon Railroad Co.*, 13 Ill. 523.
> *Philadelphia and Westchester Railroad Co.* v. *Hickman*, 28 Penn, 318.

Lord ELDON, in the case of *Adley* v. *The Whitestable Company*, 17 Vesey, 321, which was a case where a fisherman, who had violated a by-law of a corporation ot which he was a member, had been excluded from the corporation, said : " We find, from the experience of every day, that, as individuals cannot possibly hold out responsibility to the extent required in great concerns, therefore great trading companies are formed, the property of the company yielding a *profit ;* which, according to the nature and principle of the undertaking, is to be divided *among the individuals* composing the corporation, just as if they were not incorporated."

This same case came up again in the 19th of Vesey, Jr., 305, when Lord ELDON laid down the doctrine, that the corporation was liable *as trustees* to each individual stockholder for his proportionate share ; and, notwithstanding the difficulties and obstacles which were interposed there, he said, that, " wherever there is a legal right vested in a party, he must, in some court, have the means of enforcing that right. It may, perhaps, be out of the power of any court *effectually* to meet *all* the human resistance, that may, where there is a great number of parties, be applied, to baffle justice—but the court must not, for that reason, desist from doing anything ; and parties may, in the end, grow extremely weary of that resistance, which they never ought to have interposed."

Prima facie, all stockholders, at any particular period, are equally interested in the property and business of a corporation. They assume the same liabilities, are *entitled* to the *same rights,* and are *equal owners of the property.* When, therefore, the directors undertake to distribute among the stockholders any portion of the funds or property of a corporation, whether it be called profits or not, all the stockholders are entitled to an equal share in the fund, proportionate to their stock ; whether they have been stockholders for a longer or shorter period.

Unless *the charter* gives the directors power to discriminate between the stockholders, at different periods, in the distribution of profits, they are *all* entitled to share therein.

Jones v. *Terre Haute R. R. Co.,* 29 Barb., 359.

Stockholders, who are *citizens of other States* than that under whose laws the corporation is chartered, may file a bill in equity against it, in the court of the United States.

> *Paine* v. *Indianapolis R. R. Co.*, 6 McLean, 395.
>
> *Dodge* v. *Woolsey*, 18 How, 331.
>
> *Louisville R. R. Co.* v. *Letson*, 2 How. (U.S.), 558.
>
> *Commonwealth* v. *Milton*, 12 B. Mon., 212.
>
> *Marshall* v. *Baltimore & Ohio R. R. Co.*, 16 How, 314.

The following cases were brought by a shareholder in behalf of himself and others, who may come in and contribute to the expenses, &c.

> *Jefferson Branch Bank* v. *Skelly*, 1 Black, 449.
>
> *Wright* v. *Sill*, 2 Black, 544.
>
> *Franklin Branch Bank* v. *State of Ohio*, 1 Black, 474.
>
> *Mechanics & Traders Bank* v. *Debolt*, 18 How., 380.
>
> See   *Shrewsbury & Birmingham R. Co.* v. *London & North Western R. Co.*, 4 De Gex; Macnaughton & Gordon, 132.

VII.

When the majority of stockholders in a corporation can bind the minority.

In the case of the *Troy & Rutland R. R. Co.* v. *Kerr*, 17 Barb., 604, the court said: "As a general rule, the acts of the majority control, *when confined* to the ordinary transactions of the company, *and consistent* with the original objects of its formation. But everything relating to the organization of a private corporation, of the nature we are considering, as well as of co-partnerships, is mere matter of individual contract; and the compact, which is to clothe its members with this artificial, corporate existence, must receive *the voluntary assent of the whole.* And as there can be no compulsion in the first instance, I *do not see how there can be a claim upon the property of a member to aid a different enterprise, after a material change in the constitution of the company.*"

Angel & Ames on Corps., p. 367.

In the case of *Davies* v. *Hawkins*, 3 Maule & Selw., 488, which was a case of a company which was formed for brewing ale, and, by deed, they confided the management of the business to two persons, who were trustees of the company—who were to manage the business until others were elected to fill their places, and general quarterly meetings were to be held.

It was decided by the K. B., that one person only could not be appointed at a general quarterly meeting, in place of the two originally appointed under the deed, unless such alteration was made by the consent of *all* the subscribers. Lord ELLENBOROUGH said, that "a change had been made in the *constitution* of this company, which could not be made without the consent of the *whole body of the subscribers.* It was such a substituted alteration in *its constitution* as required the *assent of all.*"

In *Peabody et al,* v. *Flint*, 6 Allen, 52, which was a bill in equity, filed by James Peabody and another, they being stockholders in the Lowell & Salem R. R. Co., for themselves and in behalf of the other stockholders, against the company, the directors, and agents, and, also, the Lowell & Lawrence Railroad Company, charging them all with fraud and conspiracy, to prejudice and sacrifice the Lowell & *Salem* Railroad for the benefit of the Lowell & Lawrence Railroad. The two stockholders were the owners of but a few shares out of many thousand. The case was characterized by the true spirit of modern consolidations, and it was contended, by the defendants, "that the plaintiffs have not, and never had, any remedy for such injuries as they complain of; that conceding the truth of the allegations, that the directors of the Salem & Lowell Railroad Company, either by themselves, or with the *consent and connivance* of a majority of the stockholders combined, either among themselves or with the Lowell & Lawrence Railroad Company, or its directors, or with any of the other defendants, to defraud a minority of the stockholders of the Salem & Lowell Railroad Company, and in pursuance of this combination *di l the acts* alleged, and so dealt and managed as to destroy the value of the stock, as set forth, yet the only relief which the minority can have, is the imperfect one of selling out their stock for what it will bring in market."

In commenting upon this position, CHAPMAN, J., said: "This doctrine is said to result from the nature of corporate property, which, being owned absolutely by the corporation, is under the absolute control of a majority of the stockholders, and of such directors as they choose to elect. Their decisions and acts, it is said, are final, and the minority are bound to submit to them.

But this doctrine, if correct, would place the property of stockholders in a corporation in a perilous condition. For it would enable the managers of one corporation to get the control of another by the purchase of a majority of its stock for the purpose, and then to manage its affairs in such subservience to the interests of their own corporation, as to render the stock of the minority worthless, and avail themselves of its value without compensation. The demurrer concedes, for the purposes of this discussion, that the managers of the Lowell & Lawrence Railroad Company have thus acted, in respect to the minority of stockholders in the Salem & Lowell Railroad Company. It requires no great sagacity to see how similar frauds may be practiced in behalf of many other railroads against connecting or rival roads, so that a system of railroad connections *may become a system of frauds.* If it may be practiced with impunity between railroad corporations; it may, also, be practiced between manufacturing corporations, and a managing majority may, at their pleasure, sacrifice the interests of the minority for the benefit of another corporation owned by them. The same remark is true in respect to several other classes of business corporations. The question thus presented is of great importance, because there is no known practicable method of establishing and managing railroads except by means of corporations; and many other great enterprises and branches of business which require, for their successful prosecution, a large and permanent investment of capital, are, also, usually and most conveniently established and managed by means of corporate organizations."

In the case of *Lloyd* v. *Loaring*, 6 Vesey, Jr., 773, 777, which was a suit by three persons in behalf of themselves and all the other members of a lodge of freemasons, which a majority of the members had undertaken to consolidate with another lodge, Lord ELDON said: " If I consider them as individuals, the majority had no right to bind the minority. One individual has as good a right to possess the property as any other, unless he can be affected by some agreement."

In the Chamberlain of London's case, 5 Co., 63, it was held, that the inhabitants of a town, " as a community of known description, recognized by law, (thereby acting as a corporation) might make ordinances or by-laws for the reparation of the church or highway, or of any such thing, which is for the general good of the public, and, in *such* a case, a greater part shall bind the whole ; but if it be *for their private profit,* as the well ordering of their common of pasture, *or the like*, there, without a custom, (that is, without some law *to that* effect,) they cannot make by-laws; and if there be a custom, then the greater part shall not *bind* the *less*, if it be *not warranted* by the custom."

In other words, the majority can never sell out or dispose of the interests of the minority, without a special grant from the legislature for that purpose, and the minority must have acquired their rights, or joined the association or corporation, with that distinct understanding and agreement.

Chancellor KENT upheld this doctrine, and these principles, to the fullest extent, in the case of *Livingston* v. *Lynch*, 4 Johnson's Ch., 594, where a certain number of persons had formed an association, under the laws of New York, and had subscribed articles, which a *majority* afterwards undertook to change and abrogate. In deciding the case, he said that there was not a doubt upon his mind that the articles "were *of the character* and authority of *permanent constitutional provisions*, binding upon all the members when adopted *by all*, as a solemn private contract, and that they *can only* be abolished* by *the like concurrent will* by which they were adopted. * * *

"We are not to intend, without express words, that each of these tenants in common, especially where the interests were so unequal and so momentous, surrendered his invaluable right, founded on settled principles of law, not to be controlled, in the government of his individual interest, without his consent." He then adds: "The *general principle* of law *is*, in such private associations, the *majority cannot* bind the *minority*, unless it be by *special* agreement." Page 595–6.

On page 597, the chancellor said: "If any one article might be abolished by a vote of the majority, so might every other article; and the rights and property of each individual member would be placed in the utmost jeopardy, at the control of others, without any security from compact, or the dictates of his own judgment.

" The *law* gives *no* such control to others over one's own property, or individual interest, *except* in the case of partnerships and of ship owners, which stand on peculiar grounds of commercial and maratime policy; and even in those cases, there is *particular protection* provided for the dissenting owner."

In *New Orleans, Jackson & Great Northern Railroad Co.* v. *Harris*, 27 Miss., 536, which was an action brought by the company against Harris, who had subscribed stock in the Canton Railway, and by *him* transferred to the plaintiff in error. The court say: " If the legislature possessed the authority to confer upon any number of the stockholders in said company, who might be the owners of a *majority of the* stock, the power to accept any proposed amendments to the charter, and by such acceptance, to bind the remainder of the stockholders, it might, with equal propriety, so far as the isolated question of power was concerned, delegate the *same right to a minority*, owning but a small proportion of the stock, or to any specified number less than a majority, or even to a single corporator. *A charter is :* 1st, *a contract, within the meaning* of the constitution of the United States, between the State granting the charter and the corporation itself, the obligation of which it is not within the power of the legislature to impair. 2d, the *contract subsisting between the members of a corporate body and the corporation, is equally within the protection of the constitution.* According to the doctrine that the legislature had the right to confer upon any number of the stockholders, who might own more than one half of the stock subscribed, the authority to accept of amendments to the charter, it is evident that the charter might be altered in its most essential stipulations, not only without the approbation, *but against the consent* of the great body of the corporators, thereby subjecting them to *duties and responsibilities not imposed by their contract with the company.* This, we think, can not be done without a clear violation of the constitution. Hence, we conclude that the act in question did not invest the stockholders, representing a majority of the stock subscribed, with authority to accept the amendment proposed to the charter.

The charter, in these cases, *constitutes the fundamental articles of the association.* It defines the rights and powers of the corporation, determines its objects, and *fixes the individual contract of the member with the corporation itself.* His contract is as clearly defined as the charter can make it. It must be conceded, that the legislature *have no constitutional power, unless reserved in the grant,* to change or alter, without consent, an act of incorporation, and thereby to *cast upon them additional obligations,* or take from them rights guaranteed by their charter. Its power over the corporation can be no greater; it can impose *no additional obligation* without his assent, or release him from any duty, against the will of the party thereby to be affected. In what respect can the power of a corporation transcend the authority of the legislature? He must have as perfect a right to stand upon his contract with the corporation, in opposition to the action of a majority, as he would to insist upon his rights under it, against the action of the legislature. This is a proposition too clear to be doubted, in all cases in which there is no stipulation, express or implied, that he shall be bound by the voice of the majority.

The incapacity of the majority to alter, fundamentally, the charter, against the consent of even a single corporator, was recognized by the Vice Chancellor, in the case of *Curtiss* v. *the Manchester & Bolton Canal Company,* 13 Eng. Ch. R., 131, note. In that case, an injunction was granted upon the application of *a single shareholder* in an incorporated company, restraining the company from affixing their corporate seal to a petition to parliament for an act to convert a part of the canal into a railway, and from using the corporate funds for that purpose. So, in Manly against the same company, an injunction was granted for a similar purpose. *Ib.,* 132. So, also, in *Ware* v. *the Grand Junction Water Company,* 2 Rup. & Mylne, 461, the same principle was applied to a corporation upon the application of a single shareholder.

When a person become a member of an incorporated company, by his subscription to the stock, he agrees to be bound by the terms of his contract, as defined in the charter of incorporation; he agrees to be bound by the acts of the corporation, and its officers, *performed within the scope of the charter powers.; but upon no principle can it be held, that he impliedly consents to any alteration which would work a radical change* in the structure of the association, which might *be voted* or accepted by *even a majority of the whole of the corporators, and thereby be subjected to burdens and obligations wholly foreign to the purposes and objects of the original charter.* It is our opinion, therefore, that the acceptance *was absolutely void, for want of power, on the part of the stockholders representing a majority of the stock,* to vote an acceptance of the amendatory act. It follows, hence, that the *transfer* and assignment were, *also, void and ineffectual.*

VIII.

Rights of the minority stockholders in corporations.

That the whole are bound by the majority, when their acts *are conformable to the charter, or articles of their constitution, and not inconsistent with* them, we do not deny; but when they are not thus conformable and *are inconsistent with the objects and purposes* for which the body corporate *was organized,* we say they are not bound at all, in any way. " Thus," as Angel & Ames say, in their work on corporations, section 500, " thus, when a company is authorized, by an act of parliament, to raise money for a specific purpose, only, it is not competent to any majority of the shareholders of the company to divert such money to another purpose, against the will of a *single* shareholder—*nor, indeed, would unanimity* among the shareholders, make such a diversion lawful."

And *thus* we say. Thus, neither can the Galena and Chicago Union Railroad Company sell out all of its property, money and franchises to the Chicago and North Western Railway Company, or apply its tolls, revenues, and funds to supporting that road, and paying its debts, or the debts of Kenosha and Rockford Railroad

Company, or the debts of the Peninsular and Marquette Railroad of Michigan, or any other railroad. We say that the Galena and Chicago Union Railroad Company was never organized for any *such* purpose or object whatever, and each and all of such acts are *inconsistent* with the purpose of that company, and no act or vote of the majority, whether by person or proxy, can legalize such acts, or render consistent, what is clearly inconsistent.

See *Nazro et al.* v. *Merchants Mutual Ins. Co.*, 14 Wis., 196.

This was a case where one Henry Nazro, a stockholder in the *Merchants Mutual Insurance Company*, of Milwaukee, filed a bill in behalf of himself and of all others similarly situated with himself, against the company, in which he alleged, first, that he became a stockholder in the company, as it was organized under an act of the legislature, of February 10, 1847. That after he became a stockholder that the company procured two amendments to their charter, one in 1858, and one in 1860, which acts were accepted by the company, against his protest, and which latter act of 1860, authorized an entire reorganization of the transacting of insurance business on entirely different principles from the original charter, in which he took stock. It further appeared, that the dissenting members of the corporation procured an act from the legislature, in the month of April, 1860, by which it was provided, on the application of those interested in the old company, appraisers might be appointed to examine the affairs of the company, and appraise the value of the property and assets of the company, which it owned at the time it was reorganized. And after such examination, they should report to the court the value of the same, and a judgment entered in favor of the petitioners for their porportionate and respective shares of the entire property. The court, in deciding this case, say that, " the capital stock of incorporated companies *is a trust fund*, the proper application of which courts of equity will enforce, by virtue of their jurisdiction over trusts and frauds."   *   *   *   *   " That the grant to the directors and the company, of new and distinct powers, such as are contained in the amendments to the original charter, were such as they could not have exercised, either as a matter of corporate authority or of legal or constitutional right, as *between themselves and the shareholders*, and that the shareholders might have objected to it, as a *violation of the contract under which they became members of the corporation.*"

The majority of the stockholders and directors complained bitterly of the minority; and their acts in the premises were characterized as willful and uncompromising, and the act under which they proceeded, as most harsh and oppressive. But the court said, that " the trustees and assenting members, or, what is the same, the company under its new organization, being themselves the *innovators, and having set on foot, themselves, measures* by which the *dissenting* members have been deprived of the chartered rights and privileges, *on the faith of which they invested their money, ought not to object* to any fair proceeding by which *they seek a return of it. Their claims are most equitable, and every principle of natural justice would seem to require that they should be protected.* The amendatory acts were, in effect, a grant of authority to the trustees to organize a *new company for the same general purpose, but upon entirely different principles*, with the privilege of such members of the old company, as wished, to *convert their premium certificates into the stock of the new. The new company was to take the place of the old, which was to cease, and such holders of premium certificates as refused to convert them into stock, were to have no management of its affairs. The result is, that the new organization has, without their consent, become possessed of so much of the funds of these dissenting certificate holders, which it is against conscience for it to retain.* The act, therefore, is *nothing more than a special remedy to enforce the performance of a duty, which courts of chancery, upon principles of natural equity, would have enforced without it.*"

It is a proceeding, on the part of the *dissenting members*, to get their own. The trustees, by their conduct, have made a distribution necessary and proper. *They have appropriated the property without the consent of the owners.*

Const. v. *Harris*, 1 Turner & Russell, 496.

Great Western v. *Rushout,* 10 Eng. Law & Eq., 72.

Attorney General v. *Norwich,* 9 Eng. Law & Eq., 93.

In the case of *Ward* v. *Societies of Attorneys,* 1 Collyer, 375, it appeared that out of one thousand three hundred and thirteen shares, all voted to acquiesce in an important change to the charter, *except the owners of twenty-one shares. They* filed their bill, and the court enjoined the directors and corporation.

It was argued, in this case, that it was unreasonable *that the wishes of the great majority* of the members of this society should be thwarted by the proceedings of *a few individuals;* it is more to the interest of the society that it should be devoted to professional improvement, than it should be engrossed in considering the profits of the shares. In the former case, it may command the confidence of the public, but in the latter, it cannot.

Notwithstanding this argument, the vice chancellor, on page 380, said, that "THE LAW allows individuals to acquire a beneficial interest in the preservation of such a body, so lawfully constituted, and *I am not aware of any principle of law or equity which can enable that lawfully constituted interest,* thus obtained, to be taken away without the *consent of every person interested,* unless by means of a condition, to which the original creation was subject."

NOTA BENE.—*Preston* v. *the Grand Collier Dock Co.,* 11 Simons, 327.

This was a case where Preston, the owner of *twenty* shares out of *nine thousand,* brought a suit against the Grand Collier Dock Company, and various other persons, and the court *held,* that *a bill,* by a member of a numerous incorporated company, on behalf of himself and all the other members, except the defendants, praying that a transaction in which the defendants had been the actors, but which had been *sanctioned, unanimously, at a meeting of the company,* might be declared null and void, *was sustained,* although some of the members, on whose behalf the bill was filed, had been present and voted at the meeting.

" The minority of the shareholders, or one of them, may file a bill on behalf of the whole body, though at a meeting a large number may have sanctioned the act, if it be illegal; if not, it would be impossible for a shareholder, in such a case, to obtain relief, that does not apply to the other part of the objection, that the directors are not made the defendants." Parker V. C. In case of *Winch* v. *the Birkenhead, Lancashire & Cheshire Junction R. R. Co.*, 13 L. & Eq., on page 518, he said, 19 Eng. L. & Eq., 361 :

" I think that this bill is correctly framed by one, on behalf of himself and all the other shareholders. It is not necessary to refer to any authority, further than the very forcible language of Lord CRANWORTH, in the case of *Beman* v. *Rufford*, 1 Sim. (N. S.), 550, in which it is said, that any one shareholder may come, in behalf of all, to prevent, what he calls, an infringement of the law of the concern. I do not think it is necessary that the directors should be made parties. The act that is sought to be restrained is, the the act of the company. It is quite sufficient if there is an order restraining the company. The company, itself, cannot act, except by means of its officers.

" It appears to me that the suit is properly framed, by the relief being sought against the company alone."

> *Bagshaw* v. *the Eastern Union Railway Co.*, 7 Hare, 114 ; 2 Mac. & G., 389.
>
> *Bromley* v. *Smith*, 1 Sim., 8.
>
> *Preston* v. *the Grand Collier Dock Co.*, 11 Sim., 327 ; 1 Stockton, 401 ; 13 Barb., 567.
>
> *Coleman* v. *Eastern Counties R. Co.*, 10 Beav., 1.
>
> *Ward* v. *the Society of Attorneys*, 1 Coll,, 370.
>
> *Adley* v. *Whiteable Co.*, 19 Vesey, 305.
>
> *Methodist Book Concern case*, 16 How., 288.
>
> *Smith* v. *Swamstedt*, 26 Conn., 456.
>
> 11 Georgia, 569.
>
> 31 Ala., 612.
>
> 28 Penn., 379.
>
> 1 R. I., 312.

Angel & Ames on Corporations, Sec. 312.
40 N. H., 540.
33 Maine, 132.
21 N. H., 81.
24 Barb., 187.
43 N. H., 517.

The principle is, that any shareholder in a corporation may sue to prevent the corporation from doing an act *ultra vires*.
1 Chand., (Wis.,) 286.
15 Ill., 255.

The case of *Dodge* v. *Woolsey*, 18 How., 341, is directly in point.
30 Penn., 1.
28 Penn., 379.
Adrience v. *Mayor of N. Y.*, 1 Barb., 19.
Milhau v. *Sharp*, 15 Barb., 244.
Wood v. *Draper*, 24 Barb., 190.
Christopher v. *Mayor of N. Y.*, 13 Barb., 567.
DeBaun v. *Mayor of N. Y.*, 16 Barb., 392.
1 Simon, 550.
23 How., 396.

A *single shareholder* can enjoin a corporation, when it is misapplying its funds, or violating its charter.
In *ex parte* Booker, 18 Arkansas, 338.
This was an application for *a mandamus to compel the judge to grant an injunction against the officers of a railroad company, for violating its charter, in appropriating funds to different purposes than those contemplated by the charter.*

Justice HANLY says:
"It was a question of serious doubt, until comparatively a recent date, whether a private corporation could, under *any* circumstances, be sued, either at law or equity, by one of its own members." (See 2 Bay. (S. C.) R., 109 ; 1 Myl. & Rup. Ch. R., 131, and note, and 18 How. U. S. R., 331.)

" *But it is now well settled, that a private corporation may be sued, either at law or in equity,* under particular circumstances, or a special state of facts." (See Ang. & Am. Corp., Sec. 390–1, and the authorities above cited; also, *Pearce* v. *Patridge*, 9 Met. R., 44; *Hills* v. *Manchester & Salford Water Works*, 5 Adolph. & Ellis R., 866.)

And a special case in which a private corporation may be sued in equity by one of its members, is, when the company *attempts to do acts which they are not empowered to do, under the acts of the legislature, from which they derived their authority* to act as such; and in such case, it has been holden that a court of chancery may restrain them, by an injunction, from the commmission of the *threatened* and *impending* usurpation. See, Ang. & Am. on Corp., sec. 391; *Ware* v. *Grand Junction Water Co.*, 1 Myl. & Rup. Ch. R., 126; 1 Beav. Ch. R., 1. In the last case cited, the objection was expressly taken, on part of the corporation, that the corporation ought not to be a party to the suit. But the Vice Chancellor, Sir James WAGRAM, said he had no hesitation in overruling the objection; that the acts of the directors (in directing the corporate moneys for a purpose different from what was originally contemplated, *against the will of a single shareholder*,) were the acts of the directors as the representatives of the company, and as such, were the acts of the company itself, and that the company would not be bound, unless it were a party in its corporate character. See, also, *Coleman* v. *Eastern Counties Railway Co.*, 10 Beav. Ch. R., 1, to the same point.

The result of the authorities, therefore, clearly is, that a corporation, when acting within the scope of, and in obedience to, the provisions of its constitution, the will of the *majority*, duly expressed at a legally constituted meeting, must govern; yet, *beyond the limits of the act of incorporation*, the will of a majority *can not make the act valid;* and the powers of a court of equity may be put in motion, at the *instance of a single stockholder*, if he can show that the corporation are employing their statutory powers for the accomplishment of purposes not within the scope of their institution. (See Ang. & Am. on Corp., sec. 393, *note* 2, and authorities there cited.

Dodge v. *Woolsey*, 18 How., 341, is perfectly conclusive upon this point.

Kean v. *Johnson*, 1 Stockton's Ch. R., 401.

This was a case where John Kean, the complainant, as the owner of 275 shares out of about 8,000, filed a bill against John T. Johnson, and sundry other persons, as directors of the Elizabeth and Somerville Railroad and the Somerville and Eastern Railroad, otherwise called the Central Railroad of New Jersey, under the following circumstances: The Elizabeth and Somerville Railroad Company was chartered on the 9th of February, 1831, by the legislature of New Jersey. In 1839, a mortgage was made on the road and franchises, &c., which was afterwards foreclosed, and all the property purchased by Stearns and Colkett, who organized a new company, and issued stock, some of which was purchased by the complainant, and which he then represented by his bill, to the amount above stated. In 1847, another company was chartered by the legislature of New Jersey, to construct a railroad from Somerville to Easton, called the Somerville and Easton Railroad Company, in which some of the individuals named in the bill were directors, and owned a large majority of the capital stock. About the latter part of 1848, the directors of the Somerville and Easton Railroad Company combined with the directors or persons in the interest of the Elizabeth and Somerville Railroad Company, to effect an amalgamation of the two companies, and of compelling the stockholders of the Elizabeth and Somerville Railroad Company to surrender their stock, and go into a new company, under one management. That to effect said purpose, they procured a supplemental act to the Somerville and Easton Railroad Company, which provided: 1. That it should be lawful for the Somerville and Easton Railroad Company to purchase the *road* constructed by the Elizabeth and Somerville Company.

2. That if payment could be made in stock, the Somerville and Easton Railroad Company could issue as much as might be required for that purpose.

3. That the purchased road should become a part and parcel of the Somerville and Easton Railroad, and that the two roads thus combined, should be known as the " Central Railroad Company, of New Jersey."

4. That no rights of any of the stock-holders or parties interested in the road should be affected, and that the consolidated road should be responsible for the claims, debts and demands of each, and that the purchase should be made by the consent of the stock-holders of the L. & E. R. R. Company.

The bill then alleged that, after the passage of this act and about the 1st of April, 1849, the individual defendants in the bill " holding a *large majority* of the stock of *both companies* and *being directors of each* and constituting *almost the entire* boards, did proceed, *using*, and proceeding, in the *names of said companies respectively*, and assuming to act as said companies, to make a consolidation," &c., &c., did procure of Stearns & Colkett, the purchasers at the master's sale, a deed, conveying all the property and appendages of the E. & L. R. R., which simply conveyed all the title which they had. The persons who are named in the bill and who were directors in both roads, and *who owned the majority of the stock*, then consolidated the two roads under the name of " The Central Rail Road Company of New Jersey," and since managed and operated the roads under the said name.

The complainant further averred that he was, and is, owner of 275 shares of stock in the Elizabethtown & L. R. R. Company, as issued by Stearns & Colkett, in the organization and formation of the new company, &c., and that Thomas Hartwell and William Thompson were owners of some stock also, but that, they, neither of them, gave any consent to the proceedings but protested and still protest against the sale and consolidation.

For these reasons he, Kean, insisted that the whole sale and consolidation was void as to himself and all dissenting stock-holders. He then made parties the *Directors* of both roads, individuals, and the corporation, and prayed that the sale and consolidation be set aside and an accounting of the earnings be had, &c.

The court in deciding this case say :

" What rights, then, had the stockholders of the Elizabethtown & Somerville Company at law or in equity *in* that corporation? Does a sale of the road, which was the scource of all their emolument, actual or prospective, whose possession was the very condition of their actual, if not technical, being, and the diversion of their capital to other employment, affect in anywise their rights? If so, by the clear meaning, almost the express words of the proviso, they had a right to dissent, and that dissent prevented the transfer permitted by the act, at any rate as far as regarded *them.* If a transfer it did not affect the rights of the dissentient, whatever other effect it might have ; I cannot divert my mind from the conclusion that a sale of their road, and the employment of the capital they invested in it to other uses, does affect the rights of every stockholder in a railroad company. As stockholders they own the road in common, to be employed in specified uses. Each owns a share in the whole, and is to have a proportionate share in its profits. They have invested a portion of their capital in it, and in it alone. They have a right in the road, and *in every dollar it earns.* The directors are the trustees, to employ the joint capital in the management of the road, and the road only, to the end that from the investment the stockholders have chosen they may reap the contemplated profits. And this is the agreement of the stockholders among themselves. They each contract with the other that the money shall be so employed. What the majority determine *within the scope* of this mutual contract, they each agree to abide by, but there their mutual contract ends, and *no majority,* however large, *has a right to divert one cent of the joint capital* to any purpose not consistent, and growing out of this original, fundamental, joint intention.

To sell the road, to abandon the contemplated investment and embark in another scheme, whether entirely different *or only more extensive than the original contemplation as apparent on the face of the charter*, is, it seems to me, clearly contrary to the rights of individual stockholders.

If they had any rights as partners or beneficiaries, it would seem to be this, that their money should be devoted to that use, and never employed in any other, nor returned to them before they desire it. The mere statement of the proposition seems to me to prove it. No argument, however lengthened, can add to the force of the naked position.

The general principle here asserted has frequently received the sanction of the courts both of England and this country. It is the same, whether applied in the case of private associations or *incorporations*. " It is not, I apprehend," says Lord ELDON, " competent to any number of persons in a partnership, (unless they show a contract rendering it competent to them) formed for specific purposes, if they propose to form a partnership for different purposes, to effect that formation by calling upon some of the partners to receive the subscribed capital and interest and quit the concern." And again, he says in the same case, " Those who seek to embark a partner in a business not originally part of the partnership concern, must make out clearly that he did expressly or tacitly acquiesce." *Natusch* v. *Irving*, Appendix to Gow on Part. 376, Am. Ed., 1830. *And see also the decision of Kent, C., in Livivingston* v. *Lynch*, 4 Johns. Ch. R. 573. So in incorporations. Nothing is more certainly settled than that any fundamental alteration of a charter, or material deviation from or extension of a road, in the case of railroad companies, interferes with the rights of the corporators, and that no majority, *however large*, can compel any individual stockholder to submit. Thus, in such cases, if the stockholder has not paid his subscription, he is freed by such deviation from liability on his contract to do so. *New Haven & Conn. R. R. Company* v. *Croswell*, 3 Hill, 383 ; *Union Lock & Canal Co.* v. *Towne*, N. H. Rep. 44; *Middx. T. Corp.* v. *Locke*, 8 Mass. 268; *Same* v. *Swan*, 10 Mass. R. 385. The opinions of the able judges who decided these cases, present the principle with remarkable clearness and force. The late distinguished Judge WOODBURY, in *Union Locke* v. *Towne*, states the ground of his judgment thus : Every individual owner of shares, whether a petitioner or associate, or purchaser, expects, and indeed stipulates with the other body owners as a copartner, to pay them his proportion of the expense, which a majority may please to incur in the promotion of the particular object of the corporation. By acquiring an interest in the corporation, therefore, he enters into an obligation with it in the nature of a special contract, the terms of which contract are limited by the specific provisions, rights, and liabilities detailed in the act of incorporation. To make a valid change in this private contract, as in every other, the assent of both parties is indispensable. The corporation on the one part, can assent by a vote of the majority ; the individual, on the other, by his own personal act.

However the corporation, then, may be bound by the assent to the additional acts, the defendant, in his individual capacity, having never assented to either of them, is under no obligation to the plaintiff, *except what he had incurred by becoming a member under the first act.*

But, it is contended on the part of the defendants, that, by the sale of their road, no rights of any stockholder in the Elizabethtown & Somerville R. R. Co. are effected : *that the majority of stockholders have the power and the right at any moment to sell all the property of the corporation and quit the business.* And that, if they pay over to him the profits of the business while it is carried on, and his proportionate share of the proceeds of sale, the " rights " of every stockholder are satisfied, and he can claim no farther at law or in equity. But is the doctrine contended for true ? Is it the law that a majority of stockholders in any corporation, however prosperous its business affairs may be, can, at their own mere caprice, sell out the whole source of their emoluments, invest their capital in other enterprises, and that, however the minority may desire the prosecution of the business in which they had engaged, they have no injury to complaim of, at law or in equity, so long as they obtain their proportion of the proceeds of the sale. On principle, this position seems to me unsound. If it be true, a minority is entirely in the power of a majority, and the moment a rich man, or a few rich men, see what they deem a better investment for their money than the corporation in which they are already stockholders, they may compel the poorer members of the company to abandon profits satisfactory to them, and either risk the little they have, according to the views from which they differ, or take back the money to lie profitless on their hands, until they find another investment; or, more nearly to approach the case in hand, as asserted by the complainants, if a rich man, or a number of rich men, possess a controlling interest in two roads whose termini meet—one already successful, the other not built or needing nursing care—they may compel the poorer stockholders either to abandon or postpone the profitable use of their share of the capital, or take back their money and give up an investment, which perhaps their own enterprise suggested, and their own perseverance recommended to the attention of others, and hazard the finding of a new investment and a repetition of the same destruction of it. If such were the law, corporations would soon be few ; for seldom would capitalists, whatever their comparative wealth, invest in enterprises so readily rendered profitless at the caprice, or in obedience to the interests of any man, or set of men, rich enough to control the majority of stock. That the majority should have the power claimed for them, does not seem to me to be the contract between the stockholders, for there is a contract as already shown, in the case of every corporation, between them. That contract is, that their joint funds shall, under the care of specified persons, generally called directors, be employed, and that for certain, specified purposes. Sometimes the duration of such employment is limited in the charter; and then, until that time, it must continue so employed, unless, perhaps, in case of clear loss. Sometimes no time is fixed by the charter at which the proposed use of the capital shall cease, and then the contract between the parties is, that so long as the affairs of the company are prosperous, it shall go on unless all consent to the contrary.

It can hardly therefore, I think, be argued, with justice, that a majority of the stockholders had a right, upon principle, to sell out all the property of the company from which its profits were to be realized, and abandon the business, and that the minority's rights are satisfied by a division to them of the value of their stock.

In *Byron Stevens* v. *the Rutland & Burlington R. R. Co. et al.*, 29 Vt., 545.

In this case, the Rutland and Burlington Railroad Company were incorporated by an act ot the legislature, passed in 1843, for the purpose of building a railroad " from some point *at Burlington*, thence southwardly, through the counties of Addison, Rut-land and Windsor, or Windham, *to some point on the west bank of Connecticut river.*" *This road they constructed* in accordance with the provision of their charter, and the legislature then (in 1850) passed an additional act authorizing them to *extend* their road from their present terminous, in Burlington, northwardly, &c., " to any point or points in the town of Swanton, in the county of Franklin ;" which act the company voted to accept as an amendment to their charter, and were proceeding to carry out its purpose. To *this* amendment, and to the acceptance ot *it by a majority* of the stockholders, and to the *proposed* action of the corporation under it, the *complainant,* who had previously become a member of the corporation by subscribing and paying for *five* shares of its capital stock, *did not assent, and brought his bill in chancery to enjoin the company from building the proposed extension.* *Held,* that the proposed extension of the the road *beyond its originally designated* northern terminus, was a *fundamental change* from the original purpose of the company's incorporation and organization, to a participation in which *the complainant could not be bound against his consent, by the additional* act of the legislature, and the acceptance of *it by a majority of the stockholders ;* and that, therefore, *he was entitled to an injunction, restraining the company from applying the funds, obtained by them, for the general purpose of their original creation, or the income of their road already built, towards building said extension ; or from using or pledging their credit for that purpose.*

" It is an admitted principle, that, in partnerships, and joint stock associations, they can not, by a vote of the majority, change or alter their fundamental articles of co-partnership or association, against the will of the minority, however small, unless there is an express or implied provision in the articles themselves, that they may do it. It is equally well settled, that a court of chancery will, upon the *application of an individual member* of a partnership, or joint stock association, restrain, by injunction, the majority from using the funds or pledging the credit of the partnership or association, in a business not warranted, and not within the scope of their fundamental articles of agreement.

Courts of equity treat such proceedings, by a majority, *as a fraud* upon the other members, which they will neither sanction or permit. To prevent the commission of fraud, by injunction, has been one of the *earliest and most appropriate heads of equity* jurisdiction, as well as to relieve against it, when committed.

It was upon this principle that Lord ELDON, when High Chancellor, upon the application of a humble individual member of a company, which had been organized for the purpose of carrying on a fire and life insurance business, restrained the company, by injunction, from embarking, also, in the marine insurance business; though the applicant had paid into the funds of the company only one hundred and fifty pounds, as a deposit upon fifteen shares, and the company gotten up by the Rothchilds of England, and composed of six or seven hundred individuals, with a capital of *five millions sterling.* (See *Natusch* v. *Irving et al.,* Gow on Part., Appendix, 576.) The *same principle* was applied to *a corporation* by the Vice Chancellòr, and by Lord Chancellor BROUGHAM, in the case of *Ware* v. *the Grand Junction Water Company,* 2 Russ. & Mylne, 461, S. C. 13, Cond. Ch. Rep., 126. The Vice Chancellor, upon the application *of a single shareholder, restrained the corporation, not only from embarking their funds and credit* in a matter *beyond* the provisions of their charter, but, *also, from applying* to parliament for a change in the charter, which would warrant it.

It is, and must be, admitted, that the legislature has no constitutional power, unless it be reserved in the grant, to change or alter an act of incorporation *without consent,* and thereby cast upon the company new and additional obligations, or take from them rights guaranteed under the original charter. And, indeed, this the legislature have not attempted to do. It is, also, equally true, that it is a part of the law of corporations, that they act according to the voice of the majority. But it is to be remembered, that this is not a suit in which the plaintiff seeks to protect himself in any *corporate* right, but in his own *individual right, growing out of the fact of his having become a corporator by his subscription, and its payment, to the capital stock of the company.* One of an aggregate corporation may contract with the company, as well as a third person; and the rights of the individual so contracting, are not more distinct and independent in the one case, than in the other. The plaintiff, by his subscription, assumed to pay to the corporation, and only *for the purpose specified in the charter*, its amount, according to the assessments; and there was, at the same time, a *trust* created, and an implied assumption, on the part of the corporation, to apply it to that object, and none other. The corporation, also, assumed upon themselves to account to this corporator for his share of the dividends, when this road should be completed, and put in operation, and for his share of the capital stock, though not *in numero.* The charter, in this case, gives to the State the right to purchase out the road of the corporation, after a given number of years, upon certain terms therein specified. The relation between each original shareholder and the corporation is the same. The obligation of the contract between the legislature and the corporation, after an acceptance of the charter, is no more sacred than that which is created between the corporation and the individual corporator. Does any one suppose the legislature could, without the consent of parties, absolve a corporator from liability on his subscription to the corporation, or modify it? and can they do the reverse of it?

The franchise granted to this company was territorial; and an extension of the termini, necessarily, is an extension of the franchise. It can not remain the same thing in substance, until it can be established that a part is equal to the whole. Besides, the company may increase the capital stock to such an additional sum as shall be necessary to construct the extension.

It is *not necessary that the business should be changed in kind, to change the original purpose. If this is not a change in purpose, it would not be to extend the road in one direction to the Canada line, and in the other to the Massachusetts line; and there would be no limits to the control which the corporation might acquire over the individual corporators, and this, too, without their consent,* except what arises from the confines of legislative authority.

Shall it be said that the legislature and the corporation have power to embark this corporator in a speculation to which he has never consented? If it can be done in one case, it can in another. But, having paid his funds into the corporation, he has a right, in chancery, *to compel a faithful performance of the trust by the corporation, in conformity to the original charter, and to keep them within its purview.* No one can suppose, that, upon the payment of his subscription, the *personal identity of the plaintiff was merged in the corporation, or that he ceased to have distinct and independent rights.* In *Rex* v. *Eastern Counties Railway Company,* 1 Railway Cases, 509, the King's Bench issued a mandamus, upon the application of a *minority,* against the company, directing them to proceed in the construction of a railroad, which had been chartered between two points, the corporation having stopped short of one of the termini, and voted to go no further. In the case before us, it must follow, if the plaintiff is not bound by the conjoined effect of the act of 1850, and a majority vote of the corporation, the defendants can stand on no better ground than a voluntary association, who are about to go *beyond* and *aside* of their original articles, against the will of a minority.

In case of public associations and corporations, the *public good* requires that the voice of the majority should govern, and hence, the power is more favorably expounded than when created for private purposes; and it would seem that *public convenience* required the adoption of such a rule. But in the *case of private associations and corporations it is not the doctrine, that a majority can bind the minority in a matter beyond and aside of their original articles of association, or charter of incorporation,* unless it be by special agreement giving such power, which must be a part of the original association.

If, in a case like the present, the majority cannot bind the minority, it is plain that there *is an equity in this bill*, and that the defendants can stand in no better situation than if they had, by a vote of the company, proceeded to build the extension, and to apply the funds and credit of the corporation to that purpose, without any additional act of the legislature.

To give courts not only the power to enforce, but, also, the power to make, or even modify, in one iota, a contract fairly made, would be the *rankest despotism.*

Gifford v. *N. J. Railroad Co.*, 2 Stockton's Ch. Rept., 174.

The New Jersey Railroad and Transportation Company, by their charter of March 7th, 1832, were authorized to construct their road from New Brunswick to some point on the Hudson River, opposite New York ; and, also, to purchase the turnpike roads and bridges on the line of the route, and all or any of the stock of such companies, and to construct such bridges over the Passaic and Hackensack, with the consent of the bridge company, as might be necessary for enjoying the privileges of the act of incorporation.

The New Jersey Railroad Company agreed with the proprietors of the bridges over the rivers Passaic and Hackensack, to buy the stock of such of the stockholders of the latter company as desired to sell. Out of 1,000 shares of the Bridge Company, the New Jersey Railroad Company purchased 932 shares.

In October, 1853, the New Jersey Railroad Company agreed with the Morris and Essex Railroad, to build, with the consent of the Bridge Company, over the Passaic river, a bridge, &c. In December 30th, 1853, the Bridge Company, at a meeting for that purpose, gave their consent to the New Jersey Railroad Company to build the bridge in question, by a vote of all the stockholders present at the meeting. The complainant, who is a stockholder in the Bridge Company, and the owner of ten shares of stock, having mistaken the hour of the meeting, did not reach the place of meeting until after the adjournment, and offered a written protest against the proceedings of the meeting, which was not received, on the ground that the meeting had adjourned.

The complainant filed his bill for an injunction to restrain the New Jersey Railroad from building the bridge, on the ground, that it will impair his vested rights as a stockholder in the Bridge Company, and depreciate his stock. It is a bill filed by a *single* stockholder dissenting from the act of a majority of the corporation.

It is well settled, "that a court of equity will interfere on behalf of a single stockholder, if he can show that the corporation are employing their statutory powers, funds, &c., for the accomplishment of purposes not within the scope of their institution, and an injunction, in such cases, will be granted."

Grant on Corporations, 290.
Ward v. *Societies of Attorneys*, 1 Coll., 370.

The legislature may give additional powers, from time to time, to corporations; and acts of the corporation, in pursuance of such authority, are binding, *unless they conflict with the vested rights*, or impair the obligation of contracts, according to the provision of statutes, or the constitution of the State.

By the supplement to the charter of the Newark and Bloomfield Railroad Company, passed March 26th, 1852, sec. 3, it is enacted, that, nothing in this supplement shall be so construed as to impair, in any manner, any reversionary interest, or vested rights, which the State, or any incorporated company or companies, or any individual may possess, under the charter of the Bridge Company. This provision is, also, in effect, contained in the article of the constitution, restraining the legislature from passing any act impairing the obligation of contracts.

What are the vested rights of a stockholder of the Bridge Company? They are, in regard to this question, and the value of his stock and interest in the franchise of exclusive tolls, and, as ancillary to this, an interest in the exclusive right of building bridges over the rivers Passaic and Hackensack. Any act of the incorporation impairing these rights of a stockholder, without his consent, either expressed or implied, could not be binding on him under the above provision, except in a proceeding authorizing the taking of private property for public uses upon making compensation.·

See, also— *Bliss* v. *Anderson,* 31 Ala., 612.

In the case of the *Queen* v. *the Eastern Counties R. R. Co.* 1 Eng. Railway Cases, 384, the court say : " *Another argument against our interference* was drawn from the *power* given to *general meetings* of the company to decide *upon the expediency of all measures,* to be adopted for executing the act of the Parliament ; but we must consider the real nature of this application. It is *not* a complaint by a *majority* of the proprietors against the governing body, but by a *minority against the conduct of the company itself,* which they charge substantially with a breach of faith towards *them,* by stopping short of a *bona fide* execution of that purpose which induced them to become subscribers. They (that is the majority) strongly urge upon *us,* that all the sacrifices which *they* may have made in furtherance of *their own interests* may go unrequited, *or* even may entail upon *them additional loss* by giving advantages to others in which they cannot share. To *say that a majority* of the whole body *are satisfied* with the dividends they are *likely to receive* and are unwilling to risk more expenditure, is *obviously no anwer* (at all) to them (the minority) or to the public, who created their great powers for different purposes, or to Parliament which was induced to grant them, by the promise of public benefits, much more extensively diffused."

Nota Bene—*Colman* v. *The Eastern Counties Railway Co.,* 4 Eng. Railway Cases, 390.

Any one dissenting stockholder may restrain the company from executing a contract which exceeds its powers.

Zabriskie v. *Cleveland & C. R. R. Co.,* 23 How. (U. S.) 381.

A corporation cannot by a vote of the stockholders, without the individual assent of the holder, oblige him to receive their bond, instead of money, for the interest upon such certificate.

McLaughlin v. *Detroit & C. Railway Co.,* 8 Mich. 100.

Neither can a majority of the members of a corporation under the constitution of the United States, divest the interest of a dissenting stockholder, by a transfer of the whole of its property to another company, to *be paid* for in the shares of such other company.

Lauman v. *The Lebanon Valley R. R. Co.,*
30 Penn. 42.

IX.

The Jurisdiction of a Court of Equity in cases arising between the members of a corporation and the corporation itself. Any individual share-holder can enjoin a corporation of which he is a member from misapplying its funds or from exceeding its powers.

" It is now no longer doubted, either in England or the United States, that courts of equity, in both, have a jurisdiction over corporations, at the instance of *one* or more of their members, to apply preventitive remedies by injunction to restrain those who administer them from doing acts which would amount to a violation of charters, *or to prevent any misapplication of their capital or profits, which might result in lessening the dividends of stockholders or the value of their shares,* as either may be protected by the franchises of a corporation, if the acts intended to be done create, what is in law denominated, a breach of trust. And the jurisdiction extends *to inquire into,* and to enjoin, as the case may require that to be done, any proceedings by individuals in whatever character they may profess to act if the subject of complaint is an imputed violation of a corporate franchise or the denial of a right growing out of it, for which there is not an adequate remedy at law."

Dodge v. *Woolsey,* 18 How. 341–485.
2 Russ. & Mylne, 480.
2 Russ. & Mylne, 470.

Colman v. *Eastern Counties R. Co.*, 4 Railway Cases, 492.

Bagshaw v. *Eastern Counties R. Co.*, 7 Hare Ch. R. 114; also in 6 R. Cases, 130.

Ang. & Ames on Corp. (4th Ed.) 424, and cases there cited.

Mechan. & Traders' Bank v. *Debolt*, 18 Howard, 380.

Mechan. & Traders' Bank v. *Thomas*, 18 Howard, 384.

Bacon v. *Robertson*, 18 Howard, 485.

Verplanck v. *Mercantile Insurance Co.*, 1 Edwards, 84.

Taylor v. *Salmon*, 4 Mylne & Craig, 134.

Bissell v. *Michigan Southern & Northern Ind. R. R. Co.*, 22 N. Y. 274.

Winch v. *The Birkenhead, Lancashire & C. Junc. R. R. Co.*, 13 Law & Eq. 513.

Beam v. *Bufford*, 1 Sim. (N. S.) 550.

Ang. & Ames on Corp., Sec. 312, pp. 366–7.

Robinson v. *Smith*, 3 Paige, 233.

Barmester v. *Norris*, 8 Eng. Law & Equity, 487, 490, 491.

Hichens v. *Congreve*, 4 Russ. 562.

Putnam v. *Sweet*, 1 Chand. (Wis.,) 286.

Bagless v. *Orne*, 1 Freeman, (Miss. Ch.) 173.

Hersay v. *Veazie*, 11 Shep, 12–13.

1 Edwards, 24–513.

1 Craig & Phillips, 1.

2 Atk. 400.

1 Ves. & Bea. 226.

York & North Mid. L. R. R. Co. v. *Hudson*, 19 Eng. Law & Eq. 361.

7 Beavam, 176.

Beman v. *Rufford*, 1 Sim. (N. S.) 550.

See also—*Jefferson Branch Bank* v. *Shelly*, 1 Black, (U. S.) 449–436.

Wright v. *Sill*, 2 Black, (U. S.) 544.
Woods v. *Draper*, 24 Barb.
1 Parsons Select Cases in Eq. 180.
De G. & S. 562.
1 Phil. 790.
1 Simons, 550.
Ang. & Ames on Corp., Sec. 312, pp. 367–8.
See also—*Peabody* v. *Flint*, 6 Allen, (Mass.) 55–6.
Hood v. *N. Y. & N. H. R. R. Co.*, 22 Conn. 510.
Allen v. *Curtis*, 26 Conn. 460–1.

When the corporation is in the control of the directors who have committed the alledged breach of trust, a stockholder may bring his bill against them and make the corporation a party.

Robinson v. *Smith*, 3 Paige, 231–2.
Ang & Ames, p. 305.
Bayless v. *Orne*, 1 Miss. (Freeman) 176–175.
Taylor v. *Salmon*, 4 Mylne & Craig, 141.
Webb v. *The Manchester & Leeds R. Co.*, 4 Mylne & Craig, 120—141.
Nota Bene—*Peabody* v. *Flint*, 6 Allen, 55–6.

See as to the right of a shareholder to bring suit by bill in equity—

Ang. & Ames on Corp., Secs. 391–392–393.
Ang. & Ames on Corp., Sec. 749.

The sound doctrine of equity is, that the capital or property and debts due to banking, trading, and other moneyed corporations, constitutes a trust fund, pledged to the payment of the dues of creditors and stockholders; and that a court of equity will lay hold of this fund, into whosoever hands it may pass, and collect and apply it to the purposes of the trust.

The same doctrine seems to have been established by the United States Supreme Court in the case of—

Curran v. *State of Ark.*, 15 Howard, 312.

Bacon v. *Robinson*, 18 Howard, 480.

See also—2 Kent Com. 307, *Note a.*

Hightower v. *Thornton*, 8 Georgia, 493.

Rhode Island Cases.

Hodges v. *New England Screw Co.*, 1 R. I. 312.

The Supreme Court of the U. S., in noticing this case, in deciding the case of *Dodge* v. *Woolsey*, 18 Howard—on page 343—call special attention to the language of the Rhode Island Judges—in which they say expressly that they consider the jurisdiction of the court over corporations for breaches of charter, at the suit of share-holders—still an open question.

C. J. Green, in deciding this case, commences his opinion by admitting that, in a case like the present, that the jurisdiction by a court of chancery, is undoubted and says:

" We think the directors of the Screw Company are liable in equity, as trustees, for a fraudulent breach of trust. The jurisdiction of a court of equity over such a case was affirmed by Lord Hardwick, in the case of *The Charitable Corporation* v. *Sutton and others*, (2 Atkins, 404,) in 1742, and has been exercised both in England and in this country ever since. In the case of the *Att'y. General* v. *Utica Insurance Co.*, (2 Johns. Ch. Rep. 359) Chancellor Kent recognizes the jurisdition as well settled. In *Robinson and others* v. *Smith and others*, (3 Paige, 222,) and in *Cunningham* v. *Pell and others*, (5 Paige 608,) the same doctrine is affirmed and acted on. So, also by Vice Chancellor McCoun, in *Verplanck* v. *Mercantile Insurance Co.*, (1 Edwards, 84.) The cases on this point are so numerous that we deem any farther reference unnecessary.

The primary party to sue for such fraudulent breach of trust, is the corporation; because the corporation is the party injured. *Robinson and others* v. *Smith and others*, (3 Paige, 222.) But if the corporation refuse to sue, the stockholders may sue in their individual names. *So if the corporation be under the control of the guilty directors, the stockholders may sue.* 3 Paige, 222;) Ang. & Ames on Corp., 304–5.

In the present case, the defendants, who are charged with the fraudulent breach of trust, *are the directors* of the corporation and control its action.   We think, therefore, that the present bill so far as it seeks a remedy against directors, comes within the settled jurisdiction of the court, and that the plaintiff, under the circumstances, is the proper party to sue.

CONNECTICUT CASES.

Hood v. *N. Y. & N. H. R. R. Co.*, 27 Conn., 510, is directly in point.

Allen v. *Curtis*, 26 Conn., 461.

In this case, the court, after referring to the charge made in the declaration, that the directors, after being elected, through deceit and fraud, wasted and made worthless the stock of the plaintiff, said : " The charge, if sustained, calls for the severest denunciations and penalties of the law, and more so at this time, if possible, when the want of integrity in the managers of too many of our banks, railroads, and other corporations, is spreading alarm and distress throughout the country, and calling in question the character of all corporations for financial and commercial purposes and the expediency of creating such corporations.   Doubtless, some of them (the defendants) are implicated in the charges made against them.   Doubtless, some of them are implicated, and are, moreover, guilty, if public rumor or judicial investigation may be trusted ; nor can we doubt, from what has been publicly disclosed on the subject, that there is criminality somewhere, which really merits a criminal arraignment and an ignominious punishment."

The court then proceeds to show that, " if, for any cause, the *corporation* is unable to bring suit, or if, through fraud and collusion, the directors refuse or neglect to bring suit, in the corporate name, and will not seek redress, a ground will be laid for invoking the interposition of a court of equity," &c.

The Charitable Corporation v. *Sir Robert Sutton et al.*, 2 Atkins, 401.

This was a bill in chancery, filed by the complainants, asking for satisfaction for a breach of trust, fraud and mismanagement from the defendants, who were directors. The corporation, it appears, had been chartered by an act of Parliament for the purpose of loaning money to poor persons, on pawns and pledges, in order to assist them, and was managed and controlled by the defendants, who were directors.

The jurisdiction of the court below was denied, and it was contended that the court could not interfere in the affairs of a private corporation in this way; but Lord HARDWICKE said, that the defendants, who were the directors and managers, "by accepting a trust of this sort, were obliged to execute it with fidelity and reasonable diligence, and *it is no excuse to say*, that they had no benefit from it, but that it was merely honorary; and, therefore, they are within the case of common trustees." See, also, *Coggs* v. *Bernard*, 1 Salk, 26.

Other objections were urged against any decree being made against the defendants personally for their negligence and mismanagement, but the Lord Chancellor said, page 406, that, "he would never determine that a court of equity cannot lay hold of every breach of trust, let the person be guilty of it either in a *private* or public capacity." He further said that, "the tribunals of this kingdom are wisely formed, both of courts of law and equity, and so are the tribunals of most nations; and for this reason there can be no injury, but there must be a remedy in some or all of them; and, therefore, I will never determine, that frauds of this kind are out of the reach of courts of law and equity, for an intolerable grievance would follow such a determination." And he, being of the opinion, that the case was most eminently one for the interposition of a court of chancery, solemnly decreed, that the directors should, and were, liable for all losses which had occurred by reason of their fraud and negligence, and ordered the master to make an examination of the officers of the company, and report to him for final judgment.

Francis Putnam et al. v. *Alanson Sweet et al.*, 1 Chandler' Rep. (Wis.,) 286. Where two separate and distinct parties are acting in the accomplishment of a measure injurious to others, who have rights in the same matter, though they may be acting separately, and without concert, to carry their plan into effect, *all the parties so acting may be joined in a bill, by the aggrieved party, as defendants*, and an objection, by demurrer, on account of such alleged misjoinder, will not be sustained.

Though it may be necessary, in proceedings against a corporation, to oust it of its jurisdiction and franchises, for the proper officer of the State to be the actor, by information or *quo warranto, yet, where one or more have obtained, through fraud, the possession of a corporation* created by law, and assume to exercise its functions, and *are possessed of its franchises, the court will entertain a bill, filed by parties aggrieved by such an act, as a matter of private right.*

Where a corporation is *in esse, in facto*, it is necessary that the corporation should be party in a suit to oust those who are alleged to have fraudulently possessed themselves of its franchises; and it is erroneous to dismiss a bill filed, where a corporation should have been a party. In such a case, leave to amend should be granted. It is competent for any number of persons, who have an interest in the stock of a corporation, to file a bill in behalf of themselves and all others standing in like condition, though all are not participants in filing such bill.

This is a case of contributors to a common fund, for equal profit and at equal risk; so far they stand as partners in a joint stock company. Neither are they corporators, for there is no organized corporation. The corporation may never be organized; and for all purposes of equitable jurisdiction, they stand together in the relation of a partnership. But the cases make the analogy stronger than this. In England, these joint stock companies, without being strictly incorporated, are licensed, and their powers and duties defined by act of parliament, as *quasi* corporations. And the *courts* of equity there deal with them as partnerships, and sustain such bills as this. *Gray* v. *Chaplin*, 2 Sim. & Stu., 267. *Hichens* v. *Congreve*, 4 Russ., 562. And even in the case of a regular corporation, *Adley* v. *Whitestable Co.*, 17 Vesey, 315.

We see no sound distinction between these cases and the case before the court. They are equally cases of subscribers to the stock of companies organized under act of the legislature; and the only difference is in this, that here there is a capacity to become a corporation, which capacity, however, has never been and may never be exercised. We think, therefore, that if there were no other ground of jurisdiction in this court over this case, it would take it on the general ground of jurisdiction to regulate and control partnership relations.

Equity takes exclusive jurisdiction of the administration of trusts, express or implied; this is one of the most comprehensive grounds of equitable jurisdiction, whenever one interested with the administration of the property, has abused or is about to abuse such trust, equity will grant relief to the *cestui que* trust. (2 Story's Eq., 228–29–30.) We assume, that the funds subscribed to the stock of this company are a trust fund; of which the complainants and their fellows are *cestui que trusts*, and the commissioners, in the first instance, the trustees. The funds were the complainants' funds, when paid; remained beneficially theirs, after paid, although they became vested in the commissioners, and the commissioners held them for the use of the complainants. The commissioners had the legal title; the complainants the equitable and beneficial ownership. This is the exact definition of a trust. (2 Story's Eq., 230.) Nor is it any new doctrine, that corporate funds are a trust in equity, which the court will control and preserve.

> 2 Story's Eq., 498–9.
> 2 John's Ch. R., 386, 389.
> 3 Mason, 311.
> 3 Paige, 222.
> 8 Peters, per Story J., 286.
> 2 Atk., 2000–6.

Where a corporation transcends its legislative powers and performs an act clearly illegal, and where the necessary effects of such an act would well be to impose a burden on the property of any corporator, the court has power to interfere.

> *Christopher* v. *Mayor, &c., of New York*, 13 Barb., 567.

Courts of equity have, through a long train of decisions, established their jurisdiction over corporations charged with a misapplication of funds, regarding them as trusts, also, treating them as partnerships ; and in very many cases, upon the ground of fraud, commencing with the celebrated declaration of Lord HARDWICKE in *the Charitable Corporation* v. *Sutton*, and running through all the decisions down to our own day. ·

> See—   *Brown* v. *Vandyke*, 4 Halst. Ch. R., 795.

Another objection taken on the part of the company was, that the company ought not to be a party to the suit. That applies to the demurrer by the company. This objection I have no hesitation in overruling. *The acts of the directors of which the bill complains, were the acts of the directors as representatives of the company, and, as such, were the acts of the company itself.* The object of the suit, amongst other things, *is to restrain the company from doing the acts complained of ;* and the company would not be bound in this suit, unless it were a party in its corporate character. This frame of suit is admitted by the court *as the only means of binding the company, in a case in which the question arises between some of its own members, whether that which the company is about to do, or has done, is a lawful act.* In truth, the only regular way of suing the company is as a corporation ; but *in a case where a dispute arises between the members of the company as to the legality of the acts done, or intended to be done, by the managing body of the company, and a suit become necessary, the court, as the only means of trying the question, allows some of its members to sue the others ; but still, it is the company against whom the question is raised.* I do not think there is any question or doubt upon that in any of the cases.

> *Bagshawe* v. *the Eastern Union Railway Company*, 6 English Railway Cases, 130.

See, also—   *Sears* v. *Hotchkiss*, 25 Conn. 171.

The right of a member of an incorporated company to sue the corporation is well settled.

> *Barnstead* v. *Empire Mining Co.*, 5 Calf., 299.
>
> See, also— Ex parte Boker, 18 Ark. 338.

In the case of *Jefferson Branch Bank* v. *Skelly*, 1 Black, 449, Justice WAYNE said, " that a stockholder in a corporation has a remedy in chancery against the directors of a bank, to prevent them from doing acts which would amount to a violation of its charter, or to prevent them from any misapplication of its capital which *might lessen the value of the shares*, if the acts intended to be done shall amount to what the law calls a breach of trust ; also, that a stockholder in a bank, or other corporation, had a remedy in chancery against individuals, in whatever character they profess to act, if the subject of complaint is an *imputed* violation of a corporate franchise, or the denial of a right growing out of it, for which there is not an adequate remedy at law, and if the stockholder, who complains, be a resident of another State than that in which the bank or corporation has its habitat, that he may then resort to the courts of the United States for a remedy."

See, as to allowing a suit to be commenced in this way and upon the principles stated in this bill, *Wright* v. *Sill*, 2 Black (U. S.), 544, in which Judge WAYNE said : "These questions come before this court the first time, in the *Piqua Branch of the State Bank of Ohio* v. *Knoop*, 16 How., 369, and were resolved in the affirmative. They have since been repeatedly before this court, and have uniformly been decided in the same way."

> *Dodge* v. *Woolsey*, 18 How., 331.
>
> *Mechanics & Traders Bank* v. *Debolt*, 18 How., 380.
>
> *Jefferson Branch Bank* v. *Skelly*, 1 Black, 436.
>
> *Franklin Branch Bank* v. *State of Ohio*, 1 Black, 474.

In Ang. & Ames on Corporations, p. 367, the following doctrine is laid down:

" As a court of equity never permits a wrong to go unredressed merely for the sake of form, if it appears that the directors of a corporation refuse in such case to prosecute, by collusion with those who have made themselves answerable by their negligence, or fraud, *or if the corporation is still under the control of those who must be the defendants* in the suit, the stockholders, who are the real parties in interest, will be permitted to file a bill in their own names, making the corporation a party defendant. And if the stockholders are so numerous as to render it impossible, or very inconvenient, to bring them all before the court, a part may file a bill in behalf of themselves and all others standing in the same situation. The jurisdiction of chancery, in such cases, proceeds, in case of joint stock corporations, upon the same principle applied to charitable corporations in England. The directors are the trustees or managing partners, and the stockholders are the *cestuis que trust*, and have a joint interest in all the property and effects of the corporation ; and no injury that the stockholders may sustain by a fraudulent breach of trust, can, upon the general principles of equity, be suffered to pass without a remedy."

Again, on pp. 467–8–9–70 of Ang. & Ames on Corporations :

" That in cases where the legal remedy against a corporation is inadequate, *a court of equity will interfere, is well settled;* and there are cases in which a bill in equity will lie against a corporation by one of its members. It is a breach of trust towards a shareholder in a joint stock incorporated company, established for a certain, definite purpose, prescibed by its charter, if the funds or credit of the company, are, without his consent, diverted from such purpose, *though the misapplication be sanctioned by the votes of a majority ;* and therefore, he may file a bill in equity against the company, in his own behalf, to restrain the company, by injunction, from any such diversion, or misapplication. The language of Lord BROUGHAM, in the case of a bill filed by a member of a water company against the company, was, ' It is said that this is an attempt on the part of the company to do acts which they are not empowered to do by the acts of Parliament. So far I restrain them by injunction. Indeed, an investment in the the stock of any corporation, must, by every one, be considered a wild speculation, if it exposed the owners of the stock to all sorts of risks in support of plausible projects not set forth and authorized by the act of incorporation, and which may posssibly lead to extraordinary losses.' "

If the managers of a corporation are about to engage in an enterprise not contemplated by the charter, or apply the corporate funds or credit to any other than the purposes therein specified, a court of equity will interfere by injunction at the instance of the stockholders.

> *Smith* v. *Bangs*, 15 Ill. 401–2.
> *Bagshaw* v. *Eastern Counties R. Co.*, 7 Hare 114.
> *Beman* v. *Rufford*, 6 Eng. Law & Eq. 106.
> *Coleman* v. *Eastern Counties R. Company*, 10 Beavan, 1.

Although the result of the authorities clearly is, that a corporation, when acting within the scope of, and in obedience to, the provisions of its constitutions, the will of the *majority* duly expressed at a legally constituted meeting, must govern; yet *beyond the limits of the act of incorporation*, the will of the majority cannot make an act valid; and the *powers of a court of equity may be put in motion, at the instance of a single shareholder, if he can show that the corporation are employing their statutory powers for the accomplishment of purposes not within the scope of their institution.*

The case of *Abbot* v. *American Hard Rubber Co.*, 33 Barb. 578, decides expressly, that a stockholder and creditor in a corporation is entitled to an injunction and a receiver in a case where the trustees have undertaken to sell to a new company, in which they were largely interested, substantially the whole property and interest of the corporation.

Cohen v. *Wilkinson*, 1 Macnaughten & Gordon, 481.

This was an application on behalf of the defendants, the directors of the Direct London & Portsmouth Railway Company, and of the Direct London & Portsmouth Railway Company, to reverse an order made by the Master of the Rolls, on the 4th of June, 1849, whereby it was ordered that an injunction should issue to restrain the defendants from applying the capital or funds of the Direct London & Portsmouth Railway Company, or any part thereof, in or towards the construction of a railway from the Croydon & Epsom Railway, commencing by a junction therewith in the parish of Epsom, to Leatherhead, in the county of Surrey, only, or any otherwise than for the purpose of making and completing a railway from the Corydon and Epsom Railway, to the parish of Portsea, in or near the town of Portsmouth, in the county of Southampton, in pursuance of the powers then vested in them by act of parliament; and that the injunction so granted be dissolved.

The Lord Chancellor observed that the main point in the case, namely, the *right of an individual member of a company to restrain that company from applying its funds to a purpose different from that to which he had subscribed, was one well settled in this court ;* that the question therefore reduced itself to this—was what the company here contemplated doing, the purpose for which the plaintiff has subscribed? in short, could it be said that the line of railway proposed to be constructed between Epsom and Leatherhead, a distance of four miles only, was equivalent to the construction of a railway between Epsom and Portsmouth. His Lordship remarked that a railway from Epsom to Portsmouth, might, in the estimation of the plaintiff, have been a good speculation while the construction of a line for the four miles which the company proposed making, might have been considered a very bad speculation. His Lordship then added—the injunction which has been granted, while it leaves it entirely open to the company to complete the whole work, very correctly restrains the defendants from applying the funds of the company to the construction of a portion only of that work, a purpose clearly different from that to which the plaintiff subscribed.

Coleman v. *the Eastern Counties Railway Company,* 4 Railway Cases, 513. The managing directors of a railway company, with the view of increasing the traffic on their line, entered into a contract with a steam packet company, that they would guarantee the proprietors of the steam packet company a minimum dividend of five per cent. on their paid up capital, until the company should be dissolved, and that, upon a dissolution, the whole paid up capital should be returned to the shareholders, in exchange for a transfer of the assets and properties of the steam packet company.

One of the shareholders filed a bill in behalf of himself and all the other shareholders who contribute, except the directors, against the company and the directors, and obtained an injunction, *ex parte* to restrain the completion of the contract :

Held, on motion to dissolve the injunction, that an objection for a want of parties to a suit so framed, was not sustainable. That directors have no right to enter into or pledge the funds of the company in support of any project not pointed out by their act, although such project may tend to increase the traffic upon the railway, and may be assented to by the majority of the shareholders, and the object of such project may not be against public policy. That acquiescence, by shareholders, in a project, for however long a period, affords no presumption that such project is legal. That an objection, stated by affidavit, and remaining unanswered, that the plaintiff was proceeding, at the instigation and request of a rival company, did not deprive him of his rights to an injunction; and the motion to dissolve the injunction was refused with costs. The learned judge says:

" To look upon a railway company in the light of a common partnership, and as subject to no greater vigilance than common partnerships may be, would, I think, be greatly to mistake the functions which they perform, and the powers of interference which they exercise with the public and private rights of all individuals in this realm. We are to look upon those powers as given to them in consideration of .a benefit, which, notwithstanding all other sacrifices, is, on the whole, hoped to be obtained by the public ; but the public interest being to *protect the private rights of all individuals, and to save them from liabilities beyond those* which the powers given by the several acts necessarily occasion, *those private rights must always be carefully looked to.* I am clearly of opinion, that the powers given by an act of parliament, like that which is now in question, *extend no further than what is expressly stated in the act,* except where they are necessarily and properly acquired for the purposes which the act has sanctioned. How far those powers may extend which are necessarily or conveniently to be exercised for the purposes intended by the act, will very often be a subject of great difficulty. But I apprehend that it has nowhere been stated that railway companies have power to enter into transactions of all sorts and to any extent. Indeed, it is admitted, and very properly admitted, that they have not the right to enter into new trades and a new business not pointed out by the act ; but it is contended that they have a right to pledge the funds of the company, without any limit, for the encouragement of other transactions, however various and extensive, *provided, only, they profess that the object of the liability* occasioned to their own shareholders by such encouragement, is to increase the traffic upon the railway, and, thereby, the profit to the shareholders. Surely, that has nowhere been stated ; *there is no authority for any thing of that kind.* What has been stated is, that these things, to a small extent, have frequently been done since the establishment of railways. Be it so : but, unless what has been done can be proved to be in conformity with the powers given by the special acts of parliament, they do not, in my opinion, furnish any authority whatever. *There is no project, however wild, which the shareholders, or the persons liable in respect of those companies, have not acquiesced in, from one cause or another, either from cupidity and the hope of gaining extraordinary profits beyond their first anticipations, or from terror of entering into a contest with persons so powerful.* In the absence of legal decisions, I look upon the acquiescence of shareholders in these transactions as affording no ground whatever for the presumption that they may be in themselves legal."

In *Salomons* v. *Laing*, the same learned judge said (6 Railway C., 301): " A railway company, incorporated by act of parliament, is bound to apply all the moneys and property of the company for purposes directed and provided for by the act of parliament, which, in truth, was the motive and inducement for the granting extraordinary powers given by all these acts of parliament; when these purposes are fully performed, any surplus which may remain, after setting apart the sum to answer contingencies, may, if not applied in enlarging, improving or repairing the works, be divided among the shareholders. The dividends, which belong to the shareholders, and are divisible among them, may be applied by them, severally, as their own property; but the company itself, or the directors, *or any number of shareholders assembled at a meeting, or otherwise,* have no right to dispose of the shares of the general dividend, which belong to the particular shareholder, in any manner contrary to the will, or without the consent or authority of that particular shareholder. *Any application of, or dealing with, the capital, or any part of the capital, or any funds or money of the company, which may come under the control or management of the directors or governing body of the company, in any manner* not distinctly authorized by the act of parliament, is, in my opinion, an *illegal application or dealing;* and I am of opinion, that, if it involve the company, or the shareholders of the company, *or any of them,* in liabilities to which the shareholders, or any of the shareders, never consented, relief may and ought to be given in this court."

"A corporation, in the exercise of its franchises, will not be allowed to make use of any fraud or deception in order to evade responsibilities; and all persons who are guilty of fraud are proper parties to a suit.

It is certainly true that the law will strip a corporation or individual of every disguise, and enforce a responsibility according to the very right in despite of their artifices.

And it is equally certain that, in favor of the right, it will hold them to maintain the truth of the representations to which the public has trusted, and estop them from using their simulation as a covering or defence."

The York & Maryland R. R. Co. v. *Winans,* 17 How., 40.

It is a fraud, not only on the shareholders, but also on the legislature, that a company should be permitted to obtain its capital stock for a particular and special purpose, and then apply it to another.

> *Bagshaw* v. *Eastern Union R. R. Co.*, 6 R. Cases, 127.
>
> *Coleman* v. *Eastern Counties R. Co.*, 4 R. Cases, 513.
>
> *Chapple* v. *Cadell*, Jac., 537.
>
> *Reg* v. *Eastern Counties R. Co.*, 2 R. Cases, 260.
>
> *Blakemore* v. *Glamorganshire C. Co.*, 1 My. & K., 154.
>
> *Gray* v. *Chaplin*, 2 S. & S., 267.
>
> *Natusch* v. *Irving*, Gow on Partnership, Appendix, 398.

In the case of *Bagshaw* v. *the Eastern Union Railway Co.*, 6 Railway Cases, 129, which is directly in point, Bagshaw was the owner of two scrip certificates, only, out of a capital stock of over 300,000 *pounds* sterling, and he, as owner in behalf of himself and all others similarly situated, enjoined the company from applying the funds of the company to build some branch roads not specified in the charter, and the court, in deciding the case, said :

" No majority of the shareholders, however large, could sanction the misapplication of the capital. *A single dissenting voice* would frustrate the wishes of the majority. Indeed, in strictness, *even unanimity would not* make the act lawful."

See, also— *Burmester* v. *Norris*, 8 Eng. L. & Eq., 487.

In the case of *Salomons* v. *Laing*, 6 R. & Canal cases—above quoted—Salomons was the owner of 149 shares out of a capital of 1,420,000 pounds—the case is directly in point—and it was there contended, first, that the majority in interest ought to control—and that a shareholder who possessed so little interest ought not to be allowed to bring suit—and—second, that it was erroneous to make both companies and their directors parties ; but the court held that the complainant brought his suit properly, and, that all who were *particeps criminis* were proper parties ; and that in all illegal transactions the will of the majority could never bind the minority.

In deciding this case, on final hearing, Lord LANGDALE said—that " whether it was alleged in words or not it is perfectly clear that both the parties to this transaction (in the case at bar both the C. & N. W. R. Co., and G. & C. U. R. R. Co.,) are guilty of fraud and collusion. They are guilty of fraud against the legislature who gave them their powers for purposes entirely different from those which they are exercising ; and they are guilty of collusion, in together uniting and combining for the purpose of completing that fraud. But it is not necessary to say that they have been guilty of fraud and collusion ; it is enough to say they are parties to the same *breach of trust*, one in paying and the other in receiving moneys for a known illegal purpose ; which moneys are now or ought to be in the hands of the Portsmouth Co. The question before me is whether the Portsmouth company ought to be made a party to this suit, which seeks a declaration of rights and the re-recovery of these moneys which the Portsmouth company have received with knowledge that they were trust moneys, and which ought to have been applied to a purpose entirely different.

I have *not the least* doubt that they are properly made parties to this suit—they have themselves received the moneys, knowing the purpose to which they were to be applied. Knowing, therefore, the persons to whom they rightly belonged (to-wit, the stockholders of the Brighton Co.,) they get them out of the hands of the persons who had the management of them, for the purpose of applying them to other and quite different purposes. I think there is no doubt that the Portsmouth company are proper parties to this suit."

Where a bill is filed for relief in respect of a fraud alleged to have been committed by several persons, it is not necessary that all the persons charged with the fraud should be made defendants.

Sedden v. *Connell*, 10 Simmons, 81.

The power of the corporation, being limited by its charter, could

not be extended by the stockholders—hence, the sale of the G. &
C. U. R. R. and all its property, even by a majority of the stockholders, would be illegal and void against all who did not consent.

> *Hood* v. *N. Y. & New Haven R. R. Co.*, 22
> Conn. 507.
> *Andrews* v. *Union Mutual Fire Ins. Co.*, 37
> Maine, 2.
> *N. Y. F. I. Co.* v. *Ely*, 5 Conn. 560.
> *Phoenix Bank* v. *Curtis*, 14 Conn. 443.
> *Welland Canal Co.* v. *Hathaway*, 8 Wend.
> 484.

Directors can't make a sale of the whole entire property of every
character and kind.

> See—*Rollins* v. *Clay*, 33 Maine, 139.

Neither can the shareholders of a corporation delegate their
powers to another company and allow it to be worked and controlled by such company. See—

> 1 Shelford on Railways, p. 251.
> *Beaman* v. *Rufford*, 1 Sim. (N. S.) 550.

A corporation may institute a suit for setting aside transactions
fraudulent against it, although carried into effect in its name by
members of the governing body. The members of the governing
body are agents of a corporation, and if they exercise their functions for the purpose of injuring its interests and alienating its property they are personally liable for any loss occasioned thereby.

> 1 Shelford on R's. 284–5.
> 1 Cr. & P. 1.
> 2 Mylne & Craig 621.
> 1 Swanst, 265.
> 1 Ves. & B. 226.

A corporation cannot, except with the consent of the legislature,
.(and by the authorities above cited), by the consent, also, of all the
stockholders, alienate its property and relinquish the control and
management of its affairs to another company.

> *York & Maryland & C. R. R. Co.* v. *Winans*,
> 11 Howard, (U. S.) 30.

In *Abbot* v. *American Hard Rubber Company*, 33 Barb. 589, Allen, J., says: " A bare statement of the case shows as conclusively as an elaborate argument could establish it, *that the transfer was without power, and a violation of the trust* and confidence reposed in the trustees *and directors of the corporation.* It is *ultra vires.* It would be strong evidence of fraudulent intent, under the circumstances, that a bare quorum of the body should undertake, by their acts, so seriously *and radically to affect* the *future* of the company *and the interests of the stockholders,* but waiving that question, and conceding that their acts stand as the acts of the whole board, *I am of the opinion they were invalid for want of power. By the transfer, if allowed to stand, although the corporation still remained, in form,* with property which might be applied to some lawful purpose, the *existence of the corporation was nominal,* its substance was taken from it, and its property was valueless ; as a ' Hard Rubber Co.,' it had *no rights, no franchises, and no existence. Its very title was a misnomer, and a false pretence.*"

And Sutherland, J., says: "The purchasers *cannot* be considered *bona fide* purchasers for value, without notice, for they did not give money or value, but their notes or promises to pay ; and I must assume from the conceded facts of the case, that they knew the purpose and object for which the corporation was organized, and the only business which it had prosecuted ; and as they must also be presumed to know the law, I must assume that they *knew* that *directors, with or without the consent of a majority of the stockholders, had no right or authority to make the sale and transfer in question.*"

In the case of the *Troy & Rutland R. R. Co.* v. *Kerr*, 17 Barb. 601, the court said :

" As I understand the evidence, *the whole line of the railroad* of the plaintiffs has passed out of the charge of the corporation. It has been decided in England that one railroad corporation cannot lease its road, or *give up the management of its line to another, nor delegate the powers conferred* without the authority of the legislature. Those acts *are ultra vires—*"

Beman v. *Rufford*, 1 Sim. (N. S.) 550.
6 Eng. Law & Eq. 106.
Great Eastern Counties R. Co. v. *Eastern
Counties R. Co.*, 9 Hare, 313.
13 Eng. Law & Eq. 506.
1 Sim. (N. S.) 110.
16 Eng. Law & Eq. 180.

and could not be done—"*Not even with the assent of all the shareholders.*"

East Anglian R. Co. v. *Eastern Counties R.
Co.*, 11 C. B. 775.

MAINE CASES.

The powers of a corporation are derived from the law.
They *cannot be enlarged* by any act of the corporate body.

Andrews v. *Union Mutual Fire Ins. Co.*, 37
Maine, 260.
Rollins v. *Clay*, 33 Maine, 139.

A corporate body has no corporate existence beyond the limits
of the territory or state which created it.

Day v. *The Newark India Rubber Co.*, 1
Blatch. Ct. C. 628.
Caledonian R. R. Co. v. *The Helmsburg Har-
bor Trustees*, 39 Eng. Law & Eq.

Blake v. *Mowatt*, 21 Beavan, 613, is in point to show that notwithstanding the parties are in such a position that they cannot be
restored, still the court will, regardless of all consequences, set
aside a fraudulent contract.

X.

*The rights, privileges and franchises of a corporation are created by
the sovereign power of a State—and are in fact a part and parcel of it—and on grounds of public policy, therefore, they cannot
be bought and sold or bartered away like goods and chattels.*

Franchises, in kingly governments, are a part of the king's prerogative, and are esteemed royal privileges subsisting in the hands of a subject, which can only be obtained by grant from the crown, or by prescription, which presupposes a grant from the sovereign. In this country the word franchise and liberty are held synonymous, and mean *governmental* leave to use certain governmental powers and rights for the purposes, and in the manner prescribed by public authority.

In this country, therefore, as well as in England, no governmental privileges are ever conferred upon any person by construction, or implication—and no franchise is ever assignable except by express statute ; neither can it be so agreed or substantially put under the control of any but the grantee.

5 Johns. 175–6.

1 Blackf. 405.

16 N. Y. 161–8

6 Eng. Law & Eq. 106–10.

12 Eng Law & Eq. 224–8.

13 Eng. Law & Eq. 506–16.

26 Vt. 721.

12 Barb. 61.

82 Eng. Com. Law, 396–7.

3 Comst. 242.

5 Law Reporter, 107–8.

In this country there is no such thing as creating corporations by prescription or usurpation.

10 How. (U. S.) 534.

18 Johns. 229.

4 Mass. 522.

One stockholder has got just as much interest in the franchises of a corporation as another—and the *privileges* which the state confers upon a member of a corporation will be just as sacredly upheld, and his *rights*, which he thereby *acquires*, just as sacredly *protected* as any other right or privilege which he has under the constitution of the United States, or which are conferred upon him by being or becoming a citizen of this republic.

If, therefore, there should be, for instance, two thousand stockholders of a corporation—could fifteen hundred hundred sell out the franchises—and tell the other five hundred to appeal to the winds for their remedy? If the *stockholders* could not do it— could the *directors*—who are nothing but the trustees for *all* of the stockholders—do it? Or would it confer upon either, or both, any more power or authority, if the *directors* and a *majority* of the stockholders, were in collusion, and acted together, or first one assembled and resolved to sell out and then the other assembled and did the same thing? In short, could they sell out the franchises of a corporation, at all—whether the stockholders and directors acted seperately or collectively—whether in an official capacity or otherwise—we maintain that it cannot be done by any shift, slight of hand, or prestidigitation whatever. The defendants may seek to evade it by calling it " consolidation " or any other name known to man, but it does not alter the principle at all. And, if now, the franchises of a corporation cannot be sold or bartered away like merchandize or wooden clocks, can they be *mixed up, merged, combined* and *consolidated,* with any other franchises, by the majority in interest of any corporation? We maintain, that, on principle, it cannot be done—and this doctrine has been established by scores of cases in this country.

> *Commonwealth* v. *The Pittsborg & Connells-*
> *ville R. R. Co.,* 24 Penn. State Rep. 159.
> *Bruffett* v. *Great Western R. R. Co.,* 25 1ll.
> 357.

In this case, the court, (Judge WALKER,) said, that " the charter and franchises are not an incident that is annexed to, and passes with, a transfer of the property of such company. Nor does the company forfeit or become deprived of such rights by the loss of its property. If there is a cause of forfeiture, that must be determined judicially to make it effectual."

The franchises and corporate rights of a company and the means vested in them which are necessary to the existence and maintenance of the object for which they were created, *are incapable of being granted away* and transferred, by any act of the company itself, or by any adverse process against it.

> *The Susquehanna Canal Co.* v. *Bonham,* 9 Watts & Serg. 27.

The shareholders could not convey the real estate of the corporation, though they all join in the deed.

> *Wheelock* v. *Moulton & Woodstock Manufacturing Co.,* 15 Vt. 519.

In the case of *Arthur* v. *The Commercial & R. R. Bank of Vicksburgh,* 9 Smede & Marshall, 431, the court said : "The franchise itself cannot be sold or assigned without the consent of the power which granted it. It is a mere easement, a privilege granted to an artificial being, not the subject of sale. The sale, or assignment of the road does not carry the franchise with it, nor does it work a dissolution of the corporation."

> See also—*Dartmouth College* v. *Woodward,* 4 Wheaton, 637–638–663.
>
> *Clark* v. *Corporation of Wash.* 12 Wheat. 40.
>
> *Beatby* v. *The Lessee of Knowler,* 4 Peters, 168–514.
>
> *Jackson* v. *Lamphire,* 3 Peters, 289.
>
> 11 *Ib.* 546.
>
> 13 Serg. & R. 212.
>
> 15 Mass. 237.

In the case of the *York & Maryland R. R. Co.* v. *Winans,* 17 Howard, 39, which was a suit brought by Winans against the company for an infringement of a patent right, respecting cars. The defense set up was that the company was incorporated by the laws of Penn., but the stock was all owned by a Maryland company, except a few shares which were held by Pennsylvania parties— enough to make directors—and the road was operated by the Maryland company. The court, in deciding the case said, in speaking of this defence—that it " *implied* that the duties imposed upon the plaintiff by the charter, are fulfilled by the construction of the road, and that by alienating its right to use and its powers of control and supervision, it may avoid further responsibility. *But, those acts involve an overturn* of the relations which the charter has arranged between the corporation and the community. Important franchises were conferred upon the corporation to enable it to provide the facilities to communication and intercourse required for the public convenience. *Corporate management* and *control over these* were prescribed, and corporate responsibility for their insufficiency provided, as a remuneration to the community, for their grant.

The *corporation cannot* absolve itself from the performance of its obligations *without the consent* of the legislature."

The court, after thus deciding in the most clear and emphatic manner, that a corporation *cannot alienate* its franchises—and surrender up control of the corporation to strangers—says :

" It is certainly true that the law will strip a corporation or individual of every disguise, and enforce a responsibility, according to the very right, in despite of their artifices. And it is equally certain, that, in favor of the right, it will hold them to maintain the truth of the representations to which the public has trusted and estop them from using their simulation as a covering or defence."

Michigan Cases.

James v. Pontiac & Groveland Plank Road, 8 Mich. 94.

This case decides that the franchises of a corporation could not be sold on execution at common law—and could only be reached by proceedings in equity. This was an attempt to sell the franchise on execution—and the court said—that " there could be no acquiescence which would render such an act valid on the part of the shareholders.

Massachusetts Cases.

The *Middlesex Turnpike Corporation* v. *Thomas Locke,* 8 Mass. 269, decides, that where the corporation makes a fundamental change in the objects of the corporation, a stockholder would be released from his contract which was implied in taking stock in a corporation designed for a particular object.

Middlesex Turnpike Corporation v. *Swan*, 10 Mass. 385.

An agreement between railway companies without the authority of the legislature, transferring the powers of one company to the other, is against good policy, and a court of equity will prevent it.

Redfield on Railways, 418.

Great Northern R. Co. v. *Eastern Co. R.*, 9 Hare.

Johnson v. *The Shrewsburg & Birmingham R. Co.*, 19 Eng. Law & Eq. 584–6.

Troy & Rut. R. v. *Kerr*, 17 Barb. 581.

This doctrine is reaffirmed by the House of Lords in *Shrewsburg & B. R. R.* v. *L. & N. W. R.*, 29 Law Times, 186, and it has been decided in numerous cases in this country—that, where companies do, by consent of the legislature, make leases of their roads, that they cannot release themselves from their obligations to the public.

Nelson v. *The Vermont Central R. Co.* 26 Vt. 717.

Sawyer v. *The Rutland R. R. Company*, 27 Vt. 370.

Parker v. *Renssaelar & S. R. Company*, 16 Barb. 315.

The English courts have, in many instances, even restrained railway companies from carrying contracts of lease into effect.

And the reason, for all this strictness, in not allowing railway companies to become articles of commerce and merchantable property, is just this—the charter constitutes a contract between the State and the corporation—in, and by which the State grants certain privileges and immunities on its part—and the corporation contracts for the performance of certain public duties and functions on its part. Now, this contract is not in its nature assignable, so as to transfer those rights and privileges to others and release themselves from their duties and obligation ; therefore, it is, that the rights, privileges and franchises of corporations are not negotiable

—and do not pass by endorsement, in writing on their back, quite so easily as many seem to imagine.

The supreme court of the State of Illinois in the case of the *Ohio & Miss. R. R. Co.* v. *Dunbar,*........ 623, decides that a railroad company *cannot* relieve itself from liability by leasing its road.

> See also—*Chicago* v. *Rock Island R. R. Co.* v. *Whipple,* 22 Ill. 109.
>
> *Illinois Central R. R.* v. *Finnigan,* 21 Ill. 649.
>
> *Bruffert* v. *Great Western R. R. Co.* 25 Ill. 356.

Certainly no lease, whatever, could be made except by permission of the legislature, and, in that case, the lease would not relieve the company from any liability to the public.

> *City of Chicago* v. *Evans,* 24 Ill. 52.

The case of *Coe* v. *Columbus, P. & Ind. R. R. Co.,* 10 Ohio, 373, reviews this whole subject of attempting to sell or dispose of the franchises of a corporation the most elaborately of any case to be found in the books, and it holds that it cannot be alienated by any act of the corporation.

XI.

Ultra Vires.

We contend that the Galena & Chicago Union Rail Road Company was formed for the purpose which is stated and set forth *in the charter,* viz: " To construct, and during its continuance, to maintain and continue, a railroad with a single or double track, and with such appendages as may be deemed necessary, for the convenient use of the same from the town of Galena, in the county of Jo Davies, to such point at the town of Chicago as shall be determined, after a survey shall have been made of the route, to be most eligible, proper, direct, and convenient therefor; with such lateral routes as may be deemed advantageous and expedient and necessary, under the same rights and privileges, as, by this act, is provided for the constructing of the main route," and for no other purpose or purposes whatsoever; and all contracts which are made for any other purpose, such for instance, as building a railroad beyond its termini—or aiding in building one—or becoming security for, or jointly liable for the debts and liabilities of other distinct railroad corporations either in this State or any other State—or selling out its entire property to another corporation, or giving up the control of it to another corporation—or throwing its capital stock into hotch-pot, or a common fund, with any other corporation, and mixing up its earnings and expenses with any other corporation in any way—are *ultra vires* and void.

In the case of *East Anglian Railway Company* v. *Eastern Counties Railway Company*, 7 Eng. Law & Eq. 505, where a railway company was incorporated by a public act of parliament, " for the purpose of making and maintaining " a particular railway, and other works by the act authorized, " and for other purposes therein declared," the defendants, the company so incorporated, covenanted with the plaintiffs, another railway company, to take a lease of their railways, and to pay the costs of soliciting bills then pending in parliament, by which the plaintiffs were to be authorized to make extensions and branches of their railways. This was an action for breach of covenant, in not paying the costs of the bills in parliament.

JERVIS, C. J., in deciding the case, says : " This act is a public act, accessible to all ; and supposed to be known to all, and the plaintiffs must, therefore, be presumed to have dealt with the defendants, with a full knowledge of their respective rights, whatever those rights may be. It is clear, that the defendants have a limited authority only, and are a corporation only for the purpose of *making* and *maintaining the railway sanctioned by the act*, and that *their funds can only be applied for the purposes* directed and provided for by the statute. Indeed, it is not contended that a company so constituted can engage in new trades not contemplated by their act, but it is said that they may embark in other undertakings, however various, provided the object of the directors be to increase the profit of their own railway. This, in truth, is the same proposition in another form : if the company cannot carry on a new trade, because it is not contemplated by the act, they cannot embark in other undertakings not sanctioned by their act, merely because they hope the speculation may ultimately increase the profit of the shareholders.

" They cannot engage in a new trade ; because they are a corporation only for the purpose of making and maintaining the Eastern Counties Railway. What additional power do they acquire from the fact that the undertaking may, in some way, benefit their line ? Whatever be their object or the prospect of success, they are still but a corporation for the purpose only of making and maintaining the Eastern Counties Railway, and if they cannot embark in new trades because they have only a limited authority, for the same reason, they can do nothing not authorized by their act, and not within the scope of their authority. Every proprietor, when he takes shares, has a right to expect that the conditions upon which the act was obtained, will be performed, and it is no sufficient answer to a shareholder, expecting his dividend, that the money has been expended upon an undertaking, which, at some remote period, may be highly beneficial to the line. The public, also, has an interest in the proper administration of the powers conferred by the act. The comfort and safety of the line may be seriously impaired if the money supposed to be necessary and destined by parliament for the maintenance of the railway, be expended in other undertakings not contemplated when the act was obtained, and not expressly sanctioned by the legislature. If the contract is illegal, as being contrary to the act of parliament, it is unnecessary to consider the effect of dissenting shareholders ; for, if the company is a corporation only for a limited purpose, and a contract like that under discussion is not within their authority, the assent of all the shareholders to such a contract, though it may make them all personally liable to perform such contract, would not bind them in their corporate capacity, or render liable their coporate funds.

" If railway companies could embark in undertakings collateral to their main line, merely because the main line might in the result be benefited, there would be much in this objection ; but upon the view which we have above expressed, the objection cannot prevail. We know that each of the four litigant companies has a separate act of parliament ; we know that the statute incorporating the defendants company gives no authority respecting the bill promoted by the plaintiffs ; and we are, therefore, bound to say, that any contract relating to such bills is not justified by the act of parliament, is not within the scope of the authority of the company as a corporation, and is therefore void."

Waldo v. *Chicago, St. Paul & Fond Du Lac
R. R. Co., William B. Ogden, et al.,* 14
Wis. 581.

This was a suit brought by Waldo against the above named defendants to have certain conveyances of land made by the plaintiff to Wm. B. Ogden, and by the latter to Mahlon D. Ogden, set aside or declared void, and to compel a reconveyance of the land. The bill was filed Jan. 3I, 1859, and alleges that in the winter of 1856, William B. Ogden, Pease, and others, came to the county of Jefferson to canvass for subscriptions to the stock of the road, and that in order to induce the complainant and others to subscribe, that said Ogden, Pease, &c., represented that the C. St. P. & Fond Du Lac R. R. Co., had recently succeeded to all the rights and liabilities of the Rock River Union Valley R. R. Co., and that all the creditors of the latter company had come in and converted their claims into stock in the new company—that the company was in good condition and credit—that the net earnings of the finished road from Chicago, Fond Du Lac, and the La Crosse Junction for the last six months had been equal *to four and a half per cent. on the entire cost of the road,* and that the directors would have declared a *semi-annual* dividend of four and a half per cent. but they thought it best to use said earnings to carry on the road, and they had been carried to the constructive account instead of being divided among the stockholders—that the stock would soon be par and above par, &c., which things, the complainant declared, were false, and were made to get his land, and that of other citizens, for the purpose of procuring assets of the company, and that the company was on the eve of bankruptcy. It appeared that the complainant's lands were many miles from the railroad—and that after the lands had been conveyed to William B. Ogden to hold in trust for the railroad—that it had been conveyed to Mahlon D. Ogden, and that it was represented that the lands were to be sold for the benefit of the company. Large quantities of land were obtained for the company by William B. Ogden, by way of subscriptions for stock in the road, in this way, and were disposed of for the company, in order to aid the road, but the court held, citing *Clark* v. *Farrington*, 11 Wis. 306, 424, "that a railroad could not engage in any distinct and separate branch of business not authorized by its charter, for the purpose of raising funds to accomplish the *objects* for which it was created. That while the corporation, in the exercise of the power conferred upon it by its charter, might adopt any convenient means, proper in themselves, to accomplish the objects of its creation, it could not embark in the business of banking, or manufacturing, or *speculating* in *real estate* to raise money to build its road, for this would be acting outside of its charter.

The court then proceeds to show that a railroad company might exchange its stock for grading, ties, &c., or sell it for money, in order to enable it to accomplish the objects of its organization. " But, when a corporation, created for the purpose of building and operating a railroad, goes into the business of banking, or manufacturing and selling goods, *or dealing and speculating in real estate, because its corporators, or board of directors, think such adventures may be profitable*, or if a bank should go to building and operating a railroad for like reason, *it is easy to see that in each instance the corporation* is attempting to transact business which, under its organic act, it has no right or power to do. And if the corporation *might embark* in a separate and distinct business, not *contemplated by its charter, merely because it was supposed it would be profitable, and increase its means and resources, there would be no safety to the public in granting any special charters, and none to individuals who might invest in the stock of the company."*

The court then shows that the complainant was entitled to relief upon the other grounds set forth in the complainant's bill, and that the conveyances should be set aside.

In the case of *Gage* v. *the New Market Railway Company*, 14 English Law & Equity R., 57, in which the railway company, who were promoting, in parliament, a bill for an extension of their line, which, if made, would pass through the lands of the plaintiff, covenanted with the plaintiff, "that, in the event of the proposed bill passing in the then session of parliament, the company should, before they should enter upon any part of the plaintiff's lands, pay to him £4,900 purchase money, for any portion not exceeding forty-three acres, which the company might, under the powers of their act, require and take for the purposes of their undertaking; and that, in addition to purchase money, as aforesaid, the company should pay to the plaintiff, before they should enter upon any part of his said land, £7,100, as landlord's compensation, for the damage arising to his estate by the severance thereof, in respect of the lands, not exceeding forty-three acres to be taken by them."

Lord CAMPBELL, C. J., in deciding the case, says: "We, therefore, do not think that the company can be considered as having absolutely covenanted to pay £12,000 to the plaintiff in a reasonable time after the passage of the act. *If this deed could bear such a construction, we should have thought it, so far, ultra vires and void.* Here the railway are the covenanters, and if the present action lies, the capital paid up by the shareholders must be answerable for the damages to be recovered. We consider that this would be a *misappropriation* of the funds of the company, which the directors could not lawfully make."

In the case of the *Baltimore & Ohio R. R. Co.* v. *City of Wheeling*, 13 Grattan, 75, the court say: "If a company incorporated to make a railroad, should be about to make a canal; or incorporated to make a road from A to B, should be about to make one from A to C, these would be plain and palpable violations of the

charter, and would be restrained at the suit of a dissatisfied stockholder."

In the case of *Clark* v. *Farrington*, 11 Wis., 323, the court said,
in remarking upon the case of *Madison Plank Road Co.* v. *Watertown Plank Road Co.*, 5 Wis., 173 : " When the case was here
subsequently, and it appeared that the company had undertaken
to *assist* in the building of another road, then its acts were *held
void.*"

North Carolina Cases.

Wiswall v. *Grenville & R. Plank R. Co.*, 3 Jones Eq. (North
Carolina), 183. This was a bill brought by stockholders in the
Grenville and Raleigh Plank Road Company, to restrain the company, which was formed to build a plank road from Grenville to
Raleigh, from using funds to purchase stages and horses, and establish a mail route ; and the court enjoined them, and this was done
by a vote of the directors and by the sanction of a majority of
stockholders.

To the same effect precisely is the case of *Dowing* v. *Mount
Washington, &c., Co.*, 40 N. H. 230.

See, also—   Maverick, Sprague, 23.

Any one dissenting stockholder may restrain the company from
executing a contract which exceeds its powers.

Zabriskie v. *Cleveland, &c., R. R. Co.*, 23
How. (U. S.) 381.

In the case of *Rock River Bank* v. *Sherwood*, 10 Wis. 236, the
court said that, " it is a familiar principle, which runs through all
the law upon this subject, that a corporation is not only incapable
of making contracts which are forbidden by its charter, but, in
general, it can make *none* which are *not necessarily*, either directly
or indirectly, to effect the objects of its creation. So, when a corporation undertakes to make a contract entirely foreign to the purposes and objects of its creation, such contracts are void."

Penn., Del. & Md. Steam Navigation Co. v. *Dandridge*, 8 Gill.

& J. 248; *Madison, &c., Plank Road Co.* v. *Watertown Plank Road Co.,* 7 Wis. 59, are precisely to the same effect. This last case was where the company made a contract of *guaranty* in order to enable the other company to raise money, and it was held that the *contract was void.*

These cases show, that, in this State, the late Supreme Court and Court of Errors, and this court, have all concurred in holding, in accordance with the numerous English cases to which I have referred, that the *contracts of corporations, which are ultra vires,* are void and can not be enforced. Similar decisions have been made by the courts of other States and of the United States.

> *The Pennsylvania & Delaware Canal Co.* v. *Dandridge,* 8 Gill. & John 248.
>
> *Hood* v. *N. Y. & N. H. R. R. Co.,* 22 Conn. 502.
>
> *Ehune* v. *Nangatuck R. R. Co.,* 23 *id.* 457.
>
> *Mutual Savings, &c.,* v. *Meridian Agency Co.,* 24 *id.* 159.
>
> *Nangatuck R. R. Co.* v. *Waterbury Button Co., id.* 468.
>
> *Bank of Michigan* v. *Niles,* 1 Doug. Mich. R. 401.
>
> *Orr* v. *Lacey,* 2 *id.* 254.
>
> *Root* v. *Goddard,* 3 McL. 102.
>
> *Root* v. *Wallace,* 4 *id.* 8.
>
> *Dodge* v. *Woolsey,* 18 How. U. S. R. 331.
>
> *Pierce* v. *Madison & Quincy R. R. Co., and Peru & Quincy R. R. Co.* 21 *id.* 441.

If principles can ever be settled by authority; if the slighest respect is due to the opinions of other tribunals, it would seem that *no court could resist the overwhelming weight of the decisions which have been cited.*

Banet v. *Alton & Sangamon R. R. Co.*, 13 Ill. 508. The charter in this case provided for the building a railroad from Alton by way of Carlinville, in Macoupin County, New Berlin, in Sangamon County, to the city of Springfield. The suit was brought on a subscription by a person who had subscribed to the stock of the company, and was interested in land in New Berlin.

After the subscription, the route was changed by an act of the legislature, and ran direct to Springfield, saving twelve miles. The court review, at some length, the authorities in regard to the alterations of charters, and the effect upon the contract, and they came to the conclusion that a slight deviation *from* a crooked to a straight line would not release the subscriber, but they consider any act a change, which attaches to the corporation a new and different enterprise; and they cite, as an illustration, the case of the *Hartford & N. H. R.* v. *Creswell*, 5 Hill 385, and as a further illustration, they say, on page 513 : . "If the charter had been so amended as to authorize the construction of a road from Alton to Vandalia or Shelbyville, or from Springfield to Beardstown or Peoria, instead of the one originally designated, the company would be committed to a *new and different* enterprise, and the stockholders might, with much force and justice, say—*this is not the undertaking* in which we engaged, and not the stock in which we agreed to invest our funds."

NOTE.—I wonder if they would have regarded it any change in the "*undertaking*" of a Galena, &c. U. R. R. stockholder if they had been told that they had "*consolidated*" on to them, all the railroads between Chicago & Lake Superior, and twenty or thirty millions of dollars besides?

This case, although holding that *the* deviation in question was not a material one, contrary to the decision of many courts, yet establishes and illustrates principles broad enough to cover all the questions involved in the suit at bar.

When the case of *Newhall* v. *G. & C. U. R. R. Co.* 14 Ill. 274, came before the court, it was contended that the railroad company had no right to build lateral roads, (which the court defined to be branch roads built between the two termini, and branching from the main trunk), although that power was given in the most explicit and unmistakable manner—and it was urged that if they could build such roads they might build a railroad from Chicago to Cairo, or Shawneetown, or all over the State. The court, in deciding the case seemed to regard such a thing as a most extravagant assumption of power, and said—

" When the case arises, which was supposed in argument, of an attempt to run a road to Cairo and Shawneetown, or any other *similar* apparantly *gross abuse* of the power given in this provision of the charter, using it in a way *palpably* and *manifestly* beyond *anything* which *could* have been in the contemplation of the legislature in passing the charter, it will then become the duty of this court to say whether the court shall set a limit, and what limit, to a power which the legislature has seen fit to confer, without fixing a limit. I fully recognize *the propriety*, and even *necessity* of applying the rule of *strict construction* to the powers granted *in these* railroad charters; but the rule can only be applied in cases of ambiguity or where a power is claimed by inference or implication, and is *not* expressly given by the charter."

If it would be a gross abuse of the power of the G. & C. U. R. R. Co., to *build* a lateral road from Chicago to Cairo or Shawneetown, would it not be a thing "*palpably* and *manifestly beyond anything* which *could* have been in the contemplation of the legislature imposing the charter," for that road to engage in building or operating a railroad from Chicago to the North Pole, or Lake Superior, or the upper peninsula of Michigan.

We *pause* for a reply.

XII.

DIRECTORS.

Directors of corporations are trustees for ALL *the stockholders, and are subject to all the duties, obligations, and liabilities of trustees.*

In the case of *The New York & New Haven R. Company* v. *Schuyler, Cross, et al.* 17 N. Y. 592, where the railroad company filed a bill against Schuyler and the holders of the over issued stock, to have it cancelled, the court say—

" It is well settled that the directors or managers of a corporation *are trustees* for *the holders of its stock. It is on this ground* that the *shareholders are entitled to relief in equity against* an *actual* or threatened waste *or misapplication* of its corporate funds. It seems also to be settled that a suit for that purpose must be brought in the name of a corporation, unless it appears that the directors refuse to prosecute *or are themselves the guilty parties answerable* for the wrong. If they do refuse, *or are thus answerable* the shareholders may sue in their own names, *but in such case* the *corporation must be made a defendant, either solely or jointly, with the directors sought to be charged.* (*Robinson* v. *Smith*, 3 Paige, 222, and cases there cited). I have nowhere seen it laid down that the corporation itself, considered as a mere legal abstraction, is a trustee for its stockholders ; yet it is not difficult to see that certain trust relations exist between it and them. A corporation aggregate is clothed with a legal title to its real and personal estate, franchises and privileges, *while the shareholders, as individuals,* have in them *equitable interests, the interests of each being in proportion to the amount of stock which he holds.* The corporation is entitled to receive, and does receive, the gross amount of the earnings ; upon a *trust, however*, or at least under a *duty*, to pay over to the stockholders the net profits, as dividends upon their stock. If not under all circumstances bound to make and pay over, in money, the dividends earned, it must at all events, use them for the shareholders benefit, in the prosecution of its legitimate enterprises, and subject to ultimate accountability. If these relations are not precisely defined in the books, it is because the occasion has not arisen requiring this to be done."

In the case of *Scott* v. *Depeyster, et al.*, 1 Edwards, 513, which was a bill filed by complainant for himself, and other stockholders of the National Insurance Company, against the directors of said company for the purpose of charging them personally with heavy amounts embezzled by their secretary, the court say—

"*Persons who become directors or managers of a corporation place themselves in the situation of trustees; and the relation of trastee and cestui que trust is thereby created between them and the stockholders. The former are obliged to take the same care, and use the same diligence as factors and agents.* They are answerable not only for their own fraud and gross negligence, but also for all faults which are contrary to the care required of them. Directors are to be looked upon as *bailees* of the property. And as they are persons generally having an interest in the stock, they are not bailees who are to derive no benefit from thir undertaking, and therefore, to be held responsible for slight neglect, *but they act in relation to a bailment beneficial to both parties. And the rule then is, they must answer for ordinary neglect;* and " ordinary neglect " is understood to be, the omission of that care which every man of common prudence takes of his own concerns."

In *March* v. *R. R. Co.*, 43 N. H. 529, the court said—

" Directors of railroads who have charge of other people's money, should, and must be held to exercise the same care, caution, and prudence which they would be expected to exercise in their own affairs."

The court, then, after referring to the case of *Coleman* v. *Eastern Counties R. Co.*, 6 Eng. R. Cases, 573, in which it was held that directors have no right to enter into, or pledge the funds of the company in support of any project not pointed out by their act although such project may tend to increase the traffic upon the railway and may be assented to by a *majority* of the stockholders and the object may not be against public policy, and that acquiescense by shareholders in such a project for ever so long time affords no presumption of its legality; and to *Macedon Plank R. Co.* v. *Lapham*, 18 Barb. 312, then adds on p. 533—

" In the case before us there has been a misapplication, as it would seem, of the funds—to some part of which, these plaintiffs are entitled—to purposes and objects not provided for in their contract between the defendant companies nor within the scope of the objects then in the contemplation of the parties, which is illegal and which is treated in law as a breach of trust or as a fraud upon the plaintiffs (*whatever the intention* of the directors and a majority of the stockholders in the defendant companies may have been), which is the proper subject of inquiry and for correction by this court in an *application* like the present."

The court further held in this case that it was not necessary for the plaintiff to make out a case of actual fraud and conspiracy or to charge any moral turpitude or guilt to the directors, but it was sufficient, if it appeared that the defendants were managing the roads in a manner detrimental to the plaintiff's interest, in consequence of their mistaken views of the law of their rights. And in support of this *Salomons* v. *Laing*, 6 Eng. R. Cases, 289, is particularly referred to.

In the case of *Sturges* v. *Knapp*, 31 Vt. (2 Shaw, 1), the court held that the trustees of bondholders were liable to the minority of the bondholders for a faithful discharge of their duties.

Ang. & Ames on Corporations, page 371.

" The directors of an incorporated company must take the same care, and use the same diligence, as factors or agents. They are answerable not only for their own fraud and gross negligence, but, as they are usually interested in the stock, and act in relation to a bailment of the corporate funds to them, beneficial to both parties, they must answer for 'ordinary neglect,' or the omission of that care which every man of ordinary prudence takes of his own concerns."

In *Peabody et al.* v. *Flint et al.*, 6 Allen, 36, CHAPMAN, J., says : " As between the corporation itself and its officers, it was long since held that they were trustees, and that a court of equity would hold them responsible for every breach of trust. *Charitable Corporation* v. *Sutton*, 2 Atk. 400.

The *corporation itself holds* its property as trustees *for the stockholders*, who have a joint interest in all its property and effects, and each of whom is related to it as *cestui que trust*. The corporation may call its officers to account, if they willfully abuse their trust, or misapply the funds of the company; and if it refuses to sue, *or is still under the control* of those who must be made defendants in the suit, the stockholders, who are the real parties in interest, may file a bill in their own names, making the corporation a party defendant; or a part of them may file a bill in behalf of themselves and all others standing in the same relation, if convenience requires it.   *Robinson* v. *Smith*, 3 Paige 222, and cases there cited; *Hersey* v. *Beazie*, 24 Maine 9; and *Smith* v. *Poor*, 40 Maine 415. .

If other parties have participated with the officers in such proceedings, they may, according to the established principles of equity pleading, be joined as parties.   In the discovery of frauds, and in furnishing remedies to parties defrauded, equity does not suffer technicalities to stand in its way, but seizes upon the substance of the case, and holds all parties to their first responsibility, following trust property into the hands of remote grantees and purchasers, who have taken it with notice of a trust, in order to subject it to a trust.   The objection, therefore, that a court of equity has no power to furnish a remedy in a case of this character, is untenable."

Blain v. Agar, 1 Sims. 37; 2 Sims. 289.

In *Robinson et al.* v. *Smith et al.*, 3 Paige 221, the Chancellor says:

"The directors are the trustees, or managing partners, and the stockholders are the *cestui que* trusts, and have a joint interest in all the property and effects of the corporation.   [See Wood's Just. B., 1 Ch. 8, p. 110; 11 Coke's Rep. 98, b.]   And no injury the stockholders may sustain by a fraudulent breech of trust, *can, upon the general principles of equity, be suffered* to pass without a remedy.   In the language of Lord HARDWICKE, in a similar case, *" I will never determine that a court of equity can not lay hold of every such breech of trust; I will never determine that frauds of this kind are out* of the reach of courts of law or equity, for an *intolerable grievance* would follow from such a determination."

In the *York & Midland R. Co.* v. *Hudson*, 18 Eng. L. & Eq. 365, the court said: " The directors are persons selected to manage the affairs of the company for the benefit of the shareholders. It is an office of trust, which, if they undertake, it is their duty to perform fully and entirely." And the court, in this case, held them to the strict rules of trusts.

Deeks v. *Stanhope*, 5 Eng. L. & Eq. 97.

See, also— *Borgate* v· *Shortridge*, 31 Eng. L. & Eq. 44.

National Exchange Co. v. *Drew*, 32 Eng. L. & Eq. 1.

The directors of an incorporated company cannot speculate with the funds or credit of the company, and appropriate to themselves the profits of the speculation.

Redmond v. *Dickenson*, 1 Stockt. (N. J.) 507.

See *Barton* v. *Port Jackson & Union Falls Plank Road Co.*, 17 Barb. 397.

The declarations or acts of a director will not bind or affect, in any manner, the corporation, unless they *are* within the scope of his ordinary powers, or some special agency.

Loper v. *Buffalo R. R. Co.*, 19 Barb. 310.

A director of a manufacturing company, who has assented to a dividend amounting to more than the profits, may be *sued* for such violation of duty, without joining with him the company as a co-defendant.

Hill v. *Frazier*, 22 Penn. 320.

Fidelity, by directors, to the interests of stockholders well be enforced in every thing.

Butler v. *Cornwall Iron Co.*, 22 Conn. 335.

Nota Bene—*Colquett* v. *Howard*, 11 Georgia 556.

All corporate action, as well that of the directors and agents, as of the corporation itself, is but a succession of trials, in regard to which the creditors of the corporation, in the order of their priority, are the primary, and the shareholders the ultimate *cestui qui trust.*

Sturges v. *Knapp*, 31 Vt. (2 Shares) 1.

The directors or trustees of a corporation, when not themselves the corporate body, have *no power* to assent to an alteration of its charter.

The Commonwealth v. *Cullen*, 13 Penn. State 133.

Persons acting in a fiduciary capacity, cannot purchase at sales made by themselves.

Wickliff v. *Robinson*, 18 Ill. 289.

In the case of *Koehler* v. *Black River Falls Iron Co.*, 2 Black 721, Judge DAVIS said, quoting a number of authorities, that " the directors are the trustees or managing partners, and the stockholders are the *cestuis qui trust*, and have a joint interest in all the property and effects of the corporation, and no injury that the stockholders may sustain by a fraudulent breach of trust can, upon the general principles of equity, be suffered to pass without a remedy."

They (the directors) hold a place of trust, and by accepting the trust are obliged to excute it *with fidelity, not* for their own benefit, but for *the common benefit of the stockholders of the corporation.*

2 Atkyns, 404.

3 Paige 220.

1 Rhode Island 321.

19 Eng. L. & Eq. 361.

The directors of a moneyed institution are responsibible, in an action upon the case, for improperly obtaining and disposing of its funds or other property. *Franklin Fire Insurance Co.* v. *Jenkins*, 3 Wend. 130.

Where the directors of a railway assume to do an act exceeding their power they will be personally liable.

Redfield on R. 405.

Owen v. *Van Uster*, 10 C. B. 318.

Roberts v. *Button*, 14 Vt. 195.

A member of a corporation has a right of action against the corporate body for any injury he sustains from the misconduct of its agents *or officers.*

Grag v. *Portland Bank*, 3 Mass. 385.

See, also— *Waring* v. *Catawba Co.* 2 Bay. 109.

Courts of equity will scrupulously examine the conduct of persons acting in fiduciary or trust capacities, and protect the trust property from waste, whether it arise from the actual or constructive fraud of the trustees acting with the party obtaining the undue advantage, or from the fraud of the latter alone.

> *Moore* v. *School Trustees of Term Three*, 19 Ill. 87.
>
> *Thomas* v. *Sloo*, 15 Ill. 67.
>
> *Morris* v. *Thomas*, 17 Ill. 113.

If the managers of a corporation are about to engage in an enterprise not contemplated by the charter, or apply the corporate funds or credit to any other than the purposes therein specified, a court of equity will interfere, by injunction, at the instance of stockholders.

> *Smith* v. *Bangs*, 15 Ill. 401-2.
>
> *Bagshaw* v. *Co. R. R. Co.*, 7 Hare 114.
>
> *Beman* v. *Rufford*, 6 Eng. L. & Eq. 106.
>
> *Coleman* v. *Eastern Co. R. R. Co.*, 10 Beav. 1.

We allege that the Chicago & North Western Railway Co. were very much in want of money to carry on their schemes and that they formed a *conspiracy* to get control of the G. & C. U. R. R. Co. and appropriate it to their own use—and that the persons who were elected directors of the G. & C. U. R. R. Co., knew this, —but as was said by Judge Davis, in the case of *Koehler* v. *Black River Falls Iron Co.*, 2 Black, 720-1, " Instead of honestly endeavoring to effect a loan of money advantageously, for the benefit of the corporation, these directors, in violation of their duty, and in betrayal of their trust, secured their own debts, to the injury of the stockholders and creditors. Directors cannot thus deal with the important interests intrusted to their management. They *hold a place of trust ; and by accepting the trust are obliged to execute it with fidelity, and not for their own benefit,* but for the common benefit of the *stockholders of the corporation.*

XIII.

The " consolidation " in question was a sale—the vendor being the G. & C. U. R. R. Co., and the vendee being the C. & N. W. R. Co.—and as the directors of the G. &. C. U. R. R. Co. who made the sale, were also directors of the C. & N. W. R. Co., or a large number of them were, it became a sale by THEMSELVES *to* THEMSELVES—*or if the directors of the G. & C. U. R. R. Co. were merely* AGENTS *of the stockholders, it presents a case of where the agents acted* AS AGENTS *for* BOTH PARTIES, *and is, therefore, if not absolutely void—voidable by a dissenting stockholder* WHO IS THE PRINCIPAL.

1. To prove that it was a sale you have only to look at article 12 of the consolidation agreement, (see p. 10 of this brief), which is as follows—" And the second party of the second part (the G. & C. U. R. R. Co.) in consideration of the premises, and of the sum of *one dollar to it paid* by the party of the first part, (the C. & N. W. R. Co.) the receipt whereof is hereby acknowledged, doth hereby grant, convey, assign, set over to and vest in the said consolidated company, for the purpose of such consolidation, *all* the railroads of the said party of the second part, and all the equipments, implements and materials used or acquired therefor, *and* the rights, privileges, immunities, franchises, powers, and all the lands and property, money and effects, real and personal, and mixed, and all the rights of action and things of every name or nature now held or owned by the said party of the second part, or in or to which the said party of the second part hath any right, title, interest or claim, either in law or equity."

2. And to show that the *agents* who effected this sale were the agents of both parties, and acted as such, you have only to look at the lists of directors of both corporations.

The directors of the Galena and Chicago Union Rail Road Company who made and entered into the agreement for a sale and consolidation of the road to and with the Chicago & North Western Railway Company were—

1. *John B. Turner ;* 2. *William H. Ferry ;* 3. *James D. Fish ;* 4. *Thomas D. Robertson ;* 5. *William B. Scott ;* 6. *William R. Sands ;* 7. *James W. Elwell ;* Alexander C. Coventry, Mahlon D. Ogden, Francis B. Peabody, Edwin H. Shelden and Ira Y. Munn. *And the Directors of the Chicago & North Western Railway Co. were—*

1. *John B. Turner ;* 2. *William H. Ferry ;* 3. *James D. Fish ;* 4. *Thomas D. Robertson ;* 5. *William B. Scott ;* 6. *William R. Sands ;* 7. *James W. Elwell ;* William B. Ogden, Perry H. Smith, J. J. R. Pease, A. L. Pritchard, M. C. Darling, George M. Bartholomew, Samuel J. Tilden, William A. Booth, A. H. Boody and Lowell Holbrook.

1. The qualifications of these persons to perform the duties required, will readily appear, when it is known, that John B. Turner, the former president of the company, who resigned when the issue was raised by the stockholders, that no mere branch roads should ever be built, or aid given to any wayside projects—assisted the Chicago & N. W. R. Co. to procure the proxies of stockholders for the very purpose of effecting a *coup d 'etat*—and he heads the list of proxy-holders and voted a proxy for 452 shares which did not authorize any such thing and was never designed to be so used by the party who gave it.

Furthermore, he was elected president of the G. & C. U. R. R. Co., although it does not appear that he owned any stock in the company himself at the time ; at least his name does not appear on the poll-book except as a proxy-holder.

2. Alexander C. Coventry was the confidential attorney of William B. Ogden, a member of his family and was chiefly instrumental in arranging with the bankers of New York in borrowing proxies and is now one of the attorneys of the *consolidated* company.

3.   Mahlon D. Ogden is a brother of William B. Ogden.

4.   Edwin H. Sheldon is a brother-in-law.

5.   Francis B. Peabody is a brother of A. S. Peabody of New York—a Wall street broker, who was in the consolidated ring, and helped consolidate things in New York—and he is, also, a near relative of one of the consolidated directors.

6.   Ira Y. Munn is, and was, at the time of the consolidation, the *lessee* of the Chicago and North Western Railroad Company elevator, and, as we *believe*, for the very best of reasons, had five shares of stock *transferred* to him the day before the election of directors, in order to qualify him to become a director—but was not a *bona fide* holder of stock at all.

7.   William H. Ferry and Thomas D. Robertson, once directors of the Galena *&* C. U. R. R. Co., were, as soon as they had betrayed their trust, immediately appointed to office in the consolidated company, and hold it now.

8.   The peculiarities of the other persons, who were elected directors of the G. & C. U. R. R. Co. consist in just this, that they were *each* directors in the C. & N. W. R. Co., and were largely interested in its welfare, and anxious for its preservation, but were very *zealous* in blotting out the G. & C. U. R. R. Co., and having its earnings poured into the *consolidated coffers* of the C. & N. W. R. Co., whose name and fame they were bound to protect and forever uphold.

Now, we contend, 1st, that this sale was not *bona fide* at all ; but was a sale made for the sole benefit of the C. & N. W. R. Co.—indeed it was first proposed by that company—and *they* elected a board of directors to accomplish that purpose. The whole proceeding, from beginning to end, was presided over by that company—and lobbied through by their agents. The resolutions passed at the stockholders meeting were drawn by them—proposed by them and voted by them. The bill of sale and articles of consolidation were drawn up by their attorney in New York, and presented to the Board of Directors of the G. & C. U. R. R. Co. by another of their attorneys, and the whole thing hurried through in the most undue haste.

The directors were elected at 12 o'clock on the day ; organized at 3 o'clock, and voted to sell out the entire railroad and all its property, rights, privileges and franchises, and abolish the corporation in less than fifteen minutes after they were organized as a board.

Second, we have shown that directors are *trustees* for the stockholders—not for a majority of them, but for *all of them*—and, *if they accept the office of trustees,* they must perform the duties of that office with *honesty and fidelity* ; and if they do not they must abide the consequences.

Ten or twelve millions of dollars worth of *trust* property is not to be trifled with, with impunity, or be used for the private ends of any man, or set of men, however cunning, or however attractive or remunerative their scheme may be made to appear.

The annals of jurisprudence do not, we believe, furnish a more reckless and utter disregard of the rights and interests of stockholders than these men displayed ; and there must be an immense *chasm* in the law if they are not amenable to its stearnest judgments and decrees.

Now, the same persons who were elected to manage and control the property for the stockholders, and who were in fact their trustees, had no sooner assumed office than they did, in violation of their duty and of all their obligations, sell out the entire property, and then walked off.

In the case of *N. Y. Central Ins. Co.* v. *National Protection Ins. Co.,* 20 Barb. 470, the court said—

" The rule is now well settled, both in England and in this country, that *such a contract* is voidable in a court of equity, at the election of the principal. The principle is illustrated in the case of an agent employed to sell. If such agent became himself the purchaser or agent of another, or if he be an agent to *buy,* and he become himself the *seller,* or the *agent* of another in making the sale, the principal may avoid the sale or the purchase, in equity. If he came to the court under a timely application, upon the fact being alleged and proved, the *court will presume the transaction was injurious and consequently fraudulent ; and this presumption cannot be disproved,* unless it can be shown that the principal was furnished with all the knowledge the agent possessed— gave him *previous authority to become purchaser and seller*, and afterwards assented to such purchase or sale. (*Campbell* v. *Walker*, 5 Ves. 678; 1 Ves. Jr. 278; *Massey* v. *Davis*, 2 *Id*. 317; 1 Russ. & Mylne, 58; 2 Myl. & K. 819; Story on Agency, §§ 9, 192, 211, 214, 210; Dunl. Paley on Agency, 33, 34; 1 Mason, 341; 6 Pick. 196; 2 Johns. Ch. 252; 5 *Id*. 388; Hopk. Ch. 515; 9 Paige 237, and a large number of other authorities cited.) The *rule* seems to be founded on the *danger of imposition* in such cases, and the *presumption which a court of equity indulges of the existence of fraud which is inaccessible to the eye of the court, and consequently in equity such agreements are regarded as constructively fraudulent.* (9 Paige 242; 4 Kent's Com. 438, 3d ed.) The rule is a *settled* one, and the presumption is a *reasonable* one, in a court of equity. The *principal*, in fact, has bargained for the exercise of all the *skill, ability and industry* of his agent, and he is entitled to *demand* the execution of this in his own favor. (Pars. on Cont. 74, 75.) When the agent, unbeknown to his principal, is acting equally in behalf of the other party, the presumption is not an unreasonable one. This principle, however, like the one that a trustee cannot be the purchaser of an estate, is a mere rule of equity. If the proper forms have been observed, the conveyance is good at law, and the title passes. The contract is not void but only voidable. (5 Met. 467; 5 John. 43, 48, and a large number of other authorities cited.) The rule of which we have been speaking is applicable to *all* persons placed in situations of trust or confidence with reference to the subject matter of the contract, and embraces *trustees*, executors, administrators, guardians, agents and factors, attorneys, solicitors, &c. It embraces *all* who come within the principle."

In *Abbot* v. *American Hard Rubber Company*, 33 Barb. 593, ALLEN, J., says—

"No principle is better settled than that a person *having a duty to perform for others* cannot act in the same matter for his own benefit. A trustee cannot, directly or indirectly, by himself or through the agency of another, become the purchaser of the trust estate. Neither can he purchase an interest in property, and hold it for his own benefit, when, in respect to such property, *he has a duty* to perform *inconsistent with the character* of a purchaser on his own account. *Van Epps* v. *Van Epps*, 2 Paige, 537. *Hawley* v. *Cramer*, 4 Cowen, 717. *Slade* v. *Van Vechten*, 11 Paige, 21. *De Cartes* v. *Le Bay de Chamont*, 3 *ib*. 178. *It requires no authority to establish the fact that the directors of the American Hard Rubber Company could not* have transferred the property of the corporation directly *to themselves, or to a corporation in which they were stockholders and directors.* That is, they could not act as buyers and sellers in the same transaction, whether they acted in their *individual* capacity, or *as the directors of two trading corporations.* [*N. Y. Central Ins. Co.* v. *Nat. Prot. Ins. Co.*, 20 Barb. 468.] This rule of restriction upon the powers of the trustee *invalidates every indirect*, as it does *every direct, transfer* to himself, or *for his benefit*; and the intervention of a third person as a means or channel, by and through whom, the title is transferred from the *cestui's que trust*, and eventually rested in the trustee, will not uphold the transaction and sustain the title of the latter. *Courts will look through the means to the end, and apply the proper remedy for the breach of trust.* If the circumstances clearly show that the two transfers constitute but one transaction, they will be treated as parts of a single transaction, together perfecting a transfer from the trustee *qua* trustee to himself individually.

When the thing transferred does not rest in the possession of the first transferree, but it is immediately by him passed over to the trustee, for his benefit, or to an association represented by him, in whole or in part, the law will hold it to be a transfer in violation of the trust.

The rights of *cestui's que trust* require in such cases that the law should presume that the intermediate taker of the property was but the agent and instrument of the trustee—a means of conveyance. The contrary of the presumption ought not to be proved, or even alleged. It would be unsafe to uphold a transfer under such circumstances, for the want of express proof of the actual intent of the parties, from the facts or upon their oath, that the repurchase of the trustee was an after thought. When the title remains in the intermediate grantee but for a moment, or a very brief period of time, and is at once transferred to the trustee, or for his benefit, the presumption that the two transfers were only intended to effect the one object, that of conveying the property to or for the benefit of the trustee, is as strong as is the malicious intent to kill from the deliberate use of a deadly weapon. This rule of law which makes certain cases of presumptiou conclusive, merely attaches itself to the circumstances when proved, it is not deduced from them. It is not a rule of inference from testimony ; but a rule of protection as expedient for the public good.

There were only two entire days, exclusive of the Sunday intervening, for accomplishing the whole thing. It would be wrong to permit the presumptiou of intent attaching to these circumstances to be overcome by any amount of evidence. If it could be, stockholders would never be safe against the acts of faithless trustees. But it is not necessary to comment upon them. The experiment of the acting trustees in the two hard rubber companies has the merit of boldness as well as originality. Three of them marched out of the old company, laden with spoils with which they enriched themselves as stockholders of the new, and it cannot be that their wronged and injured associates are remediless. The plaintiff is entitled to the relief demanded, and an injunction and receiver are necessary to the preservation of the property, and the protection of his interests, *pendente lite.*

Neither the directors nor a majority of shareholders in any corporation can abolish or annihilate it.

In *Wheaton et al. and the Trustees of the First Congregational Society of Syracuse* v. *Gates et al.*, 18 N. Y. 395, which was an action to set aside a certain order of the County Court, purporting to authorize the sale and conveyance of the church edifice and lot of the society, and to direct the distribution of the proceeds of such sale among the individuals composing the society, the court say : "The trustees had no authority to distribute the property of the society among its individual members, or any class of them. Their *duty was to preserve and administer* it in the promotion of the purposes for which the corporation was created. The court could not, according to the statute, approve of a plan for any application of the moneys arising upon a sale, except one which was considered to be for the interest of the society, as an association, which was to continue organized for the purposes of its creation. There is a sense in which it might promote the interests of the individuals composing this religious organization, to dissolve their connection and establish new relations, but this is not what is meant by the statute. It was *not in the power of the trustees, or a majority of the members of the society,* or the County Court, or of all these authorities together, *to abolish the corporation,* or dissolve the society. If every individual having any interest in the matter should concur, it might be done; because there would be no one to question the act. But *while any number of the members desire to continue the connection, all the others can not, by their own act, dissolve it.*"

In the case of *Abbott* v. *American Hard Rubber Company,* 33 Barb. 580, which was an action brought by one of the stockholders of the company for himself and others, to have an entire sale of the company's property by the directors, declared to be fraudulent and void—

SUTHERLAND, J., in granting an injunction at special term says: " I do not think the directors, *even with the consent of a majority of the stockholders, had a right, as against stockholders not consenting, thus, in effect, to discontinue its existence* and defeat the object of its organization. *I must assume, that these directors were chosen to manage the business of the corporation, and not to destroy and end it.*" He further said, that *the democratic* or representative principle *does not apply to an act or acts of the majority inconsistent with the continued existence of the corporation, and the very object and purpose* for which it was organized; *nor does a stockholder consent to such acts by becoming a member, because the law does justify them;* and to support the principle on which he holds the sale in question void for want of authority, he cites a large number of authorities on page 584.

In *Abbott* v. *American Hard Rubber Company,* 33 Barb. 591, ALLEN, J., says: " And can a board of trustees, at their option, thus compel their principals, the corporators, to change their business and their investments? I think not. Trustees can not by their vote and their act, change the business of a corporation organized for the making of woolen or cotton goods, into a manufactory of articles entirely different, although the business of the company may be named in the charter, in terms sufficiently general to include the substituted business. *If the trustees in this case, chosen to carry on and prosecute the business of the company, could, by a sale of the rights under which it was operating, disable the company from going on, as is here attempted, the same trustees could, without the assent of the stockholders, employ the corporate property in the wildest and most hopeless schemes. The immediate and necessary effect of the act was, to terminate the business and thus practically and effectually destroy the corporation. This they could not do. It is certain that the officers could not directly, and, without the assent of the great body of the society, dissolve it ; and a majority of the stockholders could not do it against the dissent of the minority.* (*Smith* v. *Smith*, 3 Dev. S. C. Ch. R. 557.) (*Ward* v. *the Society of Attorneys*, 1 Collyer 370.) In the case last cited, the attempt was to surrender the charter with a view of obtaining a new charter, for an object different from that for which the original charter had been granted ; and a temporary injunction was granted. The attempt here is to do by indirection what was prohibited when attempted directly ; for the answer here is, " True, we have disabled you from carrying out the original purpose of your association, but you may engage in any other business." *Boards of directors are agents of the corporation, to manage its affairs and carry out the purpose and objects of its formation, and not to inflict upon it political death. They are only authorized to do such* things as are directly or impliedly directed or authorized by the charter. (Ang. & Ames on Corp. § 280.) *The minority in a corporation are only bound by the acts of a majority when acting under the charter,* and the corporators are only bound by the acts of trustees and managers when their acts are *conformable to the organic law of the corporation,* its articles of association or charter. When the acts are inconsistent with the object and purpose for which the body corporate was organized, they are void. (Ang. &

Ames on Corp. §§ 499, 500.) An act which, to all intents, terminates the corporation, by taking from it its power to fulfill the purposes of its organization, is not consistent with the purposes of its constitution. That which changes the nature and business of a corporation from that for which it was created, does effectually destroy it for all the purposes for which it was formed. It is no longer the same corporation. An act which compels a corporation to change its business, is no less invalid and repugnant to its charter than an act that directly makes the change. A similar act was styled by Judge WILLARD, "An act of self-destruction which the law cannot tolerate." (*Conro* v. *Port Henry Iron Co.*, 12 Barb. 64.)

In the case of the *Society of Practical Knowledge* v. *Abbott* 2 Beavan 569, the court, in discussing the powers of the stockholders of a corporation, said that they had no doubt that the members of the corporation "had a right to do what they pleased with the property of the corporation, (i. e., manage their property as they pleased) without proceeding to the extent of destroying the corporation; yet, had they a right to act in a manner *totally inconsistent* with this charter of incorporation, and at the same time *continue* to act as if the charter of incorporation were valid—to hold out to the world that it was valid, and to sell shares upon that supposition? I apprehend they were bound to look to the *continuance of the corporation, and to the conditions and terms on which it was originally founded.* * * * A man with regard to *his own* estate may act as he pleases; he may take from one pocket and put into another, but that is not the case with these persons."

In the case of the *York & North Midland R. R. Co.* v. *Hudson*, 16 Beavan 491, the court said that, "directors are persons elected to manage the affairs of the company for the benefit of the shareholders; it is an office of trust, *which, if they undertake, it is their duty to perform fully and entirely.*"

The directors of a corporation are authorized, by virtue of their office, to transact its ordinary and customary business, unless the charter or by-laws otherwise determine. But they are not authorized wishout some special authority, to make sale of that portion of its estate or property essentially necessary to be retained to enable it to transact its customary business.

> *Rollins* v. *Clay*, 33 Maine, 139.
> 2 Atkins, 404.
> 3 Paige, 220.
> 1 R. I. 21.
> 6 Selden, 60.
> 19 Eng. Law & Eq. 361.

The case of the *Cumberland Coal Co.* v. *Sherman*, 30 Barb. 554, like that of the *American Hard Rubber Co.* v. *Abbott*, 33 Barb. 584, we think is perfectly conclusive as to the principles which should govern in this case. In this• case, (the 30th of Barb.) the whole doctrine pertaining to the fiduciary character of directors is examined—and the court say—

"There can be no question, I think, at the present time, that **a** director of a corporation is the agent, or *trustee* of the stockholders, and as such, has duties to discharge of a *fiduciary nature* toward his principal, and is subject to the *obligations and disabilities* incidental to that relation." (Quoting a large number of authorities.) He then refers to the remarks of Lord CRANWORTH, in his decision of the *Aberdeen R. Co.* v. *Blaikie*, 1 McQueen, 461, and says with Vice Chancellor McCOUN, in the case of *Verplanck* v. *Merch. Ins. Co.*, 1 Edw. Ch. 84—that " when a corporation aggregate is formed and the persons composing it, either by virtue of the compact or by the express terms of the charter, place the management and control of its affairs in the hands of a select few, so that life and animation may be given to the body, then *such directors become the agents and trustees* of the corporation and a relation is created, not between the stockholders and the body corporate but between the stockholders and those directors who, in their character of trustees, become accountable for any willful dereliction of duty or violation of trust reposed in them. I see no objection to the exercising of an *equity* power over such persons in the *same manner* as it would be exercised over *any other trustees.*"

He then says that the responsibility of directors is in no way diminished because he is one of a number—but " the *same* principles apply to him (to each) as one of a number, as if he was acting as a *sole trustee.* It is not doubted that it has been shown that the relation of the director to the stockholders *is* the same as that of the agent to his principal—*the trustee to his cestui que trust*; and out of the *identity* of those relations necessarily spring the *same duties*, the same danger and the same *policy of the law*."

The court, then, after examining in the most elaborate manner, the law pertaining to such a *trust* relation, says—commencing on page 569—

" It is thus seen that the rule by which agents or trustees are prohibited and rendered incapable of purchasing or dealing with the property of their *cestui's que trust,* is one of universal application, justified by a current of strong and high authorities, and is adhered to *with stern and inflexible integrity*; and the consequence of such dealing and purchasing is, that the agent or trustee is liable at any time, on the application of the *cestui que trust,* and as a matter of course and without reference to the fairness or unfairness of the transaction, the adequacy or inadequacy of the price paid, or any other equities of the agent or trustees, to have the sale set aside. Such has been the uniform administration of the law in England, and where the civil law prevails, and in this country. No reason is suggested why rules thus founded on the soundest morals, which have been maintained with such uniformity and steadiness, should now be relaxed. On the contrary, it is seen that every consideration arising from circumstances surrounding us, and the unparalleled multiplicity of corporations, which can only act by trustees or agents, and the very large proportion of the wealth of the country invested in them, and placed under the control and management of agents and trustees, forcibly demands of courts of justice a firm adherence to these principles, and a stern application of them to every case coming within the sphere of their action.

Nay, the rule, as applicable to managers of corporations, should *in no particular be relaxed.* Those who assume the position of directors and trustees, assume also the obligations which the law imposes on such a relation. The stockholders confide to their integrity, to their faithfulness and to their watchfulness, the protection of their interests. This duty they have assumed. This the law imposes on them; and this, those, for whom they act, have a right to expect. The principals are not present to watch their own interests; they cannot speak in their own behalf; they must trust to the fidelity of their agents. If they discharge these important duties and trusts faithfully, the law interposes its shield for their protection and defense; if they depart from the line of their duty, and waste, or take themselves, instead of protecting the property and interests confided to them, the law, on the application of those thus wronged or despoiled, promptly steps in to apply the corrective, and restores to the injured what has been lost by the unfaithfulness of the agent. This right of the *cestui que trust* to have the sale vacated and set aside, where his trustee is the purchaser, is not impaired or defeated by the circumstance that the trustee purchases for another.

Neither are the duties or obligations of a director or trustee altered from the circumstance that he is one of a number of directors or trustees, and that this circumstance diminishes responsibility or relieves him from any incapacity to deal with the property of his *cestui que trust*. The same principles apply to him as one of a number, as if he was acting as a sole trustee. *It is not doubted* that it has been shown, that the relation of the director to the stockholders is the same as that of the agent to his principal, the *trustee* to his *cestui que trust*, and out of the identity of these relations necessarily spring the same danger and the same policy of the law.

In the language of the plaintiffs counsel it is justly said— "Whether it be a director dealing with a board of which he is a member, or a trustee dealing with his co-trustee, and himself the real party in interest, the principal is absent. The watchful and effective self-interest of the director or trustee seeking a bargain is not counteracted by the equally watchful and effective self-interest of the other party, who is there only by his representatives, and the wise policy of the law treats all such cases as that of a trustee dealing with himself."

The indifference and even self satisfaction with which the directors appear to regard their acts after disposing of the railroad in question, with all of its immense interests, would ordinarily be amazing; but as the court said, in the Hoffmann Steam Coal Company case, in 16th Maryland 505: " The spirit of wild speculation ordinarily blinds those who are engaged in it, and subjects them to the condition in which they are *unable* to see things as others see them. Legal disabilities rarely occur to them ; it being with most of them an axiom of public or political economy, that the exchange of one article for another, at fictitious rates and without the bestowal of labor on either, increases the value of both. Men involved in transactions of this kind very frequently, *without* the slightest *consciousness* of dishonesty of purpose, do things which the law condemns, and which it declares to be of no value. It is to guard against this proneness to a non observance of what is strictly right and proper in the dealings of corporations, the law has wisely interposed its checks and prohibitions, and, we think, in the present aspect of this case, these are all sufficient to justify the action of the Circuit Court," &c.

We charge in our bill, and insist, that the persons who were elected directors of the Galena and Chicago Union Railroad Company, did not act in a *bona fide* manner towards the stockholders at all, but sold out the entire corporation in the most hasty and indecent manner, and upon this we most respectfully invoke the attention of the court. It is an old maxim, that fraud vitiates every contract, and—

If this question is to be settled by the *bona fides* of the transaction, then this court will not fail to examine every detail and see that no fraud was practiced upon the stockholders, either by the persons who were instrumental in proposing the measures, or by those who carried it into effect. If a change so radical and extraordinary is to be justified on the ground that it was a great public measure, and was to confer such immense benefits upon the public and the stockholders combined, why was not something said about it beforehand? Why was the secret confined so closely to the family circle and to the mahogany of the North Western Railway Company? Why were all the old patrons of the road turned aside, and the brother, brother-in-law, privy counsellor, and those of the exchequer appointed to administer on this great estate?

Why were men brought here who were utter strangers to the State, to the road, and all save the wants of the Chicago and North Western Railway Company, and made to play a part in this more than tragedy? What star, if it was not a star engagement, led them hither? Take the list of directors who were elected on the 1st of June last, and look them over—and if that old story is not more than verified in regard to the gathering together of the eagles, then we are mistaken. There are men there on that list who had never stepped a foot upon the soil of the State of Illinois before they came here at the time of their election—men who, it may be, were skilled in all the wisdom of the Egyptians, and trained in the highest school of *consolidations*, but, nevertheless, had never seen either of the roads that they were to manage, who knew nothing whatever of the wants and requirements of any road except that of the Chicago and North Western Railway Company, how, then, does it happen that these men, if they acted *bona fide* in all that they did, acquired information so rapidly as events show, how did it happen that these men were elected at 12 o'clock in one day, got together at three, and in less than ten minutes after they had assembled, proposed to sell out the whole entire road, to close out the consignment, and to save all bother, give it into the hands of the Chicago and North Western Railway Company to manage?

Does this thing look on its face, like a perfectly honest and fair transaction? Would not such conduct, so extraordinary and unusual challenge comment and investigation, and can they shield themselves from responsibility by any number of genuflexions or vain repetitions?

These persons, who were elected directors, were all personally men of character. But why did they not perform their duties towards the stockholders as men usually do? Why was it, that they were elected to office at twelve o'clock in the day, and at three killed the whole concern? Why was it, that the directors hurried things so? There can be but just one answer to all of this, and that is, that these men were elected for just one purpose, and *that purpose was to sell it out to the Chicago and North Western Railway Company. They never intended* to do their duty towards the shareholders of the Galena and Chicago Union Railroad Company. They were chosen to play a part in a drama which required no Hamlet to instruct them how to perform.

Several of these directors do not appear to have been stockholders at all in the road. Several appear to have had stock transferred to them so they could act as directors just long enough to make a quorum to sell it.

Several of those men were utter strangers to the road, and had never been in the State of Illinois before in all of their lives, and had never seen Chicago or a single railroad that lead into or out of it: how did it happen that these men became convinced so suddenly, that the best thing for the stockholders to do with the road, was to sell it out? Were these men inspired, and did they act and speak as they were moved? We think they did. They might have been influenced by the highest kind of inspiration, but the tally sheet shows that they drew their inspiration from Wall street, and the Upper Peninsula of Michigan. It had no higher source.

Several of these men were near relatives of the president of the Chicago and North Western Railway Company; one was the banker of the Chicago and North Western Railway; another was the private and confidential counsellor of the president of the Chicago and North Western Railway Company, and every one were very near and dear to that corporation in more ways than one.

There is no use of disguising the matter at all. That board of directors who were elected on the first day of June, 1864, and who *instantly sold it out, cannot set up either ignorance or innocence.* They knew exactly what they had been elected for, and they knew that they were not to hold their offices as directors for one year, but it was to go through the idle ceremony of becoming directors, only instantly to *betray* their trusts. Their conduct lacks every characteristic of *good faith*; and they appear in this court to-day as they did when they were elected, under the *patronage* and protection of the C. & N. W. R. Co. whose agents and instruments they were. In the language of another—

"If an institution of this kind is so unfortunate as to have in their board of managers a clique who aim to make it subservient to their individual rather than the proprietary interest, it is likely that they will contrive to get the finances under their control and place the *various departments of business in the hands of their relatives, or other personal friends,* who will understand just how far they may go in *carrying out the purpose* of the president, or party opposed to their proceedings. Measures adverse *to the proprietary interest,* if there be one or more persons in the board who aim to be faithful to their trust, will not probably be at once manifest.

"They will proceed gradually, and perhaps quiet some unsuspecting member, that otherwise might not look on with indifference, by a bit of what he may suppose a harmless realization in some projected operation, ostensibly of fair business aspect; and it is surprising how many men of fair standing among their neighbors, allow, in this way, an embargo on their actions until too late to remedy the evil, and so the mischief is fastened hopelessly on the interests of the proprietors.

"It has been suggested that men who aim to manage affairs of trust for their individual, rather than their proprietary benefit, are not likely, and indeed, are not generally good business managers, and fail to make the business of the institution as profitable as it should be. On this point it may be set down as a rule, that it is not usually their interest to have in their service a very scrupulous body of agents ; but rather their personal friends, who will, from affinity and interest, be well disposed to carry out their wishes, as more important than a competent and faithful discharge of their respective duties. In this respect *family connections,* are likely to be sought, as more confidential and reliable for their purpose, and also from a disposition to pension on the institution, members of the family, who may not be able to otherwise provide for their support.

"Men occupying positions through the influence of friends in power, are likely to depend on such influence rather than on a proper discharge of duty, and are often prone to assume, in consequence thereof, a position subversive of the discipline, harmony, and efficiency of business.

"The evils of nepotism have usually been mischievous to railway institutions, and *any* indulgence in this sort of patronage should be looked to with the most rigid *caution*, as it is most probable that managers and general officers who adopt it, are not *particularly scrupulous* for the interest of the proprietors."

We are perfectly aware that the directors, whose acts we are now passing in review, *claim* that the charter under which they acted, if submitted to a jury of cunning lawyers, would be found to contain power—authorizing them to do what they did—and therefore, they claim that it is unfair to impugn their motives ; besides, they say that they did not sell out the road at all.   They only *consolidated* it.   And it is perfectly wonderful what consolation this seems to afford them ; and as Shakspeare says of another subject—

" In religion
What damned error, but some sober brow
Will *bless* it and *approve* it with a text."

A *coup d 'etat* so complete and gigantic has seldom occurred— and now when it has passed, it is looked upon by many as a most *capital* joke.   But—

"Such is human nature, that, *some* persons *lose* their abhorrence of crime in their *admiration of its magnificent exhibitions*.   Ordinary vice is reprobated by them, but extraordinary guilt, exquisite wickedness, the high flights and poetry of crime, seize on the imagination and lead them to forget the depths of guilt, in *admiration of the excellence of the performance*, or the unequalled atrocity of the purpose.   There are those in our day who have made great use of this infirmity of our nature, and by means of it done infinite injury to the cause of good morals.   They have affected not only the taste, but I fear also the principles, of the young, the heedless and the imaginative, by the exhibition of interesting and beautiful monsters. They render depravity attractive, sometimes, by the polish of its manners, sometimes by its very extravagance; and study to show off crime under all the advantages of cleverness and dexterity."

Webster, vol. 6, p. 55.

XIV.

The doctrine of Trusts further illustrated in cases of Directors of Railroad Corporations dealing with the property of the Company, and how their acts affect stockholders, and under what circumstances they are binding upon them, and when not.

Upon this branch of the subject, we beg leave to refer the court to the able and exhaustive brief of Dobbins & Thurston, which is found in the 16th of Maryland Reports, 490, 496, and which covers the whole ground of this case, and is sufficient to afford relief to every stockholder of the Galena and Chicago Union Railroad Company who has exchanged his stock for that of the Chicago and North Western Railway Company without a full knowledge of all of the facts and circumstances pertaining to the sale and pretended consolidation.

The cases in respect to purchases by the trustee of the trust estate, or *contracts with him affecting its interest*, naturally divide themselves into two general classes:

1st. Cases in which a trustee buys or contracts with himself, or several trustees, of which he is one, or a board of trustees, of which he is one.

2d. Cases in which a trustee buys or contracts with his *cestui qui trust*, who is *sui juris*, and competent to deal independently of the trustee in respect to the trust estate.

In the first class of cases, the purchase or contract is voidable at the option of the *cestui qui trust*, without reference to the fairness or unfairness of the purchase or contract. The disqualification of the party purchasing or contracting, is a conclusion of law and is absolute. The right of the *cestui qui trust* to come in as of course, and set aside a sale made by a trustee to himself, though made at public auction, *bona fide*, for a fair price, and without showing actual injury, is fully considered and affirmed by this court, in *Mason* v. *Martin & Kemp*, 4 Md. Rep. 135. See, also, 2 Johns. Ch. Rep. 252; *Davane* v. *Fanning*, 4 How. 503; *Michaud* v. *Giroud*, and notes by English and American editors to *Fox* v. *Mackreth*, in White's Eq. Cases; 65 Law Lib. 126 and seq., where a large collection of the cases on the general subject will be found.

In the second class of cases, the presumption of law is against the validity of the transaction, with degrees of strength varying according to the circumstances, but the trustee is permitted to show affirmatively the fairness of the transaction, and to establish the other conditons necessary to its validity. 65 Law Lib. 146, and cases cited in *notes ;* 6 Ves. 627, *Lacey, ex parte.*

So great is the jealousy with which the dealings of a trustee with his *cestui qui trust* are regarded by courts of equity, so strong is the presumption of fraud which has been applied to such cases, that the distinction here drawn is not always recognized by the elementary writers (Story's Eq., sec. 30), or by the judges (2 Hare 60, *Edwards* v. *Meyrick*); but the principle of positive incapacity is applied to this second class of cases as well as to the first. See, also, 9 Ves. 247, *Coles* v. *Trecothick; id.* 296, *Hatch* v. *Hatch ;* 12 Ves. 372, *Morse* v. *Royal.*

The rule, however applicable to the second class of cases, throws upon the trustee the *onus* of rebutting the legal presumption against the transaction, and of proving affirmatively the conditions necessary to give it validity. If no such proof is established, courts of equity will treat the case as one of constructive fraud. Story's Eq., sec. 311 ; 10 Ves. 427, *Randall* v. *Errington ;* 3 Myl. 113, *Hunter* v. *Atkins ;* 2 Hare 60, 68, *Edwards* v. *Meyrick ;* 65 Law Lib. 146.

These conditions are :

1st. That the *cestui qui trust* knew that he was dealing with his trustee, and had agreed to discharge him from that relation and capacity. 10 Ves. 426, *Randall* v. *Errington ;* Story's Eq., sec. 316; 65 Law Lib. 130 ; 6 Ves. 627, *Lacey ex parte ;* 9 Ves. 234, *Coles* v. *Trecothick.*

2d. That the trustee had communicated all the information which he possessed, or could acquire, to the *cestui qui trust.* 8 Ves. *ex parte James ;* 9 Pick. 234, *Farnam* v. *Brooks ;* 14 Ves. 300, *Hugunin* v. *Basely ;* 6 Ves. 280, *Gibson* v. *Jeyes ;* 15 Ves. 40, *Harris* v. *Tremenhare ;* 11 Paige 541, *Howell* v. *Ransom ;* 65 Law Lib. 137, 149 ; Story's Eq., sec. 316, *a* ; 3 Swanst. 73, *Walker* v. *Symonds.*

3d. That the trustee derived no advantage whatever from his situation as trustee, or from any knowledge acquired in that character. 3 Mylne & Keene 113 ; *Hunter* v. *Atkins*, 65 Law Lib. 146, 371.

4th. That the trustee had advised his *cestui qui trust* in the same manner as if the dealing of the latter had been with a third party. 65 Law Lib. 133, 146 ; 6 Ves. 278 ; 3 Mylne & Keene, 113.

5th. That the price was fair, the consideration adequate. 65 Law Lib. 146 ; 6 Ves. 280 ; 16 Ves. 512, *Peacock* v. *Evans ;* 2 Hare 68 ; 4 Dessansure 652 ; *Butler et al.* v. *Haskell*, Story's Eq., sec. 321.

The principle has been held to apply to trustees, agents, executors, administrators, assignees for creditors, sheriffs, auctioneers, agents for sale, cashiers of banks, directors of corporations, and to all persons who have any general duty, or special duty, in respect to the transaction. 65 Law Lib. 137 ; 3 Beav. 49, *Greenlaw* v. *King ;* 9 Paige 241, *Van Epps* v. *Van Epps ;* id. 663, *Torrey* v. *Bank of Orleans ;* 1 Sandf. Ch. Rep. 225, *Dickinson and wife* v. *Codwise ;* id. 257, *Cram* v. *Mitchell ;* 4 H. & J. 332, *Smith* v. *Baldwin ;* 7 G. & J. 1, *Callis* v. *Ridout.* Nor does it make any difference though the purchases were at public auction, or even under the direction of a master. 65 Law Lib. 128. The principle applies equally where the trustee is not the sole purchaser, but is merely interested with others (3 Dana 266, *Mitchum* v. *Mitchum*), for, in either case, his interest, which is to buy cheap, is in conflict with his duty, which is to get the best price for his *cestui que trust*, and the policy of the law, which establishes the rule, is equally violated. See 1 McQueen 473, *Blakie* v. *Aberdeen Railway Co.*, a case strongly relied on by the appellees. The rule has, also, been applied equally where the purchaser was one of several trustees who made the sale. Story on Agency, sec. 211 ; 3 Brown's Ch. Rep. 482, *Hall* v. *Noyes ;* 3 Ves. 740, *Whichcote* v. *Lawrence ;* 3 Sandf. Ch. Rep. 592, *Ward* v. *Smith ;* 1 Paige 393, *Case* v. *Obed ;* 65 Law Lib. 141 ; 1 H. & G. 11, *Ringgold* v. *Ringgold ;* 7 G. & J. 1, *Callis* v. *Ridout.*

The directors of a corporation are agents of the company, and, as such, have duties to discharge, of a fiduciary nature, towards their principals, and are subject to the obligations and disabilities incident to that relation. 3 Paige 331, *Robinson* v. *Smith ;* Ang. & Ames on Corp. (ed. of 1858), sec. 312, page 365, and cases there cited ; 3 La. Rep. 568, *Percey* v. *Millandon ;* 1 Rhode Island Rep. 321, *Hodges* v. *New England Srew Co. ;* 1 Craig & Phillips 1, *Attorney General* v. *Wilson ;* Redfield on Railways, 494 ; 1 Younge and Coll. 325, *Bensom* v. *Heathom ;* 16 Beav. 485, *York & North Midland Railway Co.* v. *Hudson.*

A director purchasing of, or contracting with, the board of which he is a member, falls within the first class of cases above mentioned ; he is an agent or trustee dealing with several agents or trustees, of whom he was one ; he is under a positive legal incapacity so to deal with any binding effect upon the company ; he can so buy or contract, only, subject to the right of the company, at its option, to disaffirm the contract and have the sale set aside without reference to the fairness or unfairness of the transaction. The relation of the director to the stockholder is the same as that of the agent to his principal, the trustee to his *cestui que trust ;* and out of the identity of these relations, springs the same duties, the same dangers, and the same policy of the law. The number of the directors or trustees do not give such security as to justify an exception to the rule. But the true answer to this suggestion as to numbers, is, that *every* director and *every trustee* owes the *entire* duty belonging to that character. Each director is bound to give to his co-directors, and through them, to the company, the full benefit of all the knowledge and skill which he can bring to bear upon the subject; to advise and assist according to the best of his ability. The company contracts for this service, not from a part, but from all the directors, and they contract to render it. If any one of them, while this relation continues, shifts his position from a protector to an adversary, it is as clearly a violation of his duty and of the rights of the company, as if he were sole trustee. Experience shows that there is in practice, at least, as much danger of abuse and wrongs by directors towards the stockholders, as in any other class of trusts, while the vast amount of property involved in the administration of these great corporation trusts, and the large number of individuals interested in them, as stockholders, makes the application of the settled principles of equity to these cases, a matter of great public importance and necessity, and there is no reason whatever, nor any safety in relaxing, in respect to them, the rules which have become established in the courts as maxims of public policy. 1 McQuean 471; 3 Ves. 751, *Whichcote* v. *Lawrence.*

The case of an agent for sale, buying the trust estate, is regarded with especial jealousy, and as calling for a very stringent application of the rule. The foundation of this disposition is the opportunity he has of acquiring information which he may use for his own benefit, and the difficulty of ascertaining whether he has made the necessary disclosures. 65 Law Lib. 137, 128, 141; Story on Agency, sec. 211; Ross on Commercial Law, 101; 9 Law Lib. 213; Dunlap's Paleys Agency 33.

In the case of *Michoud et al.* v. *Giroud,* 4 Howard, 553, Justice WAYNE said—

" The rule of equity, is, in every court of jurisprudence with which we are acquainted, that a purchase by a trustee or agent of the particular property of which he has the sale, or in which he represents another—whether he has an interest in it or not—*per interpositam personarum*—carries fraud on the face of it.

*   *   *   *   *   *   *   *

The general rule stands upon our *great moral obligation* to refrain from placing ourselves in relations which ordinarily excite a conflict between self-interest and integrity. It restrains all agents, public and private; but the value of the prohibition is most felt and its application is more frequent in the private relations in which the vendor and purchaser may stand towards each other. The disability to purchase is a consequence of that relation between them, which imposes on the one a duty to protect the interest of the other, from the faithful discharge of which duty, his own personal interest may withdraw him. In this conflict of interest, the law wisely interposes. It acts not on the possibility, that, in some cases, the sense of that duty may prevail over the motives of self-interest, but it provides against the probability in many cases, and the danger in all cases, that the dictates of self interest will exercise a predominant influence, and supersede that of duty. It therefore prohibits a party from purchasing on his own account that which his duty or trust requires him to sell on account of another, and from purchasing on account of another that which he sells on his own account. In effect, he is not allowed to unite the two opposite characters of buyer and seller, because his interests, when he is the seller or buyer on his own account, are directly conflicting with those of the person on whose account he buys or sells.

> *Thorp* v. *McCullum*, 1 Gilman, 614, is to the same effect, precisely.

If a trustee, acting for others, sells an estate, and becomes himself interested in the purchase, the *cestui que trust* is entitled to have the sale set aside.

> *Davone* v. *Fanning*, 2 Johns. Ch. 257, and cases there cited.
>
> *Cumberland Coal Co.* v. *Shuman*, 30 Barb. 277.

Trustees can never speculate out of a trust estate.

In the case of the *Aberdeen Railway Co.* v. *Blaikie*, July 20, 1854, (1 McQueen's Rep. 461), the House of Lords held that a contract entered into by a manufacturer, for the supply of iron furnishings *to* a railway company of which *he was a director*, or the chairman at the date of the contract, *was invalid*, and could not be enforced against the company. Lord CRANWORH, in delivering the opinion of the court, says—

" A corporate body can only act by agents, and it is, of course the duty of those agents so to act as best to promote the interests of the corporation, whose affairs they are conducting. Such an agent has duties to discharge, of a *fiduciary character*, toward his *principal ;* and it is a rule of *universal* application, that no one having such duties to discharge shall be *allowed* to enter into engagements in which he has or can have, a *personal interest*, conflicting, or which possibly *may* conflict with the interests of those whom he is bound to protect. So *strictly* is this principle adhered to, that *no question is allowed to be raised as to the fairness or unfairness of a contract so entered into.* It obviously is, or may be, impossible to demonstrate how far, in any particular case, the terms of such a contract have been the best for the *cestui que trust*, which it was possible to obtain. It may sometimes happen that the terms on which a trustee has dealt, or attempted to deal, with the estate or interests of those for whom he is a trustee, have been as good as could have been obtained from any other person ; they may, even, at the time, have been better. But still, so inflexible is the rule, that no inquiry on that subject is permitted. The English authorities on this subject are numerous and uniform.

In the case of *Coates* v. *Woodworth*, 13 Ill. 654, the court say that chancery has jurisdiction to enfore a trust, and for this purpose, may appeal to the *conscience* of a trustee.

There is no instance on record where such an appeal has ever been taken in the case of any modern railway manager, and it is difficult to tell what the results would be ; but if it could produce

the proper contrition and remorse, the experiment might be worth
making, and might save many honest men from the imputation of
much miscellaneous baseness.

XV.

*By the charter of the G. & C. U. R. R. Co. none but stockholders
can be elected directors.*

*We allege that several of the persons who were elected directors were
not bona fide stockholders, but had stock transferred to them for
the mere purpose of making them directors.   This, we say, was a
fraud, both upon the charter and upon the stockholders.*

Where the charter provided that stockholders only should be
elected directors,—persons having no interest in the stock, but
fraudulently and collusively *receiving the transfer* of a share to
qualify them—are not eligible ; and the stockholders combining in
such fraud, have no power to confer upon them authority to do corporate acts.

Such fraud upon the charter, and combination to defraud the
public, will prevent those participating in it from claiming any
protection under its provisions to escape private responsibility.

Bartholomew v. *Bentley, et al.,* 1 Ohio, 38.

XVI.

PROXIES.

*We show in this case—and the records of the stockholders meetings
of the Galena & C. U. R, R. Co. show—that out of all the vast
number of stockholders of that company, there were not, at the
time of the sale and consolidation, more than 15 or 16 persons
present—and that of over 60,284 shares, only about 900 shares
were owned by those persons who were present ; and that the rest*

of the votes which they pretended to cast for the sale and consolidation, were cast by means of PROXIES, *which were obtained from most of the shareholders under the pretence that they were to be used merely for the election of directors.*

By the original charter of the G. & C. U. R. R. Co. no power is given to vote by proxy, for directors or anything else whatsoever; but it provided expressly for the *personal presence-*of each stockholder; and no stockholder could vote for any stock which had been assigned to him within thirty days *previous* to holding the election. By sec. 1, of an amendment to the charter, which was passed on the 26th of Feb., 1847, it was provided that *directors shall* be stockholders in said company, and shall be elected annually by the stockholders, either in person or by proxy, and shall hold their office for one year, &c. This is all that it said upon the subject in the charter, and relates, it will be observed, *exclusively to the election of directors.* By the first *by-law* of the company, relating to annual meetings, it is provided that the directors shall be elected by ballot, and then they provide with characteristic circumspection, that "such other business may be transacted as shall be brought before them *within the power of the company and the charter thereof."*

When a person therefore gives to another his proxy to vote for directors and such other business as may come before the meeting, is it reasonable to suppose that such authority gives to the proxyholder authority to take and sell out the entire corporation? Is that such a *business* as any honest man would ever think of coming before a meeting, called to elect directors, who were to manage the affairs of the corporation?

In *Abbott* v. *American Hard Rubber Company*, 33 Barb. 584, SUTHERLAND, J., says—

"In passing the resolutions, relied upon by the defendants as an authority, by a majority of the stockholders, to make the sale and transfer, it would appear that a majority of the shares voted on, were voted on by proxy. I *must presume*, in the absence of anything to show the contrary, that these proxies were ordinary proxies, given with reference to the transaction of the ordinary legitimate business of the corporation, and that *they did not and could not, authorize votes for so extraordinary a sale and transfer as the one in question.* Hence, the resolution cannot be said to have been, *in fact, passed by a majority* of the stockholders, and its *passage* can hardly be claimed as an authority by a majority."

In *Philips* v. *Wickham*, 1 Paige, 598, Chancellor WALWORTH said that, " the right of voting by proxy is not a general right, and the party who claims it *must* show a *special authority* for that purpose. The *only* case in which it is allowable, at the *common law*, is by the peers of England, and that is said to be in virtue of a special permission of the king. And it is possible that it might be delegated, in some cases, by the by-laws of a corporation, where express authority was given to make such by-laws regulating the manner of voting. I am not aware of any other case in which the right was ever claimed; and the express power which is generally given to the stockholders of moneyed and other private corporations, is opposed to the claims in this case, where there is no express or implied power contained in the act."

In *Taylor* v. *Griswold*, 2 Green (N. J.) 226, HORNBLOWER, C. J., says:

" The right of voting by proxy, in this case, is claimed by the applicants, first, upon general principles; and, secondly, upon the ground of an existing by-law, or the usage and practice of the company.

" FIRST. The first inquiry, then, is, whether, upon *general and common law principles, the members of any* corporation have *a right*, as a matter of course, to be represented, and to vote by proxy? This question *must be answered in the negative.* It is clear, that, when the charter is silent, and no by-laws have yet been passed regulating the mode of election, and *of voting upon other questions* that may arise in conducting the ordinary and appropriate business of the corporation, the corporators, when lawfully assembled, *must be governed by the same rules and principles that prevail in all primary assemblies.* That is, *until* a different rule has been established by some competent authority, *every ques-*

tion must be decided, and every election determined by the majority ; or, in other words, by *the major part, numerically*, of those who are *personally present*, and voting.

"To illustrate my meaning, let it be supposed, that the charter expressly authorizes the company to determine whether the members of it shall be permitted to vote by proxy or not. At the very first meeting of the company, the question is proposed : How shall members vote on this question ? In person, or by proxy ? Certainly not by proxy ; for that would be to admit proxies before there is any law to authorize their admission. This primary vote must, then, be given and determined by the majority of the corporators present and voting in person. Angell & Ames on Corporations 67 ; *Rex* v. *Foxcroft*, 2 Bun R. 10, 17 ; 2 Kent's Com., 1st ed., 236 ; *Phillips* v. *Wickham*, 1 Paige C. K. 598. And to these authorities may be added the *State* v. *Trudor*, 5 Days' Rep. 329 ; for the court, in that case, fully admit the general rule as above stated.

"It may be for the personal convenience of members, *but it can not be for the good of the corporation*, that its business or election should be conducted by proxies. The interest of the company, the good of the public, would be better promoted and more effect_ ually secured by the personal attendance of, and mutual interchange of opinions among the members, than by the action of proxies ; at least, this is the fair and legal presumption. If one member may appear and vote by proxy, at elections, and on other matters of vital importance to the institution, then all may, and so the welfare and interest of the company and of the public, be utterly neglected. In short, so far from its being incident to a corporation to make such a regulation, it is at variance with the spirit and "with the fundamental principles of our civil and political institutions." And it is confidently believed, that *not an authority can be found, nor a case produced, in support of the position, that the right of making such a by-law, is incident to a corporation of any description, public or private.*

" Speculations upon the evil consequences that *have resulted* to many of our incorporated institutions, and, especially, to our banks, by this and other innovations upon the salutary principles and rules of the common law, do not become this place, or occasion; but may well *deserve the grave consideration of another* department of government.

" No argument can be drawn from analogy between corporations, and the law and practice of partnerships, and voluntary associations, upon this point. *They* may attend to *their* business in person or by agents, or not at all, as they please. They act in their *natural* capacities, and upon their individual responsibilities. But corporations are *created* by, and *amenable to, law;* and when partners, or voluntary associations, ask for and accept a charter, they must take it with all its restrictions, as well as its benefits. They voluntarily relinquish just so much of their former natural and individual rights and powers as are inconsistent with the expressed, implied, or incidental terms of the charter. Neither is it a satisfactory argument, that if the right of voting by proxy is denied to these private corporations, many of the stockholders may never be able to vote at all. The same argument would extend the privilege of voting by proxy to public and political corporations; and the same thing may happen if proxies are allowed. *Femme coverts,* infants, and persons *non compos,* can not make proxies; at most, it is an argument *ab inconvenienti,* and is fully answered by the reasoning of the court in the case of *Rex* v. *Ginever,* 6 T. R. 732. After all, admitting that the practice of voting by proxy is not only convenient, but may be exercised with perfect safety and advantage, both as respects the welfare of the corporation and the security of the public, are we not called upon to do too much, when we are asked, in the absence of any adjudicated case amounting to authority, to establish the doctrine contended for? It is a power that can only be delegated by the supreme authority of the State, and ought not to be extended by judicial legislation. As the law now stands, the legislature can grant the privileges to such corporations as they please, and with such restrictions as in their wisdom may seem expedient; but if this court undertake, by judicial construction, to extend this right to all private or moneyed corporations, we impose upon the legislature the necessity of inserting a restraining clause in every charter they grant, unless they intend to delegate the right of voting by proxy.

"The object of the legislature was, to give *permanency and protection to the public improvement* that had been erected, and *security to the individuals who had embarked in the enterprise.* Instead of promoting and securing these legitimate designs, the *tendency,* at least, the *apparent* tendency, of the by-law in question, is to *encourage* speculation and monopoly, to lessen the rights of the smaller stockholders, depreciate the value of their shares, and throw the whole property and government of the company into the hands of a few capitalists; and, it may be, to the utter neglect or disregard of the public convenience and interest.

"I do not say that such was the design, or that such has been the effect; but, only, that the natural or probable tendency of the by-law in question is, to produce such a result.

"When discretionary power of any kind is delegated to men by statute, the common law requires of them the *personal* exercise of that discretion, and will not permit them to delegate it to another, to be exercised by proxy. This principle lies at the foundation of all the cases heretofore adjudged (except that in Conn.), and nothing short of a *special grant* of the legislature can overcome it. If the common law of the State authorized such powers as depend on *judgment and discretion* to be exercised by proxy and deputy, then the powers delegated to the judgment of arbitrators, referees, surveyors of highways, chosen freeholders, township committees, overseers of the poor, nay, justices of the peace and judges might be executed by deputy or proxy. The restraint, in these cases, rests entirely on the great principle, that power delegated to judgment and discretion, must be exercised *in person.* This principle of the common law does not seem to be denied; but its application to the members of a private corporation is resisted. All the powers they have, are delegated to them by the charter; but, then, it is said, that they own *all the stock,* and the public having no interest at stake, the members have a right to manage their affairs in their own way. But, that the public have no interest at stake in these private coporations, will appear to be a mistake of vast magnitude, if it be considered how vitally these *corporations* are connected and interwoven with the most important public interests of the State, with the public highways, with the common transportation and exchange of commodities, with paper bills, as mediums of currency, and their influence over commerce ; with agriculture, with manufactures, with education, and with religion. It is for the promotion of one or another of these great *public objects* that these acts of incorporation have been passed. Knowing the influence they can exercise over these public interests, the legislature, instead of cutting them loose from the restraints of public law, has placed them in the most rigid subordination to it, by declaring, in every charter, that they shall do no act contrary to the law of the land. They now seek to exercise powers which are delegated to their *discretion*, by deputy, which the law of the land has universally prohibited. *If we bend the law to them, we must bend it to all others ; there is no stopping place at which we can refuse ; but we have no right to stir a pebble of the common law. If the corporation really need this power, they must ask it of the legislature. They cannot assume it, nor can the court confer it.*"

But there is another thing about the proxies which were used by their holders at the time of the pretended consolidation, which is very peculiar, and that is—their power of not only voting early and often—but of their voting *viva voce*—and to prove this you need only to refer to the records which were kept by Thomas D. Robertson, James R. Young and J. B. Redfield, who were eye witnesses of this miracle, and who have certified to it in the most formal manner, under their own hands and signatures, in the following words and figures, to-wit (see pages 4 & 5 of this brief) : " A vote thereon by *viva voce* of the stockholders present, or *represented by proxy*, being ordered—we, the undersigned, did canvass the *said votes*—that votes on 33,847 shares *were cast*, being a majority of the whole number of shares outstanding. *All* of the votes so cast, were in favor of each and all of the resolutions aforesaid." In other words, although there were only about fifteen persons present when this *viva voce* ballot was ordered, they cast 33,847 votes; and they were very careful to state that this number was a majority of all the shares of the stock of the G. & C. U. R. R. Co. then outstanding. In other words, when this *viva voce* ballot was taken, this great and all important fact was kept steadily in mind, and had such an animating effect that it caused the dumb to speak, and the printed and written proxies to proclaim it, in *tones* which *could not be uttered.*

Judge HORNBLOWER, or any other judge, would, we think, find great difficulty in reconciling the vocal powers of these proxies with the principles of the *common* law, or any other law.

These proxies, *when* they *spoke*, undoubtedly *meant* what they *said.*

XVII.

It is a general rule of law, that a delegated authority cannot be delegated.

Hence, the directors of one railroad company can never transfer THEIR AUTHORITY *to the directors of another railroad company, and authorize them to manage it for them; if they did, they would be responsible to the stockholders for all the damages that could possibly arise in consequence thereof.*

The court will observe by the first article of the consolidation agreement, found on page 7 of this brief, that it was expressly provided, that "the persons who shall be directors of the Chicago & North Western R. Co. at the *time* of such consolidation, shall be directors of the said consolidated company, and *shall act* as such, until the next annual election of directors, as is herein prescribed, and until their successors are duly elected."

Now, where is the authority in the charter of the Galena & C. U. R. R. Co., *authorizing the directors*, who were elected to *manage its affairs*, to literally sell out their office in this manner?

The defendants in this case may call this transaction consolidation as much as they please—we shall call it a "sale"—for it amounts to just exactly that—nothing more and nothing less. Now, what would be thought of the conduct of the directors of any railroad company, (to say nothing of this) who should be elected by stockholders at 12 o'clock in the day, and in less than three hours afterwards, deliberately set down *and agree to transfer the entire management of the road to a rival corporation?* Suppose, for instance, that the New York Central R. R. shonld, at any annual meeting, *in imitation* of the conduct of the directors of the G. & C. U. R. R. Co., immediately set down and enter into an agreement, in writing, to transfer the entire management of their road to the New York & Erie R. R. Co., and in order to induce them to accept the office, should, for a dollar, give them the whole road and all its property to boot? Would such directors be considered as having acted *bona fide* and in good faith towards the stockholders, and could they complain if their motives were impugned, and could they expect to appear spotless before any court, under such circumstances? We think not; and we think that the universal opinion of mankind would be against them—and every man would say that such conduct was neither fair nor honest. Now, the case which we have supposed, is not one whit more extreme than the case at bar; and is, as we contend, perfectly parallel.

What does the law say in such a matter, and under such circumstances? We believe that, without some authority can be found in the charter of the G. & C. U. R. R. Co. itself, that such a contract is absolutely void, on grounds of public policy; but, if not on grounds of public policy, it certainly is so far as a dissenting stockholder is concerned—for a stockholder of any corporation has a right to have the corporation managed by a board of directors whose interest would be to take care of the property—not destroy it or sell it.

To this effect see Redfield on Railways, p. 418-9, and cases there cited in note 4, in which (in the text), he says—

"An agreement between railway companies, without the authority of the legislature, *transferring* the powers of one company to the other, *is against good policy*, and a court of equity will not lend its aid to carry such contract into effect."

And to the same effect, it has been, over and over again, decided in this country, that one railroad company cannot, by making a lease of its entire road to another, thereby escape responsibility, or avoid fulfilling its duties to the public. Now, the court will perceive at once, that if the agreement in question was a perfectly valid agreement, and the G. & C. U. R. R. Co. should pass as an entirety, by agreement, under the management of another railroad company, that it could, and would, thereby release itself entirely and forever, from all responsibilities to the public. We respectfully submit that this cannot be done.

A contract by which one railway agrees to give up to another railway a part of its profits, in consideration of securing a portion of the profits of the other company, is illegal and *ultra vires*.

> Redfield on R., p. 438.
> *Shrewsbury & Birmingham R. v. London & Northwestern R.*, 29 Law Times, 186.

A railroad corporation cannot DELEGATE *its powers to another company.* And in *Beman* v. *Rufford*, 40 Eng. Ch. Rep., which was a case where a railway company, constituted under an act of parliament, agreed with two other railway companies, that the *whole concern*, without incumbrance, when completed, should be worked by *those two companies*, who should have *perfect control*, and exercise all the rights of the first mentioned company, and should find stock, and *work the concern for twenty-one years*—held, that the agreement was illegal, as being in violation of the act under which the first mentioned company was constituted; and that, though a very large majority of the shareholders present at a meeting, had sanctioned the agreement, the dissentients might file a bill on behalf of themselves and the other shareholders against the company and its directors, to have it declared void.

It will not allow any of them to speculate as to whether it would be more advantageous to do something which the act of parliament does not authorize to be done ; and, therefore it is, that a very small number, or, indeed, *one*, of the shareholders may file a bill on behalf of the whole body, although, at a meeting of the company, a large majority of the shareholders may have sanctioned that course of proceeding which the bill complains of. The shareholders so filing this bill, say that their company, together with the directors of it, have entered into a contract with the North Western and the Midland companies to make a railroad different from that which was contemplated by act of parliament, and so to apply funds, which the plaintiff say are their funds, in a mode in which they never were authorized to be applied ; and therefore, the plaintiffs seek to restrain them.

I am clearly of opinion, both on principle and authority, that it is the province of this court to prevent the contract from being carried into effect, because, on the principle that has been laid down, this court will not tolerate that parties having the enormous powers which railway companies obtain, should apply one farthing of their funds in a way which differs, in the slightest degree, from that in which the legislature has provided that they shall be applied."

XVIII.

GALENA & CHICAGO UNION RAILROAD CHARTER—ITS HISTORY AND POWERS.

No authority for either a sale or consolidation or confiscation of the corporation and its property and franchises whatever.

The original charter of the G. & C. U. R. R. Co. was granted in 1836—long before the adoption of the present constitution of the State of Illinois—and neither the original charter or any amendment ever made to it, authorizes or empowers the directors or a majority of the stockholders, acting together or by proxy, to *sell*

*out the corporation and all of its property, or merge or amalgamate
it with any other railroad as an entirety*, or make all of the stockholders liable in any way, or in any form, or under any pretence,
or *under the color of any name*, whether it be called sale, union,
consolidation or confiscation, for the debts and liabilities of any
other railroad or railroads whatsoever, either in this State or the
State of Wisconsin or Michigan. In short, under the charter of the
G. & C. U. R. R. Co., no one of its stockholders *can be transferred*
against his will to another corporation, and be compelled to incur
its hazards and liabilities.

The reason for this is plain, and as is stated by Judge DAVIS, in the
case of *Clearwater* v. *Meredith*, 1 Wallace, 40, that, " When any
person takes stock in a railroad corporation, he has entered into a
contract with the company that his interests shall be subject to the
direction and control of the proper authorities of the corporation
to accomplish *the* object for which the company was organized.
He does not agree that the improvements to which he subscribed
should be changed in its purposes and character, at the will and
pleasure of a majority of the stockholders, so that *new responsibilities*, and it may be, *new hazards, are added* to the original undertaking. He may be very willing to embark in one enterprise and
unwilling to engage in another—to assist in building a short line
railway and averse to risking his money in one having a longer
line of transit."

Now, is there any authority given in the charter of the G. & C.
U. R. R. Co. authorizing its capital stock to be thrown into a common fund with that of the C. & N. W. R. R. Co., and with railroads with which it is doing business, in Wisconsin and Michigan,
and making its stockholders liable for their debts ?

In order that the court may examine this part of the case without referring to the various session laws of the State which contain
the charter and amendments of the Galena & C. U. R. R. Co., we
insert such parts of them here as are in any way essential to the
proper understanding of the powers of the corporation, and in
order that the court may determine what they authorize and what
they do not.

1. The charter of the Galena & C. U. R. R. Co. was granted on the 16th day of February, 1836, before the adoption of the present constitution of the State, which took place in 1847 ; and the first 6 sections of said charter are as follows—

AN ACT to Incorporate the Galena and Chicago Union Railroad Company, Approved January 16, 1836.

Section 1. *Be it enacted by the People of the State of Illinois, represented in the General Assembly,* That all such persons as shall become Stockholders, agreeably to the provisions of this act, in the Corporation hereby created, shall be, and *for the term of sixty years from and after the passage of this act,* shall continue to be a body corporate and politic, by the name of the " Galena and Chicago Union Railroad Company," and by that name shall have succession for the term of years above specified, may sue and be sued, complain and defend, in any Court of Law or Equity, may make and use a common seal, and alter the same at pleasure, may make by-laws, rules and regulations for the management of property, the regulation of its affairs, and for the transfer of its stock, not inconsistent with the existing laws, and the constitution of this State and of the United States, and may moreover appoint such subordinate agents, officers and servants, as the business of the said Corporation may require, and allow to them a suitable compensation, prescribe their duties, and require bond for the faithful performance thereof, in such penal sums, and with such sureties as they may choose, who shall hold their offices during the pleasure of the directors of the said Corporation.

Sec. 2. The said Corporation shall have the right to construct, and during its continuance, to maintain and continue a Railroad, with a single or double track, and with such appendages as may be deemed necessary for the convenient use of the same, from the town of Galena, in the county of Jo Daviess, to such point at the town of Chicago as shall be determined, after a survey shall have been made of the route, to be most eligible, proper, direct and convenient therefor.

Sec. 3. The capital stock of the said Corporation shall be one hundred thousand dollars, which shall be deemed personal property, and shall be divided into shares of one hundred dollars each. The capital stock of said Corporation may, at any time hereafter, be increased to a sum not exceeding one million of dollars, if the same shall be judged necessary to the completion of the said work, and the same shall be subscribed for and taken under the direction of the Directors of the said Corporation, wherever they shall direct one or more books to be opened for such purpose, and shall be subscribed and taken in such manner as the Directors of the said Corporation for that purpose shall order and appoint.

Sec. 4. That William Bennet, Thomas Drummond, J. C. Goodhue, Peter Semple, J. W. Turner, E. D. Taylor, and J. B. Thomas, Jr., shall be Commissioners for securing subscriptions to the capital stock of said Corporation, who shall give notice within twelve months after the passage of this act, of the time and place where books will be opened at Galena and Chicago, and such other places as they may deem necessary, in some public newspapers printed at said places, at least thirty days previous to the opening of such books, for the receiving subscriptions to the capital stock of said Corporation.

The majority of the Commissioners shall attend at the place appointed by such notice, for the opening of said books, and shall continue to receive such subscriptions to the capital stock of said Corporation, from all persons who will subscribe thereto, until the whole amount thereon shall have been subscribed, when the said books shall be closed. Each subscriber, at the time of subscribing, shall pay to the Commissioners one dollar on each share of the stock subscribed for by him, and the said Commissioners shall, as soon as the Directors are elected, deliver to them the whole amount so received.

Sec. 5. The affairs of said Corporation shall be managed by a Board of seven Directors, to be annually chosen by the stockholders, from among themselves, as soon as may be, after the stock has been subscribed. The Commissioners shall give notice of the time and place at which a meeting of the stockholders will be held for the choice of Directors. And at such a time and place appointed for that purpose, the Commissioners, or a majority of them, shall attend and act as inspectors of said election ; and the stockholders present shall proceed to elect their Directors by ballot, and the Commissioners present shall certify the result of such election, under their hands, which certificate shall be recorded in the books of the Corporation, and shall be sufficient evidence of the election of the Directors therein named.

All future elections shall be held at the time and in the manner prescribed by the by-laws and regulations of the said Corporation. Each stockholder shall be allowed as many votes as he owns shares at the commencement of such election, and a plurality of votes shall determine the choice ; but no stockholder shall be allowed to vote at any election after the first, for any stock which shall have been assigned to him within thirty days previous to holding such election.

The said Directors shall hold their offices for one year after their election, and shall elect one of their number as President of the said Board.

Sec. 6. The said Corporation is authorized to construct, make and use a single or double railroad or way, of suitable width and dimensions, to be determined by the said Corporation, on the line, course or way which may be designated and selected by the Directors, as the line, course or way whereon to construct and make the same ; and shall have power to regulate the time and manner in which goods, effects and passengers shall be transported, taken and carried on the same ; and to prescribe the manner in which the said Railroad shall be used ; by what force the carriages to be used thereon may be propelled ; and the rate of toll for transportation of persons or property thereon ; and shall have power to erect and maintain houses, toll-gates and other buildings for the accommodation and management of the said road, and transport thereon as may be deemed suitable to their interest. And they may also construct, maintain and use such other lateral routes as may be deemed advantageous, and expedient, and necessary, under the same rights and privileges as by this act is provided for the constructing of the main route. And it shall be lawful, also, for the said Corporation to unite with any other Railroad Company already incorporated, or which may be incorporated *upon any part of said road*, upon such terms as may be agreed upon by the Directors of said Companies ; and also, to construct such other and lateral routes as may be necessary to connect them with any other route or routes which may be deemed expedient."

The rest of the charter relates exclusively to the method to be pursued in obtaining the right of way, and can have no bearing here whatsoever.

It is a part of the public history of the State of Illinois, that about the year 1837, when this railroad company was chartered, and railroads first began to engage the attention of the people, that a vast system of internal improvements, consisting of canals and railroads, was projected, and a large amount of money expended in explorations, surveys and miscellaneous experiments in all parts of the State.

Among others was the project of a grand trunk line of railroad commencing in the southern part of the State, and extending in a diagonal direction across the State to its northern corner, and terminating at or near Galena. A large sum of money was expended upon detached portions of the road ; and it was at one time the pride of the State. The road was called the State Central. In 1837, the Galena railroad company wished to increase its capital stock, and the legislature granted them power to do so, but in deference to the State Central, provided, in section 3, of that act, as follows—

"Sec. 3. Should it appear impracticable for the said Company to construct the same Road the whole distance contemplated by said act, or that it would be more advantageous to the Company, or the public interest, that the said Road should be connected with the

State Central Railroad, then the said Company are authorized to terminate the said road at such point as shall be deemed most practicable—and may intersect and connect the said Road with the said Central Railroad in its course to Galena : *Provided*, Nothing contained in the provisions of this act shall authorize the said Company to have, purchase, receive, or hold any land upon any line of any Railroad authorized to be constructed by the State, nor to construct any Railroad upon or near the same line, or any Railroad authorized to be constructed by the State.

"NEWTON CLOUD,

"*Speaker of the House of Representatives, pro. tem.*

"W. H. DAVIDSON,

"*Speaker of the Senate.*

" Approved, 4th March, 1837.

" JOSEPH DUNCAN."

The Illinois Central, when it was chartered, embraced about the same territory that the old State Central R. R. did ; and, as it was obliged by its charter to build through from Cairo to Dunleith, it was thought that two separate roads would not pay ; as the route from Freeport, in Stephenson county, to Galena, was, at that time, considered a very difficult and costly line. Accordingly, those interested in the Illinois Central & Galena R. R. Co. came to a definite understanding upon the subject, and it was arranged between the two roads that the Illinois Central should build through to Dunleith, and that a permanent running arrangement should be entered into by which the G. & C. U. R. R. Co. would receive its legitimate proportion of all the business of the line west of Freeport, which should be destined for Chicago ; and accordingly the Galena road built through to Freeport, and there stopped. (See charter of Illinois Central Railroad Company—11th section.)

In 1847, the charter was still further amended, fixing the number of directors, and providing how they should be elected ; the first section of which is as follows—

" Sec. 1. *Be it enacted by the People of the State of Illinois, represented in the General Assembly,* That the Board of Directors of the Galena and Chicago Union Railroad Company shall hereafter consist of such number of Directors as shall be determined upon from time to time by the Stockholders of said Company, at any meeting thereof for the choice of Directors: *Provided,* That such number shall not be less than seven, nor more than thirteen ; *said Directors shall be stockholders in* said Company, and shall be elected annually by the stockholders, either in person or by proxy, and shall hold their offices for one year, and until their successors shall be elected and qualified. But any vacancy occurring in said Board between elections may be filled by the Board at any legal meeting of the Directors ; and the person so elected to fill the vacancy shall hold his office until the next annual meeting."

After the G. & C. U. R. R. Co. had completed their main line through to Rockford, it was thought advisable to construct a branch line through to the Mississippi river ; and accordingly, a line was surveyed through to Dixon ; but some of the stockholders doubted the power of the company to do this under their charter, and one Newhall brought suit to prevent them from proceeding—a full report of which suit can be found in the 14th of Ill. Rep. 273. About this time a number of persons residing in the Rock River Valley, procured a charter for a road to be built from what was called the Narrows, on the Mississippi river, near Fulton city in Whiteside county, to strike the Illinois Central at Dixon, the powers of which are contained in section 2 in said act, which is as follows—

" *AN ACT to incorporate the Mississippi and Rock River Junction Railroad Company.*

" Sec. 2. The said corporation shall have the right to survey, locate and construct, and, during its continuance to maintain and continue a railroad, with single and double track, and with such appendages as may be deemed necessary for the convenient use of the same, *from the Narrows of the Mississippi River, in Fulton*

City, Whiteside county, and State of Illinois, to a point on the Northwestern branch of the Central Railroad, north of Rock River by the way of Sterling, in said county of Whiteside, should *said branch of said Central railroad,* when definitely located, run east of said town of Sterling, and to locate and construct the same on such line, course or way as may be designated and selected by the directors of said corporation whereon to construct and locate the same, and may also prescribe the manner in which said railroad shall be used, by what power the carriages to be used thereon may be propelled, to regulate the time and manner in which goods, effects and passengers may be transported and carried on the same, and the rates of toll on the transportion of persons and property thereon."

See Session Laws of 1851, page 254 of Private Laws. This is all the power that is given in any way in regard to locating and building a railroad.

The persons interested in this enterprise caused a survey to be made and exhibited considerble signs of vitality, and the result of the suit brought by Newhall being in doubt, and the managers of the G. & C. U. R. R. Co. being desirous of pushing their branch road through as speedily as possible, entered into some negotiations with those parties in order to control the line, and made some contract with them for that purpose; but the power of the Galena & C. U. R. R. Co. to make a union or consolidation with said company being doubted by all parties, the negotiations were postponed from time to time, and contracts of various kinds and characters were considered, and a lease in some shape, was, we believe, executed. But while these negotiations were in progress, the Supreme Court of Illinois decided the Newhall case in favor of the G. & C. U. R. R. Co., which was to the effect, that, under their charter, they had power to build lateral roads, as provided in their charter, which roads, they defined to be " branches from their main line, within reasonable limits."

The legislature of the State, having also during or about this time convened, a further amendment was procured to the charter, authorizing the capital stock to be increased to five millions of dollars ; and by the second section thereof it was provided—

" That said company is hereby authorized, under its charter, to extend the Western Branch of said road to *Dixon*, in Lee county, and may connect *said branch* by lease, purchase or consolidation, with any railroad extending to the Mississippi river, *at or near Fulton* or Albany, *or said* company may extend their said branch by *way* of Sterling, in Whiteside county, to *said* river, at or near Albany, as aforesaid."

This act was approved Feb. 25, 1854.

Here the power to consolidate is expressly given, but it is also *expressly limited*, and it cannot be pretended for a moment that *this* power of consolidation has any bearing on this case at all, because it was meant to accomplish a certain, specific and distinct thing, and is not a general power at all ; and, as the sequel shows, was not used after it was obtained.

After the case of Newhall had been thus decided, and after the legislature had thus given *express* authority for the company to build through to the Mississippi river, by way of Sterling, the company proceeded with their line ; and, although, an arrangement had been made with the Mississippi River & Rock River Junction R. R. Co. which was satisfactory, it is believed that not a rod of the Galena branch was actually built under that charter ; but the whole subscription to the capital stock of the Mississippi & Rock River Junction R. R. Co. was cancelled, and, by agreement, all favorable to the route came in and took stock in the Galena & C. U. R. R. Co., to complete the line ; and, as subsequent events showed, their confidence was not misplaced.

Now, this is a full and complete history of the great original sin of this road, which, it is considered, it committed in the Eden of its days, and which is now brought up with more authority than Genesis in judgment against us.

The logic which links us to the depravity of this act pursues us with great persistency, and we find no escape whatever from its consequences except through the portals of Wall street or the Upper Peninsula of Michigan.

Our infallibility is now ended ; and in the language of the inspired writer of the answer in this case, we are henceforth, in consequence of our fall, to be called the " said consolidated Galena & C. U. Railroad Company." The serpent entered our garden when we crossed Rock river, and in this first consolidation we are now to find a " charm of powerful trouble."

We had always supposed that we knew ourselves well, and that our identity was perfect ; but it now appears that we early underwent transformation, and have only been existing in a *purely consolidated state* ever since.

This information is certainly valuable, and we will avail ourselves of it in considering further the effects it may have in determining the right of the company to make the *present* consolidation.

If the question had been asked the managers of the G. & C. U. R. R. Co. in 1854–5, what their object was in entering into any negotiations at all, with the Miss. & Rock River Junction R. R. Co., *they would have said that* it was simply to obtain an unbroken, continuous line through to the Mississippi river, and nothing else.

When the Newhall case was decided, as we have stated, *then* the power of the company itself to complete its line under its own charter became established, and it had no occasion to make use of any borrowed powers at all. The defendants in this case have attached to their bill a certain paper writing, purporting to be articles of agreement for a union and consolidation of the Mississippi & Rock River Junction R. R. Co., with the Galena & C. U. R. R. Co., with certain *conditional* resolutions attached ; but it does not appear that those articles were ever executed, or that the conditions of the resolutions were ever complied with ; and as the president, in his annual report, does not define what he means by the term consolidation, or explain what its scope and comprehension was, we are at this time unable to determine whether it meant any more than simply *transferring of the subscription* list of the Miss. & Rock River Junc. R. R. Co. to that of the G. & C. U. R. R. Co. and a union of their interests, or not ; but we are assured by those conversant with the transaction, that *it was of no higher type* of consolidation than that. But few then living would, we think, have believed that the G. & C. U. R. R. Co., which then was attacked with consolidation in so mild a form, would one day perish from a disease, the seeds of which were then planted so carelessly in the system.

There was, it is true, *much apprehension* by the stockholders, as to the policy of this branching system; and the President of the road, Hon. John B. Turner, refers to it in his annual report of June, 1855, in the following language: "Many of the eastern stockholders have expressed apprehensions that ' the construction of so many branches' would prove unprofitable, and injure the hitherto productive character of the stock. This company has constructed no branch but the one to Beloit, and this, *unlike eastern branch roads*, will be a part of a through line from Chicago to Madison, the capitol of Wisconsin, and to the pineries north, where the connecting roads in that State are completed." This explanation did not, however, allay the apprehension which had been excited; and to such an extent was the feeling carried that *it resulted in the retirement from the management of the road* in two or three years after this time, of the president and most of the managers who were engaged in it, and *they continued in retirement until June* 1, 1864, when they were again inducted into office *by the C. & N. W. R. Co.*, only to destroy the G. & C. U. R. R. Co., which they were to manage.

We do not say that Hon. John B. Turner, a man whom, individually, we respect, was instigated by anything like revenge, but it does look very much as if he yielded without objection to the schemes of a class of designing men whose rapacity and ambition knew no bounds, and, who, regardless of all consequences, like that imperial company under the British crown, " which commenced with the erection of a factory on the shores of India, *overthrew kingdoms*, and from their *ruins* ' consolidated ' an empire."

There is no evidence before this court that the law of 1855, which has been produced here, purporting to confirm the consolidation (whatever the character of that transaction which is termed consolidation was) was ever accepted by the company, or was ever acted upon by the company at all, much less was ever sanctioned by the complainants in the case. On the contrary, we believe it is susceptible of the highest proof that it never received the sanction of the stockholders at all, in any form ; and until that is shown, it amounts simply to a *proposition* made to the company, and if accepted by the directors, *would not bind the dissenting shareholders.*

Some attempt has been made to draw conclusions unfavorable to the complainant's position in this case, by referring to a clause in the 6th section of the original charter of the Galena & C. U. R. R. Co. which reads as follows : " And it shall be lawful, also, for said corporation to unite with any other railroad company, *already* incorporated, or *which may be incorporated upon any part of said road*, upon such terms as may be agreed upon by the directors of said companies."

Now, let us examine this provision for a moment, and subject it to the legal tests already laid down and established in the construction of these charters.

1. It is provided that this railroad company may " *unite.*"— Unite what ? its capital stock and all its rights, privileges and franchises ? Is that what was intended by this term ? Is this term so plain and unambiguous that the court can tell instantly what it means, and can say that it comprehends all of these things ? Does it not mean, rather, that it may, in order to make running arrangements with connecting and continuous lines of railroads, unite with them in running their cars over each others roads, just as is and has been done by this road, for years, over the Illinois Central R. R. that connects with it at Freeport. But *ambiguous* as the term *is*, let us see in the second place, when, and with what, it can *unite.* This is answered by the context, which says, that it can unite, 1st, with any other railroad company *already incorporated*— that is, with any railroad company which was in being at the time when *it* was chartered—*i. e.*, in 1836. Now, as the C. & N. W. R. R. Co. had no existence at that time, and scarcely exists now, it will not be pretended that the legislature meant any union with any such corporation.

But in the 2d place, it is said, " or which may be incorporated, upon *any part of said road.*" Now, what does this mean, " any part of said road ?"   Does this mean any road which may be incorporated with the intention of building a road through the northern part of Illinois, and thence through Wisconsin and Michigan ? Is that what this clause *says ?*   If the legislature meant this, why did they not say so?   Usually, when the term, " part of a road " is used, we take it literally to refer to the superstructure, the track, and road bed ; and when the term, "any part of *said* road " is used, we refer it to some road before mentioned and referred to. We do not include in it, any idea of counties, countries or States —it means no such thing, and never did ; therefore, until the defendants in this case show that the Chicago and Northwestern Railway Company has been, in the first place, incorporated, and in the second place, " incorporated upon a part of the said Galena & C. U. R. R. Co.," we shall contend that there is not the slightest authority whatever in the charter of the G. & C. U. R. R. Co., to authorize any union or consolidation whatever, with any distant and distinct corporation.

Corporate powers can *never* be created by implication, nor extended by construction."

" In the construction of a charter, to be in doubt is to be resolved ; and every resolution which springs from doubt is against the corporation.   This is the *rule* sustained by all the courts in this country and in England."

See p. 25 & 26 and 35 & 36 of this brief.

In the language of another—

" Here is a law, not designed for the general government of our own citizens alone, who may be supposed to be familiar with our legislative history, and with the general sentiments of their representatives, but *it is also a proposition for a contract, addressed to capitalists throughout the world,* ignorant as they *must* be of all these extraneous circumstances, and who must *necessarily* rely alone *upon the terms of the law* to determine the nature and character of the proposition.   In such a case, justice to them and justice to the integrity of the State, require that we should look *to the terms of a law for its meaning,* and inquire how it was fairly understood by those to whom it was addressed, and who have acted upon it, and who have thus become parties to it.

Now the result of this examination shows—

1. That there was no power whatever in the original charter of the G. & C. U. R. R. Co. to *transfer* its stockholders to that of another corporation, under any pretence whatever, and make *the* corporation or its stockholders liable for the debts of said distinct and independent corporations, by the order or direction of any board of directors, or any set of its stockholders or proxy-holders whatever, whether living in Wall street or in this State.

2. Neither is there any power which has ever been conferred upon said G. & C. U. R. R. Co., by any amendment or amendments whatever, which authorizes its board of directors or any number of stockholders or proxy-holders to *prescribe the terms* upon which the said corporation may or may not exist, or to prescribe the terms upon which its stockholders shall continue members of said corporation ; neither is there any power whatever, *by any law, which can compel the minority of stockholders to sell out or transfer their stock to any man or set of men, or any corporation or set of corporations which has existed or ever will exist; without such power and authority is specifically and expressly granted before or at the time when a person became a member of the corporation.*

3. The G. & C. U. R. R. Co. never built a rod of railroad under the charter of the M. & R. R. J. R. R. Co. or any other company ; and the pretended consolidation which it made with the M. & R. R. J. R. R. Co. in 1855, was simply *an arrangement* by which those who were trying to build a railroad from Fulton City, in Whiteside county, to Dixon, in Lee county, gave up their organization and took stock in the G. & C. U. R. R. Co., and the G. & C. U. R. R. Co. then proceeded to build its own line through to the Mississippi river under *its own* charter, and by virtue of *its own powers.*

4. If the G. & C. U. R. R. Co. did make some arrangement with the M. & R. R. J. R. R. Co. in 1855, under the name and style of consolidation, in 1855, by which the M. & R. R. J. R. R. Co. abandoned their project, is that any reason whatever for the G. & C. U. R. R. Co. to *sell out its entire railroad company,* and become responsible for the debts of a half a dozen railroad corporations in Illinois, Wisconsin and Michigan, amounting to twenty or thirty millions of dollars ?

5. We are not now complaining of any transaction which took place *years ago ;* but we are complaining of the sale and " consolidation " of the G. & C. U. R. R. Co, which took place on the 1st of June, 1864, whereby the entire G. & C. U. R. R. Co. as a corporation, and all its property, and all the rights and interests of its stockholders, is attempted to be *confiscated* and *appropriated* to the use of the C. & N. W. R. Co. This is the issue which is here presented to this court, and is the only real issue in the case.

6. If what the defendants in this case claim is true, *to-wit :* that the G. & C. R. R. Co. did once make a consolidation with some parties who had projected a line of railroad but had not built it, does it follow that it can then go on forever and consolidate its property, franchises and privileges with any railroad corporation in any State in the Union ? If it can, then on the same principle, any company of adventurers who organize a railroad company in Maine, could, in this manner, gradually extend their powers, like a cordon, across this continent, and bind up the States themselves.

Finally, under any and every aspect in which this subject can be viewed ; whether in the light of the past or present, we contend there is nothing whatever in the history of the G. & C. U. R. R. Co., or any other railroad that ever existed, which can furnish the slightest justification for the conduct of those directors of the G. & C. U. R. R. Co. betraying their trusts and in conspiring with the C. & N. W. R. Co. to take and *appropriate* it to the C. & N. W. R. Co. There is nothing in the charter of the G. & C. U. R. R.

Co. or any of its amendments authorizing it, and instead of digni-
fying the transaction, by the term " consolidation," it would be
much more appropriate to call it (not by any technical or *professional* name) but by its real and *right* name—*confiscation*; and
then argue it upon *its* merits and not upon the merits of something which has no relation to it, whatever.

XIX.

*Unauthorized contracts are illegal contracts, and upon the grounds
of* PUBLIC POLICY *they should not be sanctioned.*

In the case of *Bissell* v. *Southern Michigan & Northern Indiana
Railway Company*, 22 N. Y. 285, Judge SELDEN said—

" The contracts of corporations, which are not authorized by
their charters *are illegal*, because they are made *in contravention
of public policy*. That contracts which do in reality contravene
any principle of public policy are illegal and void, is not and cannot be denied. The doctrine is *universal*. There is no exception.
Although the unauthorized contract may be neither *malum in se*
nor *malum prohibitum*, but, on the contrary, may be for some be-
nevolent object, as to build an alms-house or a college, or to purchase and distribute tracts or books of instruction; yet, if it is a
violation of public policy for corporations to exercise powers which
have never been granted to them, such contracts, notwithstanding
their praiseworthy nature, are illegal and void. Those, therefore,
who hold that corporations are liable upon their contracts, notwithstanding they were made without authority, are *forced* to contend,
that no principle of public policy is violated by such contract.
" This is the ground which they *do* take, and which, it is obvious,
they must necessarily take, in order to sustain their position. Here,
then, we have an issue made up, which, if I am right, is decisive of
the question under consideration.
" What, then, is the argument, by which it is sought to be shown

that there is no principle of public policy involved in this question of the liability of corporations for their unauthorized acts? It is said that a private corporation is simply a chartered partnership, possessing certain attributes conferred by its charter for the purpose of enabling it the more conveniently to transact its business; that, even in incorporated partnerships, the articles of copartnership always specify the objects of the association; and that when such associations choose to become incorporated, those objects are, for the same reason, specified in the charter; that the charter simply takes the place, in this respect, of the articles of agreement, in the case of an incorporated partnership; that, as the objects of such associations, although incorporated, are of a private nature, there is no question of public policy involved; and that no public interest requires that the transactions of the corporation should be kept within its chartered limits.

" If we admit the soundness of this argument, and assume that the directors of a corporation are not under any public obligation to keep within their chartered powers, but are to be regarded simply as the agents of the corporators, so that any excess of power on their part amounts simply to a breach of trust toward their principals, it would not follow that the corporation is liable upon its unauthorized contracts. But I apprehend there are serious objections to this view of the nature of corporations, and of the effect of their charters. In the first place, if there is no public interest involved, how is it possible to justify the creation of private corporations at all? Such corporations are endowed with valuable franchises and privileges which give them great advantages over mere private citizens, whether individual or associated. The grant of such privileges upon the principles for which some of my associates contend, would be a pure piece of legislative favoritism, which should be indignantly condemned. In this country, if in no other, it is held to be the duty of the government to protect the people in equal rights and privileges, and not to use its power for the special benefit of its favorites. Every privilege or advantage given to one man or set of men is necessarily at the expense of others; and it is against the fundamental principles of our government that this should be done, unless required by interests of a public nature. No doubt these principles are frequently violated, and corporate powers and privileges are conferred which no public interest demands; but, nevertheless, such interest is the ostensible reason for the grant in every case.

"Take, for instance, the very class of corporations in question here, *viz:* railroad corporations—which are mere private associations, organized by their members with a view to their personal profit and emolument; and yet their creation is considered so much a matter of public interest, as to invoke the power of eminent domain, by which the property necessary for their purposes is forcibly taken from its owners as a public use. The same is true of telegraph and plank road incorporations. But, although the interest of the public in the creation of corporations of this class is made a little more obvious by the necessity which exists of taking from others property which is specific and tangible, for the purposes of the corporation; yet the same principle is applied to all corporations; for in all, some value, corporeal or incorporeal, is taken from a portion of the community and given to the corporators.

" Will it be said, that, although the public have an interest in the creation of corporations, it has none in the precise extent of the powers conferred, and that no public policy is concerned in their being strictly confined to the exercise of such powers? It is, obviously, impossible to support such a position. The franchises and privileges given to corporations belong to the public; and it would be just as reasonable and just as logical to contend that, under a patent for one hundred acres of land, the patentee might take possession of two hundred, without infringing any public interest.

" Every additional power given to, or usurped by, a corporation, extends its advantages over persons unincorporated. If a bank is permitted to trade in merchandise, it comes in competition with others so employed. If a railroad company is allowed to build and sail ships, it comes in competion with those engaged in commerce; and so of every other branch of business.

" The importance of limiting corporate bodies to the exercise of those powers, and the enjoyment of those privileges and franchises which have been specifically conferred upon them, must, I think, be obvious. They are rapidly multiplying. Their privileges give them decided advantages over mere private unincorporated partnerships. They have large capitals and numerous agents, and are capable of entering into combinations with each other. They are not only *formidable to individuals*, but might even, under some circumstances, become formidable to the state. They are, or should be, created, as we have seen, for public reasons alone ; and the legislature is presumed, in every instance, to have carefully considered the public interest, and to have granted just so much power, and so many peculiar privileges, as those interests are supposed to require.

" By making this principle of the common law the subject of an express and positive enactment, the legislature has shown that it considered this restriction upon corporations to be a matter of public interest and importance.

" The rights of stockholders in corporations are abundantly protected against every unauthorized assumption of power, or any breach of trust on the part of their managing officers. If the violation of duty or breach of trust is only threatened, a court of equity will prevent it by injunction, and if committed will afford the proper redress.

" If this conclusion is right, it inevitably follows that the assumption of any unauthorized power by a corporation is a violation of public policy and public right, and therefore, illegal.

" When the want of power is apparent upon comparing the act done with the terms of the.charter, the party dealing with the corporation is presumed to have knowledge of the defect, and the defence of *ultra vires* is available against him. But such a defense would not be permitted to prevail against a party who cannot be presumed to have had any knowledge of the want of authority to make the contract. Hence, if the question of power depends not merely upon the law under which the corporation acts, but upon the existence of certain extrinsic facts, resting peculiarly within the knowledge of the corporation officers, then the corporation would,

I apprehend, be estopped from denying that, which, by assuming to make the contract, it had virtually affirmed.

"A question, analogous to this, arises, where public officers who have done something in contravention of the statute under which they act, are afterwards sought to be estopped from setting up that their act was unauthorized. It was insisted by counsel in the case of *Regina* v. *White*, 4 Ad. & Ellis, N. S. 101, that, for public reasons, affairs so situated were not estopped ; but Lord DENMAN said : We have held that this is true only of a statute, the contents of which are publicly known ; such a statute is to have effect, whatever dealings may take place ; but when the persons acting, whether trustees for public purposes or not, have done any act which was not known to the parties with whom they were afterwards dealing, such an act can not prevent the estoppel arising from the subsequent dealing." This doctrine, which was also held in the case of *Doe ex dem Levy* v. *Horne*, [3 Ad. & El. N. S. 757,] will be found, when carefully examined, to sustain the exception which I have suggested in the case of corporations.

"It is, in my judgment, not only entirely clear upon principle, but abundantly settled by authority, that the contract of a corporation, if unauthorized by its charter, is an illegal contract, and that the corporation is not estopped from setting up this illegality in defense to an action brought upon it."

X X .

THE CHICAGO AND NORTH WESTERN RAILWAY COMPANY.

We have, thus far in this discussion, avoided all reference to the powers of the Chicago & North Western Railway Company, as they are nowhere defined in any written code or charter. It *has no* special charter whatever in the State of Illinois, and is claimed as a *habitat*, alternately, of Wisconsin, Illinois and Michigan. Its *real* origin is unknown ; but the highest authority which we have yet heard claimed for the grant of this corporation is, that it has been recognized as a corporation *de facto*, in some crafty and cunning statutes which were passed for foreclosing mortgages, building bridges, &c., which were not understood by the legislature when they were passed, and the powers of which are now only revealed by argument, and the keenest exercise of modern dialectics. To contend, in advance with these powers, would be like engaging the powers of the air.

Its history, so far as known, is nothing but one continued series of aggressions; and to go back to its origin would be like exploring a graveyard. Its organic law, if it has one, is a regular Golgotha, and is composed of nothing but the skull and bones of charters.

Whenever its charter is produced, we will examine its provisions; and as it will be necessary to show some " claim and color of title " for its powers, we shall wait until that period arrives. But, in the absence of any organic law, we have a right to insist that it shall not take anything by implication, but shall, if a corporation of Wisconsin or Michigan, be confined to those States, and not exercise or assume any other powers than those *expressly* given to it.

Trustworthiness, it seems to regard as a positive injury to any railroad corporation; and, in the answer which it has put in, in this case, it seems to deny the very existence of such a virtue, and expresses the belief, that, if it ever did characterize the management of the old Galena & Chicago Union Railroad Company it only produced a positive injury.

The language of the answer is as follows: " These defendants deny that the said consolidated G. & C. U. R. R. Co. had been for many years so managed and controlled that it had acquired a great reputation throughout the United States for trustworthiness, but on the contrary thereof, these defendants are informed and *believe*, that the market price of the capital stock of said corporation was impaired rather than increased by the *reputation* which it acquired for trustworthiness."

This doctrine, it will be observed, is the doctrine of *total depravity* " consolidated," and will take rank with the most approved theories of those who regard virtue as an abstraction. If it becomes a question of whether it will pay or not, time alone can tell; for it is yet to be tested on a scale sufficiently gigantic to show its results.

XXI.

PENINSULA RAILROAD COMPANY OF MICHIGAN.

The history of this road, to a stockholder of the Galena and Chicago Union Railroad Company, is in deed most extraordinary; and shows, as clearly as the most elaborate argument can, the utter absurdity of making the Galena & Chicago Union Railroad Company responsible, jointly, with it for its debts and liabilities, through the medium of the Chicago & North Western Railway Company.

In the 1st place, it is more than four hundred miles distant from the nearest point of the Galena & Chicago Union Railroad, and neither connects with the Galena & Chicago Union Railroad or with the Chicago & North Western Railroad, and can only be reached by traversing the entire length of the State of Wisconsin from South to North, and then crossing Green Bay, and then a further journey across the Peninsula of Michigan.

2. It was organized in 1863, by parties directly interested in the Chicago & North Western Railway Company, and to aid those parties in carrying out *their own private enterprises*, and was aided and assisted from beginning to end, by the Chicago & North Western Union Railway Company.

3. Its President has been, and was, up to the 21st day of October, 1864, when it was consolidated with the Chicago & North Western Railway Company—William B. Ogden—the President of the Chicago & North Western Railway Company.

4. That, in order to build said road, they procured the following law to be passed by the legislature of the State of Michigan :

Act No. 229—Session Laws of Michigan, 1863.

An act supplementary to an act, entitled " an act to provide for the incorporation of Railroad Companies," approved February 12th, 1855.

Section 4. The Directors of any railroad, as aforesaid, may sell or *dispose of, or pledge unsubscribed shares of the capital stock, in payments of real estate,* purchased for the use of the road, or for contract work upon it, or *for other valuable consideration to the company* in lieu of money or bonds.

The certificate of the secretary and treasurer of the company, attested by its seal, that *certain shares* of stock described therein by the number of the certificate, value and number of shares, had been, *by order of the directors of the company issued to the parties named as full paid stock shall be proper proof of the fact ; and such certificates from the company shall be rendered in the annual* report of the State Treasurer, and the specific tax paid thereon according to law."

And did by means of said law induce a great many parties to take the stock and funds of said railroad company, at a great discount, and then did afterwards declare the stock and bonds full paid stock.

5. That this company was authorized to issue four millions of dollars of stock ; but whether it has issued that amount of stock is not now known, but it has issued a very large amount. That it has issued and sold for a small per cent on the dollar, a large amount of bonds, which are claimed to have the power of voting at any election for directors, in the same way and manner that *that* franchise is executed by the bondholders of the Chicago & N. W. R. Co.

6. That, on the 21st day of October, 1864, William B. Ogden and James Young, being respectively the president and secretary, of *both* the Chicago & North Western Railway Company *and* of the Peninsula Railway Company, made a consolidation of the Peninsula Railway Company with the Chicago & North Western Railway Company—the papers being executed by them *as presi-*

dent and secretary of both companies—in, and by which articles of consolidation, the Galena & Chicago Union Railroad Company, as mingled and mixed up with the Chicago & North Western Railway Company, *becomes responsible for all of its debts and liabilities;* and the stock and bonds which had been issued—and sold at *about twenty-five cents on the dollar, came in on the same terms* with that of the Chicago & North Western Railway Company's stock—and in addition to several millions of dollars of stock issued by the Chicago & North Western Railway Company, and a large amount for other consolidated purposes—increases the stock several millions more, and renders it absolutely certain, that, with all of the increase of freights, tariffs and business of every sort, character and kind, that the entire consolidated corporation, will, at no distant day, fall, like the Tower of Babel, amid the confusion of tongues, which it is creating, and will create, among the innumberal host of debtors and creditors, scrip holders, stockholders, and bondholders which it is gathering around it.

It is perfectly useless to attempt to convince any one that the G. & C. U. R. R. Co. and its stockholders were benefited by heaping up this immense debt upon them ; but yet, the defendants in this case, boldly advance to the charge, and, undismayed by any combination of difficulties, seek to overpower, if not overawe, all opposition, by a display of the trophies of their conquests.

No man can, under the various arrangements, agreements, consolidations and undefined powers, claimed by the Chicago & North Western Railway Company, tell what its stock is, or point to a single law, by which its powers are defined with the least accuracy, whatever, either in the State of Illinois, Wisconsin or Michigan.

In order that the court may see how the capital stock of the Chicago & North Western Railway Company is increased by the consolidation of the Peninsula Railroad Company with it, and to show how the stock of a Galena & Chicago Union Railroad Company stockholder would be effected, if compelled to become a corporator in this new consolidated company, we append, hereto, an abstract of the articles of consolidation made between the Chicago

& North Western Railway Company and the Peninsula Railroad Company of Michigan.

The articles commence with numerous whereases, among which, it is specified, that the two contracting parties are authorized, by acts of the legislatures of the several States, " to effect a union of their respective roads and properties, and to form, by consolidation of their corporate rights and franchises *one joint stock company*, and have agreed so to do, upon the terms and conditions hereinafter mentioned and contained." The articles then provide in detail, for a consolidation of all the rights and privileges and property of each company, making each responsible for all the debts and liabilities of each other. They then provide—

" Art. 5. The common stock of the party of the first part, is hereby declared to be valid stock in the consolidated company, and the preferred stock of the party of the first part is hereby declared to be valid preferred stock in the consolidated company, with the same preferences over the common stock, which now belong and appertain to the said preferred stock. *Provided*, however, that nothing herein contained, shall be construed to impair any of the provisions hereof, in respect to the ' Chicago & North Western Railway Company, Peninsula Special Stock,' hereinafter mentioned, or to create a preference over such stock, in respect to the income or earnings of the said Peninsula Railroad, as now built, and to be built northerly from Escanaba.

" Art. 6. Holders of capital stock of the party of the second part, are hereby authorized, upon surrendering their certificates to the proper officers of the consolidated company, to demand and receive from the same consolidated company, certificates for a like number of shares of a special stock, which is hereby agreed to be *created and issued* by the said consolidated company, which special stock shall be designated, ' Chicago and North Western Railway Peninsula Special Stock ;' and the stock of the party of the second part, is hereby declared to be entitled to all the rights herein granted, reserved or secured to the said special stock hereby provided for, with the same object as if such exchange had been actually made, until the holders thereof shall have been required by the consolidated company on a notice of less than thirty days, to make such exchange; which notice, to bind a particular holder, shall be given by depositing the same in the post office, in the city of New York, addressed to such holder, and by publication in at least one newspaper of the said city. And such requirement, shall not operate in any way to impair or effect the right of any holder of bonds of the party of the second part, to convert the same into stock of the party of the second part; but such conversion may be made directly into the said special stock.

" ART. 9. On and after the first day of January, one thousand eight hundred and sixty-five, (1865) all capital stock of the said party of the second part, and also, all the said ' Chicago & North Western Railway Company Peninsula Special Stock ' hereafter issued, shall be exchanged for, *and convertible into, the preferred and common stocks of the consolidated company,* hereby formed at and after the rate of *one share of the preferred stock* of the said consolidated company hereby formed, and one share of the common stock thereof for every two shares of the said Peninsula special stock, or of the present stock of the said party ot the second part, (with scrip certificates for fractional amounts less than a share) which exchange and conversion shall be at the option of the holder of the stock so authorized to be converted. *Provided,* however, that upon three-fourths of the whole aggregate amount of the present stock of the party of the second part and the said Peninsula special stock, by this agreement provided for, being changed and converted into such common and preferred stock of the consolidated company hereby formed, it shall become obligatory upon the holders of the balance of the said stocks, so provided to be converted, to exchange and convert the same into the common and preferred stocks of the consolidated company, at the rate aforesaid, upon being requested so to do by the said consolidated company, and that dividends, after such requisition on any stock not converted, shall cease until the same be so converted. And, *provided* further, that, in order to enable any such holder to make the change and conversion aforesaid, he must first surrender up the certificate or certificates held by him, which he desires so to convert. *Pro-*

vided, nevertheless, and it is hereby expressly declared that, in respect to all the said stock of the party of the second part and the said Peninsula special stock, which shall have been converted under this provision, the same shall be transferred and kept alive for the benefit of the consolidated company, in any dividend or distribution of profits which may be made, so long as any part of the said stock of the party ot the second part of the said Peninsula special stock shall remain unconverted.

" Art. 10. This agreement is hereby declared to be an agreement between the party of the first part and of the consolidated company hereby created, with the class of stockholders of the said consolidated company herein designated as holders of the aforesaid Peninsula special stock, within the meaning of an act of the legislature of the State of Wisconsin, entitled ' an act to amend the charter of the Chicago & North Western Railway Company, approved March 26th, 1864,' and for the purpose of more effectually securing and preserving to the stockholders of the said special stock, and of the present stock of the party of the second part (which, as aforesaid, is hereby delivered and agreed to be a special stock of the consolidated company with all the rights of the special stock, aforesaid), all the rights, powers, authorities, and direction by these presents reserved, granted to or conferred upon the said holders, or intended so to be ; the holders of the said special stock and of the present stock of the party of the second part, so far as unconverted, may each year elect or appoint a committee of three persons, who shall be called the Peninsula committee for each year, and shall continue until their successors shall be appointed, and shall be the general representatives of the holders of such special stock ; and in case of any disagreement between the consolidated company and the said committee, in respect to the division of earnings arising from the joint business, as to what constitutes ' net earnings,' or any other question, such difference shall be submitted to three arbiters ; and *William B. Ogden,* Edmund H. Miller and *William A. Booth* shall be such arbiters, who shall act by a majority of such number, and who shall keep their number full by appointment in any vacancy, which appointment shall be made by

the surviving or continuing arbiter or arbiters, and in every such
case the decision of such majority shall be binding on the parties
hereto. *Provided nevertheless*, that the passenger rates on through
business of the said Peninsula Railroad shall not be reduced below
three cents a mile without the written consent of the said arbiters,
nor shall the said special stock be increased beyond the amount
now authorized by the party of the second part, and such additional amount necessary for the conversion of bonds issued or to
be issued and secured by the aforesaid deed of trust, without the
consent of a majority in interest of the holders of such special
stock, to be expressed in writing, or at a meeting duly held, or the
consent of the Peninsula committee aforesaid, or a majority of
them.

" Art. 11. The said consolidated company hereby formed under the name of the Chicago and North Western Railway Company aforesaid, shall *assume, and does by these presents assume, the
payment of the bonds aforesaid of the said party of the second
part*, commonly known as the 'First Mortgage Sinking Fund
Land Grant convertible bonds of the Peninsula Railroad Company
of Michigan,' issued, or to be issued, in conformity with the provisions of the deed of trust aforesaid, and of all interest accrued
and to accrue thereon according to the tenor thereof, and of the
coupons thereto attached, and also, of all contributions to the sinking fund, for the redemption thereof provided by the deed of trust
aforesaid, and the said consolidated company shall observe, keep
and perform, and does hereby promise and agree to observe, keep
and perform, all and singular, the requirements, matters and things
by the deed of trust last aforesaid provided to be observed, kept or
performed by the said Peninsula Railroad Company of Michigan,
and that the provision in the said bonds contained for the conversion thereof into stock of the second part, shall apply to the conversion thereof into the aforesaid special stock.

" Art: 12. The holders of the said Chicago and North Western
Railway Company Peninsula Special Stock, and of the present
stock of the party of the second part, shall have the right to vote
in all corporate meetings of the consolidated company hereby

formed, in the same manner as the holders of the stock of the party of the first part, and the holders of the bonds of the party of the second part, shall have the right to vote on the said bonds, as provided therein, at every general and special meeting of the stockholders of the consolidated company.

" Art. 14. All joint debts, guaranties and liabilities, existing against either of the parties hereto, shall be, and hereby are, *assumed, and agreed to be provided for, paid and discharged by the consolidated company hereby formed.*"

The entire agreement is most extraordinary in its provisions; and increases the stock, debts and liabilities of the Chicago & North Western Railway Company, several millions of dollars. Is it not plain, therefore, beyond anything that can be suggested, that this last act on the part of the Chicago & North Western Railway Company, is the crowning act of destruction (if allowed to stand), of all the rights and interests of the stockholders of the Galena & Chicago Union Railroad Company? Does it need any argument to prove that the addition of millions of dollars of debts and liabilities to the original Galena & Chicago Union Railway Company will produce an injury? Does it require any argument to show that this case comes within the rule laid down by this court in the case of *Clearwater* v. *Meredith*, 1 Wallace, 39–40? If it does, does not the facts and circumstances themselves, furnish the most overwhelming and convincing argument that could possibly be made?

XXII.

Expediency has nothing to do with the legal questions at issue—but was the trade a good trade—for the G. & C. U. R. R. Co.?

1. The Expediency.
2. The Trade.

In *Shrewsbury and Birmingham Railway Co.* v. *London and North Western Railway Co.*, 4th DeGex, Macnaughten & Gordon's Reports, page 132, Lord Justice Turner says:

" In determining questions of this nature, courts of justice, as I apprehend, are bound to consider *not what in their* judgment may be most for the interest of the public, but what *was the scope and object of the law*, which is said to be infringed, or attempted to be infringed? What we have here to consider therefore, is, what was the scope and object of the acts of parliament from which these companies, and other railway companies (for there is nothing in this respect peculiar to these companies) derive their powers. The great undertakings of these companies could not be carried out by private enterprise, and parliament has, therefore, with a view to the public good, authorized the constitution of large bodies, acting by directors, for the purpose of carrying them out; but these bodies have no existence, independent of the acts which create them, and they are created by parliament with *special and limited powers* and *for limited purposes*. Whether parliament has wisely limited their power, or the purposes of their incorporation, is not for us to consider. The fact of their having been endowed with such powers, and incorporated for such purposes, only shows that parliament did not think fit to intrust them with more extended powers, or to incorporate them for other purposes; and when, therefore, they exceed or attempt to exceed their powers, or to go beyond the limits of their incorporation, they are acting in contravention of the law which created them, and in opposition to what courts of justice are bound to consider to have been the object of parliament in their creation."

In the case of the *Commonwealth* v. *Erie and North-East R. R. Co.*, 27 Penn., 339, the court said that it was no justification of the violation of a provision of the charter that the public were more benefited than injured thereby.

" This is not a case," said WELLES, J., in the case of *Buffalo, C. and N. R. R. Co.* v. *Pottle*, 23 Barb., 23, " where the court are *at liberty to measure the advantages or disadvantages* to the company, or its stockholders, or the convenience of the public, but a *limitation of the franchise*."

In the case of the *Great Western R. Co.* v. *Birmingham and Junction R. Co.*, 5 Eng. R. and Canal Cases, 189, the court said :

" The great thing to be attended to in all doubtful cases is this—What is the plain truth, and justice, and honesty of the case? and if the court has that clearly laid before it, my opinion is, that it is the duty of the court rather to stretch a point, as against mere formal objections, than for the sake of mere form, *to sacrifice* the truth and justice of the case."

In that case the court considered the amalgamation as a sort of " interim machinery," the ultimate object being spoliation. In this case the machinery is called consolidation, but even that synonym cannot invest the subject with the slightest charm when the legal test is applied.

" In regard to the *expediency* of bringing this bill, the chancellor cannot, and has no right to judge. The orator has the constitutional and sole right of determining this matter, and if he thinks it expedient, we must acquiesce in it; and no plea of the public good, or *inequality* of interests involved, can justify the chancellor in denying to the orator which is clearly accorded to him by well established chancery principles. The public good is best promoted by an impartial administration of justice, according to the right of the case; and courts cannot measure the equality or inequality of interests in the litigant parties, and make that a basis for a decision, notwithstanding what has been urged in the argument."

> *Byron Stevens* v. *The Rutland and Burlington R. R. Co.,* 29 Vt., 545.

2. *Was the arrangement a good arrangement for the G. & C. U. R. R. Co.—and was the trade a good trade?*

These decisions, we suppose, are perfectly conclusive so far as the expediency of the matter affects the legal questions—but, as the answer relies almost exclusively upon showing to the court that the trade in question was a good trade for the G. & C. U. R. R. Co., we propose to consider, for a few moments, the facts pertaining to this statement, which constitutes three-fourths of the entire answer of the defendants in this case. It commences, it will be observed, with the first trial and experimental lines ever run by a corps of engineers, when laying out the road between Chicago and Freeport; and with the artlessness of a child, relates the story of its wanderings through the woods, and the great number of adventures it encountered until it reached, in due season, a beautiful stream where it sat down and surveyed the shining pebbles, and was very much pleased, and then again wandered on uutil night came, and the youthful prayer was said, and consolidation set in; and it was then borne away by angel hands, and its little grave strewn with roses, and afterwards there is seen nothing but the figure of a little lamb reposing on its grave, bearing the simple inscription—"Consolidation,"—and all is so beautiful, and fair, and innocent, that nobody would think of making a noise to disturb the sweet repose of the sleeper. This is the romance of the affair, and the court is called upon to look at the action of these two railroad companies about as childhood regards the Babes in the Woods— all innocence, and, therefore, irresponsible.

A few real facts will show how soon this more than Arcadian simplicity is dispelled, and how soon the airs of the gentle shepherd disappear.

The court will find, by an examination of the Galena and Chicago Union Railroad as it existed on the 1st day of June, 1864, that it consisted of one trunk line, which extended from Chicago to Freeport, and there connected with the Illinois Central, forming a *direct line through to Dunleith*, and that it had built and constructed just exactly two branches—one twenty miles long, starting at Belvidere and extending to Beloit, where it connects with a railroad in Wisconsin bearing the same name, which extends through to Madison; the other branch commencing at a station called the Junction, in Du Paige county, and extending through to Fulton City, a distance of about one hundred miles from that point. These are the only branches *which have ever been built by the G. & C. U. R. R. Co. in any way, shape or manner.* But, if any one was to read the answer which has been put in, in this case, they would be led to believe that the G. & C. U. R. R. Co. had built all the railroads in the North-west, or furnished funds to do it. And that the present consolidation scheme was only to carry out the purposes and objects of its creation, and that the Chicago and North Western Railway Company, and all of its branches, were, really, only the legitimate offspring of the Galena and Chicago Union Railroad, and was built for the express purpose of being, and of becoming, a part and parcel of the old G. & C. U. R. R. Co.; and to prove this, some old hand bills, maps and advertisements (which appear to have been borrowed from some historical society for the occasion) are brought forward, and which appear to have been gotten up by some ingenious yet imaginative agents of the G. & C. U. R. R. Co., when it was first opened for travel, exhibiting, in the most stunning style, by the use of diagrams and red paint, that *all parts* of the North-west was accessible, and could be reached by this route; and these things are appended, with a great flourish, to the answer, and then the argument is made, that it is *no change whatever in the general objects* of the G. & C. U. R. R. Co.; that the mere including, in the enterprise, of the Kenosha & Rockford R. R. Co., and of all the railroads in Wisconsin and Michigan, and making the stockholders in the Galena road responsible to the extent of ten or twelve millions of dollars more than their original undertaking, is nothing at all, that it is a mere *enlargement* of the original powers of the G. & C. U. R. R. Co.; that it is still a railroad, and that it concerns no body at all; that no body is hurt, and that if the complainant, and those similarly situated to him, don't like it, all they have to do is to get out of the corporation just as quick as they please, for their room is better than their company; that they might have known that this would have happened when they invested their money, and, therefore, it is not worth while to take up the time of the court with trifling with this matter any longer. Now, this is precisely the argument which is presented to this court *by the defendant's answer* (for the defendant's answer is *nothing but an argument*) and this was exactly the position that was taken in the case of *Kean* v. *Johnson*, 1 Stockton (C. R.) 401, and which the court will find answered in full on page 114 of this brief. This same argument was, also, presented to the United States Supreme Court in the case of *Clearwater* v. *Meredith*, 1 Wallace 40, and was effectually and finally answered there; and the doctrine is there laid down most distinctly, that *new responsibilities* and *new hazards* cannot be super-added to the original undertaking without impairing the obligation of the contract existing between the corporation and the stock-holders.

The counsel for the defendants say that they, the C. & N. W. R. and the various railroads connected and consolidated with them, may be regarded simply as branches or tributaries of the G. & C. U. R. R. Co. Now, there has always been a great deal said among railroad men about the policy of building branch lines, and the opinions of those who have had the best opportunities to observe their history are against them. Says a recent American engineer :

" Branch lines are expensive means of forming connections with other railways, and have often proved very useful to some parties in the management, while they have been more or less injurious to the interest of the proprietors. There are, doubtless, cases where proceedings of this kind have proved beneficial to the interest of the main line; but experience in this and other countries has shown that local interests, contractors and *jobbing managers*, are the parties most usually benefited, while, probably, in nine cases out of ten, the proprietors of the *main line* have suffered loss. It should be borne in mind, that there are *very few branches that can pay*, either directly or indirectly, for their cost. It is not to be supposed that operations of this kind are, in all cases, chargeable to dishonest management; they are, no doubt, entered upon, in some instances, in the honest expectation of promoting the prosperity of the institution ; but *they are very liable to be the occasion of a different purpose, and, therefore, any proposition of the kind should be thoroughly investigated by the directors before they are committed to the expenditure.* In this matter they will meet with many plausible representations, both in regard to branches and aid to extending lines, *from parties interested in their advancement.* These parties will generally have, or claim to have, ample local information as to facts and estimates, and, consequently, an advantage over others in the argument ; and the only safety is in taking full time to consider and scrutinize all questions involved in the propositions. Delay is generally the prudent course, *and the disaster that has so generally followed this policy*, should certainly be sufficient to *protest against hasty action*, or until after the most careful consideration of all the circumstances of the case, that may bear on the interest of the institution."

Viewed, then, as a purely financial scheme, we do not think it can stand the simplest test of the most primary principles of railroad management. But we are not to stop at the elucidation of general principles ; let us descend, for one moment, into details, and see what rules of commerce actually did govern the parties to this transaction, and what were the inducements for the C. & N. W. R. Co. to desire, with such meekness, to adopt and enforce that improved *golden* rule of—" bear ye *one another's burdens*." Was it because it wished to confer a great public benefit upon the people that it desired to link its destiny with that of the G. & C. U. R. R. Co.; or, was it because it wished to save itself from bankruptcy that it formed the scheme of seizing on the G. & C. U. R. R. Co., and appropriating ît to its own use ?

The defendants in this case have spared no pains to convince the court and the public that the trade in question was a good trade, and that instead of the G. & C. U. R. R. Co. being any benefit to them, that they really have made *great sacrifices* by uniting their road with the G. & C. U. R. R. Co., and they do not hesitate to assume an air of great superiority over the G. & C. U. R. R. Co., by reason of the trick which they played upon them in effecting the consolidation of their road in so skillful and genteel a manner. We show in our bill—

1st. (And it is a fact beyond all controversy) That up to the time of the consolidation, that the C. & N. W. R. Co., and *none of the roads* it ever *consolidated with*, ever paid a dividend to its stock holders of any sort, character or kind; that it was overwhelmed with debts and liabilities to such an extent that its stock scarcely had a nominal value in the market.

2d. We show that the Kenosha and Rockford R. R. Co. was, and had been for years, a perfect vagabond, and scarcely earned enough to defray its running expenses; that this road was purchased by the C. & N. W. R. Co., at a mere nominal amount was then consolidated with the C. & N. W. R. Co., and sold to the consolidated company for $1,400,000 of the stock of the C. & N. W. R. Co., besides several hundred thousand dollars of bonds, and was turned over to the G. & C. U. R. R. Co., for that sum, and *reckoned in as a part of the capital stock of the old C. & N. W. R. Co.* If that road did not pay before the consolidation, how can it now? And was it not a slight inducement for the managers of the C. & N. W. R. Co. to sell out the Kenosha R. R. for about five or six times what it cost them?

3d. The directors of the C. & N. W. R. Co. report the original road as taken on the failure of the C., St. Paul and Fond du Lac Co., as representing a cost in stock and bonds of $47,300 per mile, on 315 miles of road, and include the Kenosha road as herein mentioned, which cost $200,000 or $300,000 in bonds of the company, or $1,400,000 in stock ; and the extension from Oshkosh to Green Bay, 48 miles, which, according to the reports of 1862 and 1863, cost but $687,000 in round figures, including nearly $100,000 in discount on bonds from their par value, or something less than $13,500 per mile, including shave on bonds. Deducting these two pieces of road, which never yet earned interest on their money cost, and it leaves 194 miles to represent a cost of fourteen millions of dollars in round numbers, or over $70,000 per mile, after allowing half a million or more for increase of expenditures of the inferior roads subtracted. The reports of 1861, make the stock issued then, $2,864,756.81, that of 1864, $8,300,000, with a bonded debt of $6,635,000 beside, showing a small reduction, after exchanging 2d mortgage bonds for preferred stock, etc., over debt of 1861.

4th. At the consolidation of the Galena company with this company, *it* had 294 miles of road, represented by $6,030,500 stock paid in, and selling at about par, and $3,169,000 of bonded debt, making $9,199,000, or a cost of about $30,000 per mile in round numbers, with a million of value *more in equipments than the C. & N. W. R. Co.* So that it cost, as about $28,000 is to $70,000 per mile of the C. & N. W. Its stock was at par, but the C. & N. W. issued an equal amount of common stock as a bonus to it to consolidate, and a preferred stock to represent the original Galena stock. The common and preferred stock have now a market value *far* less than par, and the Galena is yoked in with a line which cannot earn two-thirds as much per mile as the Galena proper. Does not all this make it, on the whole, a bad trade for a Galena stockholder ? And is there any power which can compel him to exchange his old for the consolidated stock ?

XXIII.

The change of the name of the G. & C. U. R. R. Co. was unauthorized and void.

We allege in our bill of complaint that the directors did, by the bill of sale of the G. & C. U. R. R. Co. expressly provide, among other things, for changing its name to that of the C. & N. W. R. Co., and so far as they could did actually do this thing; this we say cannot be done—

1st. Because " The People of the State of Illinois represented in General Assembly " did enact " That *all* such persons as shall become *stockholders* (agreeably to the provisions of this act) *in the corporation* hereby created *shall be*, and for the term of *sixty years*, from and after the passage of this act, *shall continue to be*, a body corporate and politic, by the name of the ' *Galena and Chicago Union Railroad Company*,' and by *that name* shall have succession, for the term of years above specified," etc.

2d. Because this patronymic was the synonym of honor, of honesty and fair dealing, and should have been carefully preserved as an heir loom, and transmitted to the managers of all railroads as a precious legacy for the benefit of the entire railroad family ; and

3d. Because such a change was entirely *unauthorized* by the stockholders, or the legislature, and on grounds of public policy is void.

Angel & Ames on Corporations, sec. 102, say : " Though partnerships, and simply joint stock trading companies, may be at liberty to change their name or style, yet, after a company has been incorporated, such incorporated company has not the right nor the power to change its name. The *identity of name is the principal means for effecting that perpetuity of succsssion with members, frequently changing which is an important purpose of incorporation,* and the corporate name can be changed *only by the same power by which the corporate body has been created.* It is obvious likewise, that the title to shares and the right to assets would be likely to be brought into confusion if the name was subject to change."

Regina & Registrar, 10 Adol & Ell, 839.

XXIV.

Preferred and Common Stock.

The court will perceive, by examining the articles of consolidation in the case, that, in the trade which was made, the high contracting parties give to the Galena and C. U. R. R. Co. stockholders one share of preferred and one share of common stock and three dollars in money for each share of their stock, and provide that the preferred shall be entitled to a preference over the common in the dividends to be earned by the consolidated company. Now, where is the statute in Illinois that allows this *farming out of the revenues of a railroad in advance in this manner ?* If there is such a law, of course, it can be produced; and *if* there is *no such law,* perhaps it can be shown to be one of the *reserved powers and functions* of the consolidated company, and incidental to its very existence. But, upon principle, the capital stock of a railroad cannot be thus increased at all, because each share of stock represents the proportionate value of all the property, and is entitled to just that proportion of the earnings ; if the stockholders or directors, therefore, undertake to depreciate the value of the property or divide up its profits, by increasing the number who are to share it, by just that much they depreciate the stock, consequently the directors of a railroad have no power to first increase the stock, and then give one set of stockholders a preference over the others.

In the case of *Jones* v. *Terre Haute and Richmond R. R. Co.*, 29 Barb., 359, the court say :

" Prima facia, all stockholders, at any particular period, are *equally* interested in the property and business of a corporation. They assume the same liabilities, are entitled to the same rights, and *are equal owners* of the property. When, therefore, the directors undertake to distribute among the stockholders any portion of the funds or property of a corporation—whether it be called profits or not—all the stockholders are entitled to an *equal* share in the fund, proportionate to their stock, whether they have been stock-holders for a longer or shorter period. Unless *the charter* gives the directors power to discriminate between the stockholders at different periods in the distribution of profits, they are *all* entitled to share them."

To the same *effect* precisely are the cases of *March* v. *Eastern R. R. Co.*, 43 N. H., 520; and *The Mechanic's Bank* v. *N. Y. & N. H. R. R. Co.*, 3 Kern, 617, which can be found on pages 84 85 and 86 of this Brief.

Our own Supreme Court have decided that—

The dividends declared must be general on *all* the stock so that *each shareholder* may receive *his proportionate* share. The directors have no authority to declare a dividend on any other principle. They cannot exclude any portion of the stockholders from an equal participation in the profits of the company. If they should attempt to carry into effect any such understanding or to act upon *any other principle*, it would be in gross violation of the rights of stockholders, and would not for one moment bind them.

Ryder v. *The Alton and Sangamon R. R. Co.*, 13 Ill., 521.

Upon the principles here established, where does the North Western Railway Company get their authority for issuing *preferred* stock, and where is their power to make the distinction between that stock and the common stock of the company ?

By the 12th section of the articles of consolidation it will be seen that a *special* stock was provided to be issued in order to consolidate the Peninsular R. R. Co. of Michigan, but as that was a most extraordinary transaction, we suppose that no ordinary stock would suffice, but as it was a thing necessary to be done in order to fulfill its destiny—and as necessity knows no law—it may be possible that the issuing of a *special* stock was, in that instance, all right; but we submit that, without a law can be produced authorizing a railroad company to issue a preferred stock, and thereby discriminate among the owners of the share holders of the capital stock, that such a thing cannot be done; but if it can be done, then the next question to be determined is, is such stock a legal tender, and can the directors of a railroad company, or a majority of proxy holders, sell out the entire corporation and compel the dissenting ones to take it in payment of their stock? We pause for a reply.

XXV.

Extra Territorial Acts.

We allege in our bill, that, soon after the Chicago & North Western Railway Company came into the possession of the Galena & Chicago Union Railroad, that it removed its chief office to New York City; and that the president and secretary of said company *do now* reside there; *and are carrying on the said consolidated railroad from that point as their chief office;* and that the directors of the said consolidated company have met there and transacted business there, and have, as is believed, caused a large amount of bonds and stock to be issued, by votes passed by them there, and from everything that can now be learned of the said consolidated Chicago & North Western Railway Company, it is well nigh omnipresent—and as appears from the answer filed by them in this court, can be found in all lands from Minnesota to Wall Street.

We do not object to their enterprise; we only say that, if we are to be bound by their acts, that they should have some regard for law ; and we say that all extra territorial acts, by that corporation acting as a *corporation* (if there is any territory that they have not yet taken possession of), are illegal.

Angell & Ames on Corporations, Sec. 104, says—

" A private corporation whose charter has been granted by one State, cannot hold meetings, pass votes, and exercise powers in another State. It can have no legal existence out of the boundaries of the sovereignty by which it is created, must dwell in the place of its creation, and cannot migrate to another sovereignty. The case of *McCall* v. *Byram Manufacturing Company*, 5 Conn., has been regarded as deciding, that corporations whose charters were granted by one State, could hold meetings, pass votes, and exercise powers in another State. The question presented in the case was, whether the secretary of a corporation was legally appointed by the directors, at a meeting held by them in the city of New York, the charter having been granted by the State of Connecticut ; and the decision was in the affirmative. But the *directors* of a corporation *are not* a corporate body, *when acting as a board*, though they are competent to act as agents beyond the bounds where the corporation exists."

> See also—*Bank of Augusta* v. *Earle*, 13 Peters (U. S) R. 519.
> *Miller* v. *Ewer*, 14 Shep. (Me.) R. 509.
> *Farnum* v. *Blackstone Canal Co.*, 1 Sumn. (Ct. C.) R. 47.
> *Runyan* v. *Lessees of Coster*, 14 Peters (U. S.) R. 129.
> *Day* v. *Newark India Rubber Co.* 1 Blatch. (Ct. C.) R. 628.
> *McCall* v. *Byram Manufacturing Co.* 6 Conn. R. 458.

In the case of the *Ohio & Mississippi Railroad Company* v. *Wheeler*, 1 Black, 297, Chief Justice TANEY said, that a corporation exists only in contemplation of law, and *by force* of the law ; and can have no existence beyond the limits of the State sovereignty which brings it into life, and endues it with faculties and powers.

All votes and proceedings of persons professing to act in the capacity of corporators, when assembled beyond the bounds of the State granting the charter of the corporation, are wholly void.

Miller v. *Ewer*, 27 Maine, 519.

As to a railroad, owned by a company under charters from two different States, if the whole road and franchises are sold under a mortgage covering the entire line of road, and the right of redemption is given by one State, it can be reclaimed.

Wood v. *Goodwin*, 49 Maine, 261.

The by-laws of a corporation, made in pursuance of their charter, are equally binding on all the members and others acquainted with their method of business, as any public law of the State.

Cummings v. *Webster*, 43 Maine, 192.

39 Maine, 35.

The powers of a corporation are derived from the law.

They cannot be enlarged by any act of the corporate body.

Andrews v. *Union Mutual Fire Ins. Co.*, 37 Maine, 260.

18 Barb. 315.

Corporations chartered in one State cannot hold meetings, pass votes and exercise powers in another State.

Ang. & Ames on Corp. Sec. 104, p. 95.

13 Peters, 519.

Nota Bena—Miller v. *Ewer*, 14 Shep. (Maine) 509.

1 Sumner, (Ct. C.) 47.

14 Peters, 129.

1 Blatch. (Ct. C.), 628.

Freeman v. *Mechanics W. P. & M. Co.*, 38 Maine, (3 Heath), 343.

Why has the official residence of the Chicago & North Western Railway Company been removed to Wall Street? Why are not the president and secretary of that corporation in Chicago, or on the line of that great thoroughfare—the Upper Peninsula of Michigan? Are all of their freights and passengers transported thither, and is there the place to find the official residence of this great corporation? Has it all been consolidated there, and is this the meaning of this all absorbing, all comprehensive, *omnium gatherum* term, " consolidation," to lay under contribution the resources and capital of a continent, and concentrate the same into Wall Street? Is this the significance it bears? We indulge in no reflections ; but a recent well known writer, in treating of such railroad management, says—

" When the chief officers and influential managers of a company *are known to operate largely in a speculative way in the stock*, they are strongly tempted to neglect the proprietory interests committed to their trust, at any time when *their* operations in stock will thereby be promoted. And further: the men whose minds are of a speculative turn are liable, and indeed it may be said *generally do*, devote so large a share of their care and attention to objects and means of speculation, that there is not sufficient time and thought left to manage successfully the affairs of the proprietors, even if they made the best of this hastily snatched remainder. No doubt it may be set down *as a standing caution*, that if a proprietor chance to learn that the president, treasurer, secretary or superintendant, or the more active and influential directors, are engaged in large stock operations, making time sales, and corners, it would be well for him to watch a favorable opportunity to dispose of *his* interest in the institution. This method of business is only to be adopted by such managers and officers as prefer the chance of speculative results, and whose prospects will depend on the number and interest of those who may incautiously be induced to engage, on the supposition that affairs are, and are to be, conducted for the general interest of the proprietors."

XXVI.

The Bondholders.

1. RIGHTS OF BONDHOLDERS.
2. HOW THEY ARE AFFECTED BY AMALGAMATIONS.

1. *The Complainant, in this case, is not only a Shareholder, but a Bondholder, and, also, one of the Trustees of the first mortgage bonds, and he claims that he has a right as such Bondholder and Trustee, to interfere and prevent the revenues of the road from being diverted, or the securities from being impaired.*

Rights of Bondholders.

In the *Galena & Chicago Union R. R. Co. garnishee, &c.,* v. *Menzies,* 26 Ill. 121, where Menzies sued out a writ of attachment against the estate, real and personal, of the Mineral Point Railroad Company with a summons to the Galena & Chicago Union Railroad Company to appear and answer, as garnishee of the defendant. WALKER, J., says: " Money of a corporation which has been, in advance of its being earned, *set apart, by its board of directors, to the payment of interest on its bonds,* secured by a *mortgage or trust deed* on its road and franchises, and to raise a sinking fund for their redemption, is not subject to garnishee process issued by a judgment creditor of said corporation.

" Where a corporation had given a mortgage or trust deed of all its property, tolls, *incomes, franchises,* &c., to secure the principal and accruing interest on its bonds, *its revenues so pledged* are not liable to a garnishee process by its judgment creditors, after the execution by it of such mortgage or trust deed."

And the principle upon which this case was decided, was, that the *incomes and revenues* of a railroad, which have been *pledged* in advance to the payment of bonds, &c., *cannot be diverted.* Now, if this is so, is it not perfectly plain that the owner of a bond thus protected and thus provided for, could interfere to prevent the funds from being diverted? And if a bondholder can do this, cannot a trustee for the bondholders, to whom the entire legal estate is conveyed, interfere to prevent a diversion of the revenues or property which is pledged? If a mortgagee can interfere to prevent waste, cannot a trustee, whose bounden duty it is to protect the property, interfere for the same reason and in the same way?

In the case of *Sturges* v. *Knapp*, 31 Vt. (2 Shaw) 1, the court held, that the trustees of bondholders were liable to the minority of the bondholders for a faithful discharge of their duties.

Those who seek to regard this branch of the subject with indifference, and *affect* to see in these amalgamations no danger whatever to the security of the bondholders, would do well to study the history of railroads in this country as shown by actual experience.

2. Bondholders, how Affected by Amalgamations.

Said a recent veteran railroad manager of more than forty years' standing, whose observations in this country and in Europe are entitled to the highest respect:

" The stock proprietors, though first to feel the effect of such management, are not the only parties to experience the disastrous results. The bond proprietor may also suffer, especially if the bonded debt be a large proportion of the capital of the institution. This class, having no voice in the management, are usually very quiet, so long as their interest is punctually paid. It is very natural that they should feel a higher degree of safety than the stock proprietors, who may be wholly sacrificed before the bondholders feel a loss. Experience, however, has shown that they are not free from the ills and hazards of bad management. It is true, the stock must be first sacrificed, and after dividends can no longer be paid to the stock proprietors, the interest may be continued for a time on the bonds; but it rarely fails, that the policy which has destroyed the stock, will also destroy, more or less, the security of the bonds. Secured, as the bonds usually are, by a mortgage of the whole property, it would seem to be in the power of the bondholders, on the failure of the company, to take possession by foreclosure, and enter into the management as sole proprietors ; but there are difficulties in the way. In the first place, there is the difficulty of obtaining concert among the bond proprietors to act in the premises ; and, as more or less of pecuniary responsibility must be incurred, a part do not like to put themselves under engagements without the co-operation of the whole, and here they find themselves somewhat in the position of stock proprietors, a numerous body, incapable of that co-operation necessary to secure efficiency, and though some are ready and anxious to proceed, others will hold back to avoid responsibility, while they are quite ready to avail themselves of the benefits that may result from the efforts of their co-bondholders.

"Mortgage bonds of a railway corporation, which, from inadequate traffic or ill management, do not pay its stock proprietors, are far from being that quiet and reliable source of revenue that many have supposed. If the management of a railway is under speculative control, that management will be exerted to sustain the stock or the bond proprietor, as may happen to be the interest of the controlling party. If the stock controls, and the prospect is regarded doubtful as to the ultimate strength of the stock, it may lead to movements that will change this interest over to the side of the bondholder; and in the midst of a cloudy and vigorous litigation, the path of right may suddenly appear so well fortified, that further resistance will be vain, and matters are brought to an easy solution; the bondholders must, at least, be provided for, and the stockholders may take what remains. The bond proprietor is not at fault—he had no control in the management that compelled this result, and the stock proprietor must bear in mind, that if his property is wasted, it has been wasted by his representatives; and though his trust may have been abused and forfeited, it is no fault of the bond proprietor. Instances have occurred in which the bondholders have compromised their claims by delivering up the coupons, for one or more years, either gratuitously, or taking therefor new obligations of the company, secured by a younger mortgage. There may be circumstances that render this policy expedient, as from the recent operations of the railway, the undeveloped traffic may not afford the means of payment, while the future prospect is favorable for the ultimate ability to pay current interest and sinking fund; and if there is confidence in the fidelity of the management, it may be the wisest course for the bondholders. But if the condition of the company has been reduced by incompetent or *unfaithful management*, no good is likely to result from this method, as affairs will not be likely to improve, and when the time comes for payment to be resumed, the finances will be no better, the track and machinery in worse condition, and the bond proprietors no more favorably situated for securing their rights than they were when the coupons were surrendered. As a general rule, it is best for them to proceed to take possession as soon as payment fails; delay rarely works to their advantage, and promptness and efficiency in action are quite as necessary to secure their rights as those of others. It *should be borne in mind, that the same incompetent or unfaithful management that has destroyed the capacity to pay dividends to the stock proprietors, will be likely to prey on the bond proprietors as soon as the stock interest is destroyed or paralyzed,* and a new administration of affairs is necessary to secure the property."

Again, the same distinguished author says:

" Amalgamations have been made, and branch lines constructed under the *plausible idea of increasing the income of the main line, while the result has shown that, in most cases, the capital has been increased proportionably more than the net income, and the only party benefited has been some scheming contractor, or jobbing manager.*

" The financial business of railway corporations was originally cemmenced by opening books for subscription to the stock; and having secured the amount supposed to be sufficient for the undertaking, installments were called in as wanted for the work. In this way the principal capital was raised. It was regarded necessary to have, at least, half, and sometimes three-fourths, or the whole, of the amount needed in the form of stock. If bonds were issued, it was not done until the investment by stock had made a good basis for the security of the bonds. The bonds were usually sold under advertisement to the highest bidder, provided there was no restriction as to usury, and commanded par, or nearly par, for seven per cent. bonds. Gradually the old method of conducting the finances gave way to a different system. In the ardor of the railway movement, opportunity was afforded for men to enter into their management, *not faithfully to discharge a trust, but for the purpose of enriching themselves at the expense of those who confided in their supposed fidelity.* Such men have *ruined the stock,* and greatly impaired the *interest of the bond proprietors* of railways that should have been the *best investments of this kind* in the country. A small clique of such men will often baffle the efforts of a majority of fair-minded directors, and gradually deplete the proprietary interest. They enter the management with fair pretensions, and contrive to obtain sufficient, if not most, of the *proxies for elections.* Where the railway is far distant from most of the proprietors, and they know little except from reports, the *means for controlling the institution is not difficult to compass.* It is hardly worth while to go into particulars, at this time, of the process of the financiering of such men ; they have left their *marks too indelibly fixed* on the railways that have come under their financial management, to require anything more than an allusion to this source of depletion, to which railway proprietors may look for a large portion of the loss of their property. This, with the method of contracting, the construction of branch lines, and *amalgamations,* has so *over loaded* many of our railways *with capital,* that the prospect of the stock proprietors is very discouraging, if not hopeless ; and even the bond proprietors find their interest greatly depressed, and what they had regarded as very safe, has proved to be very uncertain. There can be no doubt that the old method of finance and contracting was the best. It had *sound business principles* to rest on, and by it, enterprises of a difficult and expensive nature have been carried through, and succeeded as fairly remunerating investments of capital." While, it may be added, that any railroad that is built on scrip, first, second and third mortgages, on preferred, common, and special stock, and mortgage bonds, income bonds, equipment bonds, may certainly be considered as not a *well ballasted* railroad, and, in case of accidents and reverses, might prove fatal.

XXVII.

The Consolidation is void, because not made by the unanimous consent of the Stockholders.

The result of all this investigation leads us to conclude, that, in the United States of America there can be no consolidation or amalgamation of the capital stock, and the rights, privileges and franchises of two *distinct* corporations, without the *unanimous consent* of all the stockholders, because it would impair the obligations of *the* contract which a share holder enters into with the corporation when he becomes a member of it, contrary to the 10th section of the Constitution of the United States, and, in Illinois, is contrary to the 17th clause of the Bill of Rights of the Constitution of the State of Illinois.

By the 17th clause of the Bill of Rights of the Constitution of the State of Illinois, it is provided that "*No ex post facto law, nor any law impairing the obligation of contracts shall ever be made ;*" and by the 10th section of the Constitution of the United States, it is also provided that *no state* shall pass any "*law impairing the obligations of contracts,*"—consequently, under these restrictions, no two distinct corporations in Illinois can ever amalgamate their capital stock, and make the stockholders in one become liable for the debts and liabilities of the other, without the *unanimous consent* of all the stockholders.

> *Clearwater* v. *Meredith*, 1 Wallace U. S., 39–40–41.
>
> *Kean* v. *Scott*, 1 Stockton, 405, 424.
>
> *Hartford & New Haven R. R. Co.* v. *Croswell*, 5 Hill, 386.
>
> *March* v. *R. R. Co.*, 43 N. H., 525–6.
>
> *Cumberland Coal Co.* v. *Seerman*, 30 Barb., 573.
>
> *Hoffman Steam Coal Co.* v. *Cumberland Coal Co.*, 16 Maryland, 456.
>
> *Abbott* v. *American Hard Rubber Co.*, 33 Barb., 593.
>
> Redfield on Railways, p. 622.
>
> *Fisher* v. *Evansville & Crawfordville R.* 7 Porter, 407.
>
> *Chapman* v. *M. R. & L. E. R. R. Co.*, 6 Ohio, 119.

Consolidation of Corporations.

Two or more corporations cannot consolidate their funds or enter into a copartnership, unless authorized by express grant or necessary implication.

> Angel & Ames on Corporations, sec. 272, p. 295.
> *Clearwater* v. *Meredith*, 1 Wallace, 39, 40, 41.
> *Sharon Canal Co.* v. *Fulton Bank*, 7 Wend., 412.
> *Smith* v *Smith*, 3 (Dessaus') S. C. Ch. R., 557.
> *Farnum* v. *Blackstone Canal Co.*, 1 Sumner, (C. C.) 47.
> *Boston and Lowell R. R. Co.* v. *Salem and Lowell R. R. Co.*, 2 Gray, 39.
> *Bissell* v. *Michigan S. & N. I. R. R. Co.*, 22 N. Y., 28.

This was a case where the Michigan Southern R. R. Co. was chartered to build and operate a railroad through Michigan, and the Northern Indiana R. R. Co. was chartered by the State of Indiana to build and operate a railroad through the northern part of the State of Indiana, and then, in conjunction with another railroad, they built another railroad from the Indiana State line to Chicago ; they then formed a business connection with each other, under the name of the Michigan Southern and Northern Indiana R. R. Co., to carry freight and passengers through from Chicago to Lake Erie—and the whole business of the three connected roads was managed under a consolidated arrangement. The plaintiff took passage on their cars at Chicago for Toledo, and while riding on their cars, was injured. The court sustained the action against them, but both Judge Comstock and Judge Selden, who differed widely in their reasons, distinctly say that the companies had *no right to consolidate.* p. 280–281.

> See *Bemen* v. *Rufford*, 1 Simons (N. S.), 550, (40 ch., 550).

U. S. Supreme Court.

Pearce v. *Madison and Indianapolis and Peru R. R. Co.*, 21 Howard, 443.

This was a case where two railroad corporations in Indiana, created to construct distinct lines of railroads, consolidated by agreement, and assumed the name of the M. & I. & P. R. R. Co., and under a common board of management, and operated both roads; and that while thus managed, the President of the consolidated company gave five promissory notes, in its name, for a steamboat, which was to be run on the Ohio in connection with the railroads. After the execution of the notes, and the acquisition of the boat, the corporations were dissolved by due course of law, and at the commencement of the suit, were each managing their own affairs. The plaintiff claimed that the two corporations were jointly bound.

Held, Justice CAMPBELL, delivering the opinion of the court: " That *there was no authority of law to consolidate these corporations, and to place both under the same management, or to subject the capital of the one to answer for the liabilities of the other,* and so the court of Indiana have determined."

But, in addition to that act of illegality, the managers of these corporations established a steamboat line, to run in connection with the railroads, and thereby diverted their capital from the objects contemplated by their charters, and exposed it to perils, for which they afforded no sanction. Their powers are conceded in consideration of the advantage the public is to receive from their discreet and intelligent employment, and the public have an interterest, that neither the managers nor stockholders of the corporation shall transcend their authority.

The cases of *McGregor* v. *The Official Manager of the Deal and Dover R. Co.*, 16 L. & Eq., 180, and of *Coleman* v. *Eastern Counties Railway Co.*, 10 Beaver, 1, are quoted with great approbation, and the principles established by them, fully endorsed.

In the case of *Port Clinton R. R. Co.* v. *Cleveland and Toledo R. R. Co.*, 13 Ohio, 560, the court said: "If the agreement of consolidation imposed a duty on the directors of the C. & Tol. Co., to carry into effect its provisions, this duty, like that to pursue the provisions of the charter, might be owing to all the stockholders. If so, then a suit by one or more of the stockholders, in behalf of themselves and the others, might be sustained, to restrain acts on the part of the directors, ultra vires, or involving a fraudulent breach of trust.

See also—

> *The Marietta and Cincinnati R. R. Co.* v. *Elliott*, 10 Ohio, 61–2. In this they refer to 21 How., 441.
> *Ohio & Miss. R. R. Co.* v. *Wheeler*, 1 Black., 299.

In the *Boston and Lowell R. R. Co.* v. *Salem and Lowell R. R. Co.*, 2 Gray, 39, the court say : " We are also of opinion that the several defendant copartners, having been incorporated and chartered to establish railroads between several termini, according to their respective acts of incorporation, have no right, by the use and combination of several sections of their respective railroads, to establish a continuous and uninterrupted line of transportation, by railroad, of persons and property, between Lowell and Boston ; and that the actual establishment of such a continuous line of transportation, by railroad, is substantially making a railroad, other than that authorized to be made by the plaintiffs, to their injury, and contrary to their rights conferred on them by their charter." SHAW, C. J.

In the case of the *Illinois Grand Trunk R. R. Co.* v. *Cook*, 29 Ill., 243.

This was a case where a party had subscribed to the capital stock of the Camanche, A. & M. R. R. Co., in 1857, and gave his note for it. In the year 1859, the road became consolidated with the Joliet and Terre Haute R. R. Co. The subscriber, some time after this, died ; and on the 21st of June, 1861, the note was filed as a claim against the estate in the Probate Court. The administrator then filed a bill, asking to have the collection of the note perpetually enjoined, on the ground, among others, " that the act of consolidation made a fundamental change of the company, and the consolidated company entered upon an enterprise, differing entirely from that to which the subscription was made, and that Cook was thereby wholly released from its payment."

A *demurrer* was filed to the bill, which, on hearing, was overruled, and *relief decreed according to the prayer of the bill.*

The court, on appeal, affirmed the decree, and among other

things said : " The legal power to consolidate these roads is not questioned, but it is alleged by the bill that it wholly changed the character of the enterprise.

"The truth of this allegation is admitted by the demurrer. The defendants below saw proper to admit this allegation to be true, and not to traverse the fact, and we must act upon it precisely as if it had been established by evidence. They also abided by their demurrer, and failed to obtain leave to answer. It is believed that *no court has ever* held, that a change of such an enterprise so as to render it radical, and to constitute it a different corporation *for the attainment of other purposes* than that to which the subscription was made, did not release the subscriber from its payment. Here it stands admitted that such was the character of the change, and by it, the maker of these instruments *was* released from their payment. It is admitted, that this money is sought to be collected to be applied to the *consolidation* of a road *wholly different* in its *objects* from that to which the subscription was made.

" This the *company or the legislature* have no power to accomplish."

And the decree of the court below *was affirmed*.

In the case of *Farnum* v. *Blackstone Canal Corporation*, 1 Sumner, 62.

This was a case where two corporations were chartered by the same name—one in Massachusetts and the other in Rhode Island— to build a canal, etc. On the 20th of February, 1827, the legislature of Massachusetts enacted that, after the 1st day of July, then next, the stockholders of the Blackstone Canal Co., of Rhode Island, should be constituted stockholders in the Blackstone Canal Co., of Massachusetts, with the powers, rights and privileges of original subscribers, but that the consolidation of the two companies should not take place until the provisions of the act had been accepted by both corporations. Rhode Island also passed an act accepting the terms specified by the Massachusetts legislature. It was, when the matter afterwards came before the court, contended that the laws of the two legislatures had organized out of the two corporations, a *new* corporation ; but the court held that, " although in virtue of these several acts, the corporations acquired a unity of interests, it by no means follows, that they ceased to exist as distinct and different corporations. Their powers, their rights, their privileges, their duties, remained distinct and several, as before, according to their respective acts of incorporation. Neither could exercise the rights, powers or privileges conferred on the other. There was no corporate identity—neither was merged in the other. If it were otherwise, which became merged? The acts of incorporation create no merger, and neither is pointed out as survivor or successor. We must treat the case, then, as one of distinct corporations, acting within the sphere of their respective charters, for purposes of common interest, and not as a case, where all the powers of both were concentrated in one. The union was of interests and stocks, and not a surrender of personal identity or corporate existence by either corporation."

And it will be particularly and specially observed, that no stockholder objected to the arrangement at all; but from all that appears, that the stockholders of one, voluntarily became stockholders in the other, by unanimous consent. The case which gave rise to the decision arose out of a suit brought against the proprietors of the Blackstone Canal—to compel them to reduce the height of a dam across the Blackstone river—and is important to show that a consolidation of two corporations, effected by unanimous consent, did not create a new corporation.

The Supreme Court of Illinois decided in the case of the *Marine Bank of Chicago* v. *Ogden*, 29 Ill., 268, that two corporations could not even form a partnership. If that is so, upon what principles of law can they amalgamate their capital, rights, privileges and franchises?

Baltimore and Susquehanna Railroad Company v. *Musselman*, 2 Grant's Cases (Pa.) 348. This was an action brought by the defendant in error against the company for causing the death of her husband. After suit brought, the plaintiff in error was *consolidated* with several other railroad companies, which consolidation was called the Northern Central Railway Company. The plaintiff in error suggested this consolidation, before the jury was called, and filed it. Lowrie, J., says—

"The learned judge of the common pleas was right in deciding that the act of union or consolidation of this corporation with three others, under a law which continued all its liabilities, was not such a dissolution of the corporation, as abated an action commenced before the consolidation was effected. The law says, that the liabilities shall continue, or be assumed by the consolidated company. If they were assumed, then the new company must attend to the suit, and answer the judgment, for that was one of the liabilities by which this corporation was bound; so *qua cumque via*, the suit does not abate. But, without any such provision as the above, in the law authorizing the consolidation, a court of justice would not consider the mere voluntary union of several companies into one, as equivalent to the death of either of them; or attribute to the law-making power, an intention of enabling them to discharge their liabilities in such a summary way. It is not a case of death, for the new corporation lives from the life of the old one; their several lives are transferred into it, and, unlike ordinary cases of metemsychosis, this translation is accompanied by full consciousnoss of the former state, and its liabilities. If there has been a confusion of four lives into one, we leave, for another occasion, the decision, how far this one will be considered as assuming, or charged with, the duties of its several elements."

When the State consents to the consolidation of two railroad companies, by an act of the legislature, the act of the companies in making it, is not absolutely void, *but any stockholder* who does *not* consent would be discharged from his subscription.

McCray v. Junction R. R. Co. 9 Ind. 358.

Two distinct corporations cannot form a partnership, neither can they take an estate in joint tenancy, either jointly with another corporation or with a natural person.

Telfair v. Howe 3 Rich. Eq. 235.

PENNSYLVANIA CASES.

Lauman v. The Lebanon Valley R. R. Co., 30
Penn. 42.

"A railroad corporation may abandon its charter and dissolve itself, except so far as its public duties as conservators of a highway, may limit this power ; and the legislature may release it from this limitation, and allow a transfer of its duties to other hands.

A single stockholder has no right to object to a transfer of all the property of the corporation to another company, under the authority of an act of assembly.

But, he *cannot be compelled, by law, to accept the stock of the other company in payment for the shares held by him ; and a court of equity will restrain the corporation and its officers from entering into a contract to that effect.*

The dissolution of a corporation is not a corporate act, but an act of the members of the corporation ; and its officers in affecting such an arrangement, act as trustees of the members, not as corporate functionaries.

Under the constitution, a majority of the members of a corporation cannot be authorized to divest the interest of a dissenting stockholder, by a transfer of the whole of its property to another company to be paid for in the shares of such other company, without first giving security for the interest of such dissenting stockholder."

This case seems to go upon the theory, that the corporation becomes dissolved by a sale of all its property ; but there is only one way voluntarily to dissolve it, and that is, by surrender to the government.

Ang. & Ames on Corp. Sec. 772–7.

Where the State consents to the consolidation of two railroad companies, by act of the legislature, the act of consolidation is not void ; but stockholders not consenting thereto, *are released.*

> *McCray* v. *The Junction R. R. Co.*, 9 Ind.
> 358.
> *Sparrow* v. *The Evansville R. R. Co.*, 7 Ind.
> 369.
> 12 Ind. 605.
> 13 Ind. 387.
> 16 Ind. 46.
> *Carlisle* v. *The Terre Haute &c. R. R. Co.*, 6
> Ind. 316.

The relation between a railroad company and a stockholder, is one of contract—and any legislative enactment which, without his assent, authorizes a material change in the powers or purposes of the corporation, not in aid of the *original* object, if acted upon by the corporation, is not binding upon him.

> *McCray* v. *The Junction R. R. Co.* 9 Indiana, 359.
>
> *Sparrow* v. *The Evansville &c. R. R. Co.*, 7 Ind. 369.
>
> *Fisher* v. *The Evansville &c. Railroad Co.*, 7 Ind. 407.
>
> *Carlisle* v. *Terre Haute Railroad Co.*, 6 Ind. 316.
>
> Pierce's American Railroad Law, 89–99, and cases there cited.

But the principles which must govern in this case have already been established by the United States Supreme Court, in the case of *Clearwater* v. *Meredith*, 1 Wallace, 39. In this case, Judge Davis laid down the principles of law which should govern, precisely as we contend for, and in the following language:

"The Cincinnati, Cambridge & Chicago Short Line Railway Company, whose stock was guaranteed, was, as stated in the pleadings, organized under a general act of the State of Indiana, providing for the incorporation of railroad companies. This act was passed May 11th, 1852, and contained no provision permitting railroad corporations to consolidate their stock. It can readily be seen that the interests of the public, as well as the perfection of the railway system, called for the exercise of a power by which different lines of a road could be united. Accordingly, on the 23d of February, 1863, the General Assembly of Indiana, passed an act, allowing any railway company that had been organized to intersect and unite their road with any other road, constructed or in progress of construction, and to merge and consolidate their stock, and on the 4th of March, 1853, the privileges of the act were extended to railroads that should be afterwards organized. The power of the legislature to confer such authority cannot be questioned; and without the authority, railroad corporations, organized separately, could not merge and consolidate their interests. But, in conferring the authority, the legislature never intended to compel a dissenting stockholder to transfer his interest, because a majority of the stockholders consented to the consolidation. Even if the legislature had manifested an obvious purpose to do so, the act would have been illegal, for it would have impaired the obligation of a contract. There was no reservation of power in the act under which the Cincinnati, Cambridge & Chicago Short Line Railway was organized, which gave authority to make material changes in the purposes for which the corporation was created, and without such a reservation, in no event could a dissenting stockholder be bound.

"When any person takes stock in a railway corporation, he has entered into a contract with the company, that his interests shall be subject to the direction and control of the proper authorities of the corporation, to accomplish *the object* for which the company was organized. He does not agree that the improvement to which he subscribed, should be changed in its purposes and character at the will and pleasure of a majority of the stockholders, so that new responsibilities, and, it may be, new hazards, are added to the organized undertaking. He may be very willing to embark in one enterprise, and unwilling to engage in another; to assist in building a short line railway, and averse to risking his money in one having a longer line of transit.

" But it is not every important change which would work a dissolution of the contract. It must be such a change that a *new* and different business is superadded to the original undertaking. The act of the legislature of Indiana, allowing railroad corporations to merge and consolidate their stock, was an enabling act—was permissive and not mandatory. It simply gave the consent of the legislature to whatever could lawfully be done, and which, without that consent, could not be done at all. By virtue of this act, the consolidations, in plea stated, were made. Clearwater, before the consolidation, was a stockholder in one corporation, created for a given purpose; after it, he was a stockholder in another and different corporation, with the privileges, powers, franchises and stockholders. The effect of the consolidation, ' was a dissolution of the three corporations, and, at the same instant, the creation of a new corporation, with property, liabilities, and stockholders, derived from those passing out of existence ;' *McMahon* v. *Morrison.* And the act of consolidation was not void because the State assented to it; but a non-consenting stockholder was discharged. Clearwater *could have prevented* this consolidation, had he chosen to do so; instead of that, he gave his assent to it, and merged his own stock in the new adventure. If a majority of the stockholders of the corporation of which he was a member, had undertaken to transfer his interest, against his wishes, he could have *enjoined* them. There was *no power* to force him to join the new corporation, and to receive stock in it on the surrender of his stock in the old corporation."

Applying, then, these principles to the case at bar, how is it possible that the complainant's rights and interests can be subjected to a different rule from the one here laid down ? A bare statement of the case makes it as strong as the most elaborate argument— and we shall regard these principles which have been thus established by the Supreme Court of the United States, as the law of the land until they are overruled, and as binding on corporations with millions, as upon individuals with far less interests.

XXVIII.

The doctrine of Confirmation and Ratification by Stockholders of the unauthorized acts of Directors.

In *Cumberland Coal Company* v. *Sherman*, 30 Barb. 573, DAVIS, J., says:

" But it is insisted on the part of the defendants, that the purchase was made at the request of the stockholders, and that its alleged ratification *by the stockholders* is equivalent to a *purchase from them;* and this brings me to that class of cases where the trustee buys of, or contracts with, his *cestui que trust.*

"Taking, therefore, the ground assumed in the argument, that this was a sale, in fact, made *by the stockholders,* the *cestui's que trust,* does it appear that all these requisites were complied with by the purchaser, who stood to them in the relation of confidence? The burthen is on him to establish them, and if he fails, the sale, though made by the *cestui's que trust,* may be set aside on their application.

"Has the trustee shown that he took no advantage, whatever, of his *cestui's que trust?* That he gave to them all the information which he possessed, or could obtain, in reference to the lands sold to him? I have looked in vain for any evidence that such information as he possessed was communicated to the stockholders. Did he advise them as he would have done if a third person had offered to become the purchaser? No evidence of that character is permitted. Has he shown that the price was fair and adequate? He is entirely silent on this point, and by that silence admits the truth of the allegation of the complainant, that the price was grossly inadequate.

"I can not, therefore, upon these facts and principles, say that this sale can be upheld, even if it had been made by the *cestui's que trust* directly. But, it is said, that the stockholders, at the meeting of June, 1857, ratified and confirmed the sale and contract. It must be borne in mind that, at this meeting, the stockholders were dealing with their trustee, and that all the duties incumbent on him, when negotiating a purchase from his *cestui que trust,* devolved, with equal force, on him when seeking a ratification of a sale made to him by himself, as a trustee, with the aid of his co-trustees. I am now regarding the law as applicable to a ratification made by stockholders themselves, or a majority of them. I shall hereafter consider whether a majority of the stockholders made such ratification, and whether it was competent for the majority to make the same, or to *bind the minority.*

"The rules as to confirmation of a sale to a trustee by the *cestui que trust,* are concisely laid down in Levin on Trusts (97 Law Lib. 402); they are :

" ' 1.   The confirming party must be *sui juris,* not laboring under any disability, as infancy or coverture.

" ' 2.   The confirmation must be a solemn and deliberate act,— not, for instance, fished out from some expressions in a letter; and particularly when the original transaction was infected with fraud, the confirmation of it is so inconsistent with justice, and so likely to be accompanied with imposition, that the court will watch it with the utmost strictness, and not allow it to stand but on the very clearest evidence.

" ' 3.   There must be no *suppressio veri,* or *suggestio falsi,* but the *cestui que trust* must be honestly made acquainted with all the material circumstances of the case.

" ' 4.   The confirming party must not be ignorant of the *law;* that is, he must be aware that the transaction is of such a character that he could impeach it in a court of equity.

" ' 5.   The confirmation must be wholly distinct from, and independent of, the original contract—not a conveyance of the estate, executed in pursuance of a covenant in the original deed for further assurance.

" ' 6.   The confirmation must not be wrung from the *cestui's que trust* by distress or terror.

" ' 7.   When the *cestui's que trust* are a class of persons, or creditors, the sanction of the major part will not be obligatory on the rest; but the confirmation, to be complete, must be the joint act of the *whole* body.'

" All these positions are sustained by numerous authorities, and are believed to be sound law, and of universal recognition.

" Applying these principles to the present case, has the party seeking the confirmation of the stockholders to this sale and contract, shown that these *essential prerequisites have been complied with on his part?   I do not understand it to be pretended that all the facts and circumstances* of the case were made known to the stockholders at this time.   It is not asserted that the statement made by McNaffy to the stockholders at their meeting in June, 1856, that the whole consideration of this sale, $140,000, had been paid in money, and that $112,000 thereof had been applied in the extinguishing of that amount of bonds of the plaintiffs, and which was undeniably incorrect, and well calculated to deceive and impose on the stockholders, was, in fact, untrue, and they so understood it. Can I assume that the defendant Sherman was ignorant of this report, and this incorrect statement? If he had knowledge of them, it was clearly his duty, when he sought the stockholders to obtain from them a confirmation of this sale, to have made them acquainted with the material facts as they *truly existed*. Not having done so, it was a *suppressio veri;* and whether made designedly or not, is equally fatal, and the confirmation, if obtained, will not avail him. The confirmation must not have been made in *pursuance* of the original transaction, or under the influence of that transaction [*Wood* v. *Dawnes*, 18 Vesey 125], or under the same state of circumstances which produced that transaction [*Crome* v. *Balbard*, 1 *id.* 215]. A confirmation given under the idea that the original transaction was valid when it *was not, will be set aside.* [*Roche* v. *O'Brien*, 1 Ball & Beat, 338; *Gowland* v. *DeFaria*, 17 Vesey 18; *Dunbar* v. *Frederick*, 2 Ball & Beat, 317.]

" It is very doubtful, I think, whether confirmation or ratification of June, 1857, if made with all the conditions, and under all the circumstances required, was an act either of the corporation, or of the stockholders. To make it binding on the former, there must have been, according to the charter, a quorum of the stockholders; and in corporations having stock, each share is deemed a stockholder, and a majority of shares present or represented, is a majority of the stockholders. A very large proportion of stockholders represented at that meeting were by attorney, and the power given only authorized them to vote for the election of directors. It did not authorize them to bind their principals to acts, and in reference to matters not authorized or assumed by the power. The ratification or confirmation by such attorneys or agents having no power to act in the premises, neither bound the corporation nor the stockholders for whom they thus, without any authority, assumed to act. But even if the confirmation had been legally made, and by a majority of the stockholders, which it clearly was not, when, as in this case, it was to be made by a class, the sanction of a *major part* will not be obligatory on the rest; but the confirmation, to be complete, must be the joint act of the whole body [*Ex parte Hughes*, 6 Vesey 622; *ex parte Lacey, id.* 628; *ex parte James*, 8 *id.* 337; *Davone* v. *Fanning*, 2 John. Ch. R. 264].

"Riley, a stockholder, who attended the meeting in June, 1857, says he was not aware, nor does he believe that any of the stockholders were aware, of their legal rights, or that they had any claim to have the deed and contracts, to use his own expression, 'ripped up;' that no resolution was passed or offered, at said meeting, approving said contracts and sale. It is very apparent that no actual ratification or confirmation took place, and I am unable to see that anything was done which would authorize one to be implied. Even if obtained, Sherman was dealing with his *cestui's que trust*, and standing on the original transaction, claiming its validity and binding character; and his *cestui's que trust* believing it so to be, he is debarred, on the authority of the cases already cited, from claiming any benefits from such confirmation, even if it had been made as distinctly and unequivocally as he pretends. After a most patient investigation of the facts in this case, and the numerous authorities cited in the protracted and very able arguments made by the learned counsel for the respective parties in this cause. I have arrived at the conclusion, entirely clear to my mind, that this deed of sale and contract cannot be sustained. To hold otherwise, would be to overturn principles of equity which have been regarded as well settled since the days of Lord Keeper BUDGMAN, in the 22d of Charles Second, to the present time; principles enunciated and enforced by HARDWICKE, THURLOW, LANGHBOROUGH, ELDON, CRANWORTH, STORY and KENT, and which the highest courts in our country have declared to be founded on unmistakable truth and justice, and to stand upon our great moral obligation to refrain from placing ourselves in relations which excite a conflict between self interest and integrity."

STOCKHOLDERS.

Hood v. *N. Y. & N. H. R. R. Co.*, 27 Conn,, 50.

But it is said that the directors and stockholders gave their consent, and it cannot now be denied. " The legislature has absolutely marked the limit of their power, and they cannot exceed it, under the charter; and if the directors, even *with all the stockholders at their side*, transcend the limits of the charter, and make contracts foreign to their business, they only act for themselves. The reason is, there can be no consent of the corporation. The consent of individual stockholders, however repeated, is not their consent, nor is it admissable proof to establish consent; so that, if it were true, every stockholder had expressed his consent, it would make no difference in the case. If this is not so, there are no restrictions or limitations on chartered companies, and they may do anything and everything, the directors please, which is not absolutely unlawful. The exercise of power is held to prove itself, which is absurd."

Again, the court says, this notion of their consent is altogether untenable and unjust. We know, certainly, the stockholders did not, all of them, give their consent. Some were minors, married women, executors and administrators, trustees, officers of the law in possession—some more, at the time, out of the country. So the body of stockholders was changing from day to day. Now, to hold that the entire body of stockholders gave their consent to the contract in question, and that, therefore, it is good, is absurd and puerile. But, suppose they did; this was not a corporate act, and has, therefore, no corporate character. We repeat, that the directors and stockholders have no corporate consent, but what is within the appropriate business of the charter.

1 *Leading Cases in Equity*, p. 220, the following doctrine is laid down :

The *trustee must show* that he *took no advantage whatever of his situation ;* that he gave to his *cestui que trust, all* the information which he possessed, or could obtain, upon the subject; that he advised him, as he would have done, in relation to a third person, *offering* to become a purchaser; and that the price was fair and adequate; and the onus of proving all this, is upon the trustee. *And these principles apply to all cases where confidence is reposed* (see cases cited), *and to every one, in short, who has entered into a fiduciary relation,* or assumed an obligation, by contract or otherwise, towards another, which it would be a breach of trust and confidence to violate.

The case of *Cleveland* v. *The La Crosse and Milwaukee R. R. Co., Selah Chamberlain, Moses Kneeland, et al.,* which was a case commenced by a creditor in the United States District Court of Wisconsin, to set aside the sale of some lots (2 acres) of the Co., which had been made, and also a perpetual lease of the La C. & Mil. R. R., which was made by the directors to Selah Chamberlain, and which is reported in the 7th vol. of American Law Register, p. 536. It appeared in this case that Moses Kneeland and Chamberlain were directors of the company, and that the sale of lots and the lease had been made by them, and the lease made to Chamberlain.

The court, in this case, held that " Directors of an incorporated company are trustees of the corporators, and have possession of the corporate property for the corporators and the creditors of the company, and that all property of a corporation, not sold in good faith, is liable for the payment of its debts."

The court further held that the doctrine of trusts was applicable, and the sale of the lots and the lease to Chamberlain, were void, as being fraudulent and unauthorized acts on the part of the directors, and that all of the property, and the tolls, and revenues of the road belonged to the stockholders and creditors, and could not, under any circumstances, be diverted.

In this case, the sale of the lots and the lease, were confirmed by an express resolution, yet the court set the whole thing aside.

This case is perfectly notorious throughout the entire North-West, and was litigated with great power and vigor, and is in principle precisely like the case at bar; but, notwithstanding every obstacle that was interposed, the right prevailed, and the conveyances and lease declared null and void.

The case of the *Hoffman Steam Coal Co.* v. *Cumberland Coal and Iron Co.*, 16 Maryland, 456, was a case almost precisely like that of *Sherman* v. *The Cumberland Coal Co.*, in the 30th of Barbour, involved the same parties, grew out of the same transaction, and was decided upon the very same principles, that are enunciated by Judge Davis in that case.

It appeared, in this case, that Sherman, who was one of the directors of the Cumberland Coal Co., in connection with one or two other directors, induced the Cumberland Coal Co., to sell a portion of their lands, and that he, Sherman, bought it; that after the same had been sold, that a majority of the stockholders confirmed the sale; that then Sherman, in connection with some others, formed a corporation called the "Hoffman Steam Coal Co." and conveyed the land, which he bought of the Cumberland Co., to said corporation, issued a large amount of stock, etc. A transportation contract was also made, and entered into, by and between Sherman and the Cumberland Coal Co., which put the company almost as much under the control of Sherman, as the pretended consolidation in the case at bar, puts the Galena & C. U. R. R. Co., under the control of the C. & N. W. R. Co. A bill was filed, in order to set aside the conveyances of the land, and also the transportation contract. The defendants set up, by way of defence—

1st. That the company had a perfect right to sell the land ;

2d. That Sherman had a perfect right to buy it ; and

3d. That the sale, if irregular and invalid, had been subsequently *confirmed* by a vote of the stockholders.

But the court held precisely as was held in the case of *Sherman* v. *The Cumberland Coal Co.*, in the 30th of Barbour, that directors are trustees for all the stockholders, and that as Sherman was a *director in both companies*, that he could not sell to himself, or to a company *in which he was so directly interested*, and that the confirmation having been made by the stockholders, without a full knowledge of all the facts and circumstances, was *not binding on them at all*; and, hence, the court set the whole thing aside, and declared the transaction null and void.

The principles which are laid down in this case are applicable to every stockholder of the Galena and Chicago Union Railroad Company, who has been induced to exchange their stock for that of the Chicago & North Western Railway Company, and who have confirmed the sale and consolidation, without a full knowledge of the facts and circumstances pertaining to said transaction.

Chief Justice Le Grand, in his decision of the above case, on p. 508, said:

" But it is said, however this may be, the whole transaction was fully *ratified* and confirmed by the complainant, which ratification and confirmation relieved it from all legal informality. An attentive consideration of this whole history, as detailed in the record, has not brought us to this opinion. The *law* governing questions of ratification, in cases like the present, is well settled. To render the act of ratification effective and conclusive, certain considerations are necessary. At the time of the supposed ratification, the principal must have been *fully* aware of every material circumstance of the transaction, the real value of the subject of the contract, and the act of ratification must have been an independent and substantive act, founded on complete information and perfect freedom of volition, and, in addition to all this, the *cestui que trust* must not only have *been acquainted with the facts, but apprised of the law*, how those facts would be dealt with if brought before a court of equity (see Lewin on Trust, edition of 1858, p. 615). This last requisite, it is nowhere shown in the proof, has been complied with. But, on the contrary, it is fairly to be *inferred*, that the stockholders believed they were concluded by what had been done," etc.

The following were the points and authorities of Thurston & Dobbin in the *Hoffman Steam Coal Co.* v. *Cumberland Coal Co. and Iron Co.*, 16 Maryland, 489, and which was adopted by the court, and which are applicable to all those who have, without knowledge of the facts, exchanged their stock. As to *confirmation* of actual or constructive frauds, or of *acts of persons in confiden-*

tial relations, the rules of law, applicable to such cases, *are much more strict than in the ordinary dealings between independent and equal parties*, where there is a merely technical defect of power, or where it is the policy of the law to uphold the transaction. In all dealings between persons in confidential relations, or having just emerged from them, the policy of the law is to look with great suspicion on the transaction. In the classification of the books, such transactions, however innocent, are called constructive frauds. For a general and succinct statement of the conditions necessary to make a confirmation valid, see Lewin on Trusts, 390, also edition of 1857, of same book, page 778.

1st. The *onus* of proving all the conditions necessary to make a valid confirmation, is upon the party claiming its benefit.

> Hill on Trustees, 827.
> *Bennett* v. *Colley*, 2 Mylne & Keen, 232.

2d. The confirmation must have been given by a party *competent* to make a valid act of confirmation, not by a person not *sine juris*, or a minor, etc.

> Lewin on Trusts, 390.

If the confirmation be by a body of the stockholders, it must be shown that those who united in the act were competent to bind the others. Is not the assent of all required in such a case? See, as to creditors, *Davone* v. *Fanning*, 2 Johns Ch. Rep., 264, *exparte James* 8, Ves. 337, and Lewin on Trusts, 391, as to a class of persons and *laches* as applicable to them. Should not *specific and definite notice*, that the matter was to be acted on, be required to be given to a minority in respect to a transaction, so much out of the ordinary course of business, and with a person in a situation of trust and confidence? Does not the duty of disclosure require, that a trustee, participating in calling a meeting, at which he intends to seek a ratification of such a transaction, should give express notice to the stockholders, that the matter was to be acted on? Would anything less than such notice be *uberrima fides!* It is the better opinion, that even the common law rule, in cases where the charter is silent, requires, that if the corporation is composed of a definite number, a majority of all the stockholders is necessary to form a quorum.

> Angel & Ames on Corp. (Ed. of 1858), sec. 501.

3. The act of confirmation must be deliberate, plain and distinct, (*Morse* v. *Ropal*, 12 Ves. 337), with knowledge that it will have the effect, [2 Sch. & Lef. 474, *Murry* v. *Palmer*,] and with *intent* that it should have that effect.

> *Mallony* v. *L'Estrange*, Beatly, 413.

4. The confirmation must not have been made in pursuance of the original transaction, (*Wood* v. *Downes*, 18 Ves. 125), or under the influence of that transaction, (*Crowe* v. *Ballard*, 1 Ves. 215), or of the same circumstunces which produced that transaction; (18 Ves. 125), (*Roche* v. *O'Brien*, 1 Ball & Beatty, 338), (*Gawtand* v. *De Faria*, 17 Ves. 25), otherwise, it will not be a confirmation, but merely a continuation of the original fraud.

> Lewin on Trusts, 391.
>
> *Dunbar* v. *Tredennick*, 2 Ball & Beatly, 317.

5. The party giving the confirmation, must have done so after having full knowledge of his legal rights, of his power to disaffirm the former transactions, and to be relieved therefrom on application to a court of equity.

> Lewin on Trusts, 390.
> Hill on Trustees, 525.
> Story's Equity, Sec. 345.
> *Cockerell* v. *Cholmely*, 1 Russ. & Mylne, 425.
> *Fish* v. *Miller*, 1 Hoff. R. 280.
> 2 Ball & Beatly, 317.
> 2 Sch. & Lef. 479.
> *Bennett* v. *Colley*, 2 Mylne & Keene, 242.
> 1 Vesey, (Sumner's Ed.) 320, and notes.
> *Boyd* v. *Hawkins*, 2 Dev. Ch. R. 195.

6. The party giving the confirmation must have done so after having *full knowledge* of all the material facts of the case.

> 1 Hoff. R. 280.
> *Farnam* v. *Brooks*, 9 Pick. 234.

Austwick v. *Maddeford*, 1 Simmons, 89.
Lewin on Trusts, 390, and cases there cited.
Hill on Trustees, 525–7.
65 Law Lib. 165.
2 Sch. & Lef. 474.
2 Dev. Ch. R. 195.
1 Russ. & Mylne, 425.
Bell v. *Webb & Mong.* 2 Gill. 170.

When a trustee seeks from his *cestui que trust* a confirmation, the same principles apply as in any other dealing between such parties, and all the rules heretofore stated become applicable to the attempted confirmation ; all the conditions in respect to disclosure, to take advantage of his situation to advise, and to adequacy of consideration, are to be proved affirmatively by the trustee, as in any other case of such dealings.

The defendants in this case, have omitted no opportunity of parading before the public, with marked ostentation, and impressing the statement upon the court, that, out of the large number of shareholders of the G. & C. U. R. R. Co., who held stock in that road on the 1st of June, 1864, a great majority have been induced to exchange their stock, and become stockholders in the consolidated C. &. N. W. R. Co. Would it not be quite as appropriate to explain how, and under what circumstances they did this ? The defendants here assume that all the stockholders in question, were, at the time when they exchanged their stock, fully acquainted with all of the terms of the sale and consolidation ; but have these terms *ever been made known* to the stockholders, and if so, *when, where and by whom ?*

Were the stockholders informed of the authority under which the directors pretended to act, and did they know what the debts and liabilities of the C. & N. W. R. Co. were? Did they know of the purchase of the Kenosha & Rockford Railroad by the C. &. N. W. R. Co. at a mere nominal amount, and its sale to them for $1,400,000 of stock and $400,000 of bonds ? Did they know that the Peninsula R. R. of Michigan was to be heaped upon them with all its debts and liabilities, on the terms which have been made known since the commencement of this suit?

Did the stockholders of the G. & C. U. R. R. Co., who were induced to exchange their stock know what the capital stock of the C. & N. W. R. Co. was, and can any man tell to-day? Did they know what its debts and liabilities were then, and can any man tell to-day?

Did any man know what the capital stock of the Peninsula R. R. Co. was then, and can they tell to-day? Did they know what its debts and liabilities were then, and can any man tell to day?

Were they informed of what their legal rights were, and of all of the facts pertaining to the consolidation? And were those stockholders aware when they made their exchange, that they were conveying their stock to Wm. B. Ogden and Samuel J. Tilden, *in trust for the* C. & N. W. R. Co., and that they were to keep that stock alive; and the very certificates of the capital stock of the G. & C. U. R. R. Co., uncancelled, in order to complete the consolidation, if legal, and to control the stock if illegal?

How many stockholders of the G. & C. U. R. R. Co. will now step forward and say, that they ever constituted William B. Ogden and Samuel J. Tilden their trustees for the purposes claimed by the defendants, in their answer in this case? From facts within our possession, we hazard nothing whatever in saying, that we do not believe that one out of a hundred of the stockholders of the G. & C. U. R. Co. knew anything whatever of the real facts and circumstances attending the sale and consolidation, or knew the terms upon which it was made, and that they will be filled with astonishment and surprise when they learn that they have appointed Wm. B. Ogden and Samuel J. Tilden their trustees, for the purpose of holding their stock and of *perfecting* this consolidation which it is now admitted, has not yet been completed.

A more extraordinary transaction, when taken in the aggregate and in detail, cannot be found in the history of any country, and until it has been fully completed and confirmed, both by the stockholders, with a full knowledge of their rights, and by this court in like manner, it will be a subject of doubt and distrust.

What boldness and audacity could accomplish has already been accomplished; but the law can neither be disregarded with impunity or justice be overawed by the magnitude of the interests involved. "Of Law, there can be no less acknowledged than that her seat is the bosom of God, her voice the harmony of the world; all things in heaven and earth do her homage, the *very least* as feeling her care, and *the greatest* as not exempted from her power."

XXIX.

The Consolidation, according to the defendant's own showing, is a NUDUM PACTUM.

We have hitherto treated this subject upon the hypothesis that the consolidation of the G. & C. U. R. R. Co. had actually taken place, although unauthorized. We do not intend, however, to rest this case upon that hypothesis alone, for it now appears, by the defendant's own showing, that no consolidation, whatever, has ever taken place. It now appears that, notwithstanding the G. & C. U. R. R. Co. was, on the first of 1864, *seized* by the C. & N. W. R. Co., and all of its property taken and *appropriated* to its use, by the collusion of a board of directors whose *duty* it was to *preserve and protect* it, and notwithstanding certain rites and ceremonies were performed over its body, which they called consolidation, yet it was, nevertheless, nothing but the enactment of a gorgeous pageant, and that the *entire capital stock* of that company is still preserved, and has *never been blended* with that of the C. & N. W. R. Co. at all; and so complete is this preservation maintained, that even the *very certificates of stock* are now in possession of William B. Ogden and Samuel J. Tilden, and could be put on the market and sold to-morrow without human prevention.

The theory of a consolidation is, as we suppose, that the capital stock and all of the rights, privileges and franchises of the two corporations become blended together, and when so blended *eo instanti*, that instant a new corporation is *created* by the *power* of the legislature so conferred upon them.   Now, this is the theory of the Indiana cases which are referred to by Judge DAVIS, in the case of *Clearwater* v. *Meridith*, 1 Wallace 40, and of all the cases which we have examined.   If this is so, how is it possible that the capital stock of the G. & C. U. R. R. Co. is still in existence when it has been merged into a new company?

The way and manner in which the defendants state their position, in their answer, in regard to this matter is as follows:

" These defendants further answering say, that the five millions eight hundred and two thousand six hundred and two dollars of stock of the consolidated corporation called the Galena and Chicago Union Railroad Company so exchanged for the stock of the North Western Railroad Company as aforesaid, was for the purpose of protecting and perfecting the consolidation made between said companies; if need be, assigned by the respective holders thereof to William B. Ogden and Samuel J. Tilden, in trust, with power to do all such acts and things as might be necessary in the premises, and that said William B. Ogden and Samuel J. Tilden *now hold the said stock so assigned by them as aforesaid, uncancelled in trust for the present Chicago and North Western Railway Company for the uses and purposes aforesaid.*"

Now, we care not, for our purposes, whether the capital stock of the G. & C. U. R. R. Co. is held in trust for the C. & N. W. R. Co. or not; the moment that it is admitted, that the capital stock is still in existence, and that the certificates of stock have never yet been cancelled, that moment, the pretended consolidation falls to pieces, and the whole agreement becomes *nudum pactum.* The very statement of the case by the defendants is, to them, *felo de se.*   How can the capital stock of a company exist and be extinct at one and the same time?   How can the franchises of a corporation become merged in a *new corporation* and still exist in the old?   How can a thing which is dead at the same time be alive?

The trust which is *claimed* to exist, is *self-created*, and is another of the anomalies of this most extraordinary transaction.   It is nothing more or less than an expedient, and is a provision, undoubtedly, against the contingences of this very suit. We admit the wisdom of such a provision, and admire the foresight, but it is perfectly fatal to the consolidation.

The defendants, we repeat, admit that the capital stock of the G. & C. U. R. R. Co. is *still in existence*, but is held in trust for the C. & N. W. R. Co., and was, they say, for " the *protecting* and *perfecting* the consolidation made between said companies; if need be, *assigned* by the respective holders thereof *to* William B. Ogden and Samuel J. Tilden, *in trust*, with power to do *all such acts and things* as might be necessary in the premises, and that said William B. Ogden and Samuel J. Tilden *now hold the stock* so assigned by them as aforesaid, *uncancelled*," &c.

Now, suppose that William B. Ogden and Samuel J. Tilden should, under *such* a power of attorney as is here described, throw the whole of that stock upon the market and sell it? the certificates of stock have been regularly assigned to them and they hold them; if put in circulation and sold in large or small quantities, who is to step forward and say that there is now no longer any G. & C. U. R. R. Co.? Can William B. Ogden and Samuel J. Tilden say so, when they pretend to hold five million dollars of *its stock* in trust, and that trust is a *subsisting, live trust*. If this trust has any other meaning than the one here described, we are unable to understand the force of language. If it is contended that the certificates of stock have lost all their vitality, and that the consolidation has shorn them of their strength, what are they acting as trustees for waste paper for? The court will mark well the language which is used; they do not, it will be observed, state that they have preserved for future reference or as precious relics, the old certificates of stock of the G. & C. U. R. R. Co.—that they are holding the cast off and worn out paper in trust for the paper mill; but they announce it as a fact, with ostentation and exultation, that over five millions of dollars of the stock of G. & C. U. R. R. Co. has been assigned to them by the respective holders, and that they *hold that stock* now; and we insist, that the defendants cannot escape from the logical consequences of their admission by any *finesse*, however elaborate and picturesque.

When the defendants themselves admit that the consolidation is still incomplete, and that the capital stock of the G. & C. U. R. R. Co. which the stockholders gave to the officers of the C. & N. W. R. Co. *to be* exchanged *is still in existence,* what conclusion must the court come to? Does it make any difference as to the legal effect of the matter, whether the stock of the G. & C. U. R. R. Co. is in the hands of the original holders, or whether they put their names on the back of the certificates and handed them to William B. Ogden and Samuel J. Tilden and let them hold them? This trusteeship is new—it is the *novum organum*—it is the last card, and if it does not prove a piece of news to hundreds of stockholders of the G. & C. U. R. R. Co., who have been beguiled into exchanging their stock for that of the C. & N. W. R. Co., then there is no reliance to be placed in human veracity.

But, taking this statement to be true, just as it is made, then the entire consolidation becomes a *nudum pactum.*

Stript of its verbiage, and William B. Ogden and Samuel J. Tilden have got into their possession over five millions of dollars of the capital stock of the G. & C. U. R. R. Co., for which the C. & N. W. R. Co., paid the stockholders three dollars in cash, as a bonus, (which bonus was obtained at the time of the consolidation, from the treasury of the G. & C. U. R. R. Co. itself,) and one share of common stock, and one share of preferred stock, which stock has since been watered by pouring in the stock and bonds of the Peninsula R. R. of Michigan at *par,* which were sold for, from 25 to 50 cents on the dollar.

The consolidation and amalgamation of the G. & C. U. R. R. Co., with the C. N. W. R. Co., was either a *fixed fact on the* 1st *of June,* 1864, or it was not. If it was, then the manner in which it was accomplished, and the *power* of the directors to do the deed, has been correctly discussed. If it was not so accomplished, and the capital stock of the G. & C. U. R. R. Co. *is still in existence,* then the *C. & N. W. R. Co. has no business whatever with the road,* and they can be held liable for every dollar of its earnings, which they have received and are receiving, and for a reasonable sum for its use, and for all damages arising from their management of the same.

In either aspect of the case, the acts of the defendants cannot be reconciled with the established principles of law, and are directly in conflict with the rule laid down by the United States Supreme Court, in the case of *Clearwater* v. *Meredith*, in 1 Wallace, 40.

CONCLUSION.

I.   Powerful as the corporations are, against which we contend, the *law* is more powerful.

II.   "If principles can ever be settled by authority; if the slightest respect is due to the opinions of other tribunals, it would seem that no court could resist the overwhelming weight of the decisions which have been cited."—(Selden, J.)

III.   The term, "capital stock," in an act of incorporation, means the amount contributed or advanced by the stockholders as members of the company.

The capital of every corporation is represented in the property and franchises of the corporation, and the owner of each share is entitled to a *fixed and unalterable proportion* of that capital.   It is as much *his individual property* as any other possession.

The owner of *one* share will be protected in the exercise of *all* his rights, and the enjoyment of *all* his privileges, precisely as if he owned a million.   Hence, it follows, that any attempt to create a greater number of shares by issuing additional shares or additional certificates, is not only a violation of the organic law of the corporation, but a direct invasion of the contract existing between the corporation and each individual stockholder.   Therefore, when the directors of the G. & C. U. R. R. Co. entered into an agreement with the C. & N. W. R. Co., under the name and style of "consolidation," whereby the capital stock was increased several millions of dollars beyond the amount fixed by the charter, it was unauthorized, and a direct violation of the fundamental law of the corporation, and void, as to the complainant, and all others similarly situated to him.

IV.   Neither the G. & C. U. R. R. Co. or the C. & N. W. R. Co. had any right, power or authority either to issue common or preferred stock *for the purpose of purchasing each other ;* neither of them had any right to compel their stockholders to sell out their stock against their will, or exchange it for any other product, and as no railroad stock is a legal tender, therefore the complainant cannot be expelled from the corporation of which he was a member, or be compelled to submit to any such terms as are prescribed by the articles of consolidation which are set forth in this case.

V.   The stock which is owned by a stockholder in a corporation, is *his* property.   It is *not* the property of the corporation.   There cannot well be two entire owners of the same property.   The *stockholders have the property* and the corporation the management of it.   The *corporation* is not even the trustee ;   for it *has not* the legal estate, and *no power to sell.*   It has merely the naked possession, with the perpetual legal right of using the funds for the benefit of the legal and equitable owners.

The stock, then, which a stockholder owns, being property, cannot be sold and disposed of without his consent.

The immunities of private property and the inviolability of vested rights have been asserted by political and legal writers, and *established by judicial decisions,* for three centuries.   It is, indeed, a part of Magna Charta itself.

VI.   The charter of a corporation is a contract—
1. *Between the State and the Corporation ;*
2. *Between the Corporation and the stockholders, &c.*
The legal effect of a contract is to bind all the parties to it ; to bind them to *all* the stipulations of it, and in the *capacity* in which they contracted, and to bind them *equally.*   It was intended,

then, that *both* the parties should be bound, and that, consequently, *neither* should possess the power to *liberate themselves without the consent of the other.*

> 1 N. H. 44.
> 13 Ill. 511.
> 4 Johns. Ch. 596.

VII. The original charter is the fundamental law of the association—*the constitution* which prescribes limits not only to the directors, officers and agents of the company, but to the action of the *corporate body itself;* consequently, no radical change or alteration can be made or allowed, by which *new and additional* objects are to be accomplished, or *responsibilities incurred by the company*, so as to bind the individuals composing it, *without their consent.*

> 5 Hill 386.
> 1 Wallace 39.

VIII. "When any person takes stock in a railroad corporation, he has entered into a contract with the company, that his interest shall be subject to the direction and control of the proper authorities of the corporation, to accomplish the object *for which* the company was organized. He *does not agree* that the improvement to which he subscribed should be changed, in its purposes and character, at the will and pleasure of a majority of the stockholders, so that *new responsibilities*, and, it may be, *new hazards, are added to* the original undertaking. He may be very willing to embark in one enterprise, and unwilling to engage in another—to assist in building a short line railway, and averse to risking his money in one having a longer line of transit."

> *Clearwater* v. *Meredith*, 1 Wallace 40.

IX. The charter of the Galena & Chicago Union Railroad Co. was granted in 1836, before the present constitution was adopted, and the objects which are there set forth, are declared to be simply the *construction and maintenance* of a railroad between the termini specified; and there is no authority whatever contained in said charter authorizing the directors of said corporation to *assume* the debts and liabilities of the Chicago & Northwestern Railway Company, or any other company, whatsoever; neither has the charter ever been amended in any way or manner, authorizing the company to do it; consequently, the Galena & C. U. R. R. Co. had no right, power or authority to become *surety* for the debts and liabilities of any other corporation, and any application of the earnings of said road for such a purpose, is a diversion of the revenues of said road, and can be prevented by any shareholder.

X. An assent of stockholders to amendments changing or extending the objects, or increasing the powers, or *enlarging the liabilities* of the corporation, in any matter fundamental, is *not to be presumed, but must be proved*, and it matters not what the directors or the majority of the corporation may have done on their own account, they cannot bind, by their acts, a dissenting stockholder.

> *March* v. *R. R. Co.*, 43 N. H. 525–6.
> 1 Wallace 40.
> 2 Conn. 679.

XI. The powers of corporations are not the result of syllogisms. They do not lie coiled beneath any amount of verbiage. They are not the product of subtlety or acumen; they exist, if at all, by *express* grants and *unmistakable words;* consequently, it has become an axiom that *no corporate power is ever created by implication, or extended by construction.*

XII. In the construction of a charter, to *be in doubt* is to be resolved, and every resolution which springs from doubt, is *against* the corporation. This is the rule sustained by *all* the courts in this country and in England.

XIII. Neither *privileges, powers nor authorities* can pass, unless they are given in unambiguous words, and an act giving special privileges must be construed strictly. A *doubtful* charter does not exist; because whatever is doubtful, is *decisively* certain *against* the corporation.

2 Black 723.
27 Penn. 351.

XIV. It is the duty of all courts to *construe* the charters of corporations *strictly*, and to keep them *within their chartered limits.* This rule, when once understood and *firmly enforced*, removes from corporations all temptations to engage in illegal transactions; and while it tends to promote *good morals*, and the *public policy* of the State, it, at the same time, *protects individuals* from outrage and acts of gross injustice.

XV. "It is now no longer doubted, either in England or the United States, that courts of equity, in both, have a jurisdiction over corporations, at the instance of ONE or more of their numbers; to apply preventative remedies by *injunction*, to *restrain* those who administer them from *doing acts* which would amount to a violation of charters, or to *prevent any misapplication of their capitals or profits which might result in lessening the dividends of stockholders, or the value of their shares, as either may be protected by the franchises of a corporation*, if the acts intended to be done *create* what is, in law, denominated a breach of trust. And the jurisdiction *extends to inquire into and to enjoin*, as the case may require *that* to be done, *any proceedings by individuals in whatever character they may profess to act*, if the subject of complaint is an *imputed* violation of a corporate franchise, or the denial of a right growing out of it, for which there is no adequate remedy at law."

Dodge v. *Woolsey*, 18 How 341.

XVI. If it be true, as contented for by the defendants in this case, that the majority *in interest* of a corporation can, under any and all circumstances, *will* and *act* for the corporation, and wield and control it, then, indeed, the *majority are* the corporation, and the minority are *no part* of it.

XVII.   Corporations are not subject to the right of revolution, or rebellion against the *fundamental law*, and if it be implied in the original compact, that the majority shall rule, it is *equally* implied that the majority *shall not change the organic law*, or, by a *coup d' etat*, completely overthrow it.

XVIII.   The common law is a part and parcel of the law of this State.   The right of voting by proxy was *not* allowed by the common law.   The voting by proxy, therefore, being in derogation of the common law, must, when it is permitted for a certain specific purpose, be *confined to that purpose*, and cannot be *extended to any other*.   The amended charter of the G. & C. U. R. R. Co. allows shareholders to vote by proxy for *directors only*, consequently, that right must be confined to that *specific thing*, and cannot be extended to any other question or item of business that might be brought before the corporation ; therefore, the vote by *viva voce by proxy*, by which the action of the directors in selling out the G. & C. U. R. R. Co. was confirmed, cannot, on any principles of law yet established, be sustained.

XIX.   The capital stock of a corporation is a trust fund which is held for the benefit of stockholders, and can never be legally diverted to any other purpose, whatever, than is provided in the charter.

The directors who manage and control the capital stock and the affairs of the corporation are trustees for all the stockholders, and are subject to *all the duties, obligations and liabilities of trustees ;* consequently, when they are elected, and *assume* the duties of their office, they must discharge them with fidelity and in *good faith,* and they can not sell out the corporation and all of its property, or seek to obliterate said corporation ; if they do, all of their acts will be set aside at the suit of any dissentient stockholder, on the well settled principles of trusts, and as a fraud upon their rights.

Koehler v. Black River Falls Iron Co., 2
Black 720–1.

XX. The complainant in this case in his capacity as a stockholder and bondholder has a right to interfere and prevent the earnings of the company from being misapplied, or the property from being injured; consequently, he has a right to ask this court for an injunction to prevent the iron from being taken up and carried away, and the property from being mortgaged.

XXI. In order for this court to decide the matter in controversy it must take into consideration and determine—

1st. What is "consolidation?"

2d. Has it any positive and well understood meaning which conveys to the mind any *exact* impressions whatever, so that any one can *assume*, when that word is used, *what* it includes or excludes without resorting to the circumlocution of settling disputed facts?

3d. If this term is yet in a transition state, and its definition depends so much on circumstances, would not each separate and distinct aggregation of facts and circumstances have to be examined before determining what their legal effect would be ?

4th. The peculiarities of *the* " consolidation"—so called—will appear by examining carefully the way and manner in which it was accomplished.

First. It was accomplished by *fraud.*

Second. It was accomplished without any notice to any body of any character or kind, and by the *collusion of the directors of the G. & C. U. R. R. Co.*, most of the *same persons acting as directors of the C. & N. W. R. Co.*

Third. It was accomplished by the directors of the G. & C. U. R. R. Co. in less than three hours after they were elected, and *in less than fifteen minutes* after they had organized as a board.

FOURTH. The directors *being trustees for all* the shareholders, *violated* all their duties, and wantonly *betrayed* their trust, and such violation of their trust renders their acts void.

FIFTH. The proxies by which the persons present pretended to act, did not authorize the demolition of the corporation, and a *majority in interest* have no power to sell out a minority, and compel them to part with their property on such terms as they may dictate or prescribe, any more than they can legalize highway robbery or theft.

XXII. The consolidation in question was nothing more or less than a sell, or sale, for, by the 12th article of the articles of agreement, which were made and entered into, by and between the Chicago & North Western R. Co., as party of the *first* part, and the G. & C. U. R. R. Co., as party of the *second* part, and which can be found on page 11 of this brief, it was provided as follows: "And the said party of the second part, in consideration of the premises, and of *the sum of one dollar* to it paid by the party of the first part, the receipt whereof is hereby acknowledged, doth hereby *grant, convey, assign and set over* to, and *vest* in, said consolidated company, for the purposes of such consolidation, *all the railroads* of the said party of the *second* part, and *all the equipments* and materials used or acquired therefor, and the rights, privileges, immunities, franchises, powers and all the lands and property, money and effects, real and personal and *mixed*, and all rights of action and things of every name or nature, now held or owned by the said party of the second part, or in or to which the said party of the second part hath any right, title, interest or claim, either in law or equity."

Did human ingenuity ever draw a more complete and comprehensive bill of sale than this? So perfect is it, that *nothing* is omitted; not even those things which were, or are, *mixed*.

XXIII. The vendor was the G. & C. U. R. R. Co., and the vendee the C. & N. W. R. Co., and as the directors of the G. & C. U. R. R. Co., who made the sale, were also the directors of the C. & N.

W. R. Co., or a large number of them were, it became a sale by *themselves to themselves ;* or, if the directors of the G. & C. U. R. R. Co. were merely agents of the stockholders, it presents a case where the agents acted as the agents of both parties, and is, therefore, if not absolutely void, voidable by a *dissenting stockholder*, who is the principal.

33 Barb. 593.

XXIV. It the sale and consolidation of the G. & C. U. R. R. was unauthorized, what is the duty of this court? "The answer would seem to be plain and obvious, that no court of justice can, in its nature, be made the handmaid of iniquity. Courts are instituted to carry into effect the *laws of a country ;* how, then, can they *become auxiliary* to the consummation of *violation* of law ?"

Bank of U. S. v. *Owens*, 2 Peters, 538.

XXV. Unauthorized contracts are illegal contracts; and, upon the grounds of public policy, they should not be sanctioned.

XXVI. A corporation exists only in contemplation of law, and *by force* of the law, and can have no existence beyond the limits of the State sovereignty which brings it into life and endues it with faculties and powers. Consequently, no corporation can transport itself as a corporation to another State, and there pass votes and transact business as a corporation in its corporate capacity. By the comity of States its *existence* is recognized, and its *agents* accredited from one to the other; but it is against public policy for a corporation to migrate bodily from one State to another, and then and there exercise their *corporate* functions; hence, the acts of the directors of the C. & N. W. R. Co. in meeting together in New York city and passing votes to issue stock and bonds, are illegal and *extra territorial.*

XXVII. The Galena & Chicago Union Railroad Company was formed for the purpose which is stated and set forth *in the charter*, viz.: "To construct and during its continuance, to maintain and continue a railroad with a single or double track, and with such appendages as may be deemed necessary for the convenient use of the same, from the town of Galena, in the county of Jo Daviess, to such point at the town of Chicago as shall be determined, after a survey shall have been made of the route, to be most eligible, proper, direct and convenient therefor ; with such lateral routes as may be deemed advantageous, expedient and necessary, under the same rights and privileges as, by this act, is provided for the constructing of the main route," and for *no other* purpose or purposes whatsoever ; and all contracts which are made for any other purpose, such, for instance, as building a railroad beyond its termini, or applying the revenue and income of the road in aiding in the building of one, or becoming security for, or jointly liable for, the debts and liabilities of *other* distinct railroad corporations, whether in this State or any other State, or selling out its *entire* property to another corporation, or giving up the control of it to another corporation, or throwing its capital stock into hotch-pot, or a common fund, with any other corporation in any way, are acts which are *ultra vires,* and *any* stockholder can prevent them.

XXVIII. The pretended "consolidation" of the G. & C. U. R. R. Co. with the Peninsula R. R. Co. of Michigan, four hundred miles distant, and across two States, needs no summary—the act speaks for itself.

XXIX. The "consolidation" of the G. & C. U. R. R. Co. with the C. & N. W. R. Co., if not a sale, was nothing more or less than a *confiscation* of all its property *by* the C. & N. W. R. Co., and the appropriation of the same to the uses and purposes of that road.

XXX. The Galena and Chicago Union Railroad Co. had no right to issue preferred stock for any purpose, neither had the C. & N. W. R. Co., for the purpose of making a consolidation ; consequently, all the stock which has been issued by the condensed railroad company, called the C. & N. W. R. Co., is nothing more or less than an *over issue* of stock, and is illegal and void.

XXXI.   The franchises of a railroad company cannot be sold and disposed of except by the authority of the legislature of the State that granted them, and *all of the persons* who are interested in the same.   It may be taken and condemned by the power of eminent domain, but *it cannot be transferred from one set of persons to another* at the will of a majority of stockholders or by the action of any legislature.

> *Bruffett* v. *Great Western R. R. Co.*, 25 Ill.
> 356–7.

XXXII.   The charter of the G. & C. U. R. R. Co. was granted by the legislature of the State of Illinois to the persons therein named, and to their successors, to exist as a corporation for sixty years. It contained no provision that it might be changed, altered or amended, and when once accepted and acted upon, *could neither be altered by the State, or by the act of the majority of the stockholders*, however great and however powerful, in defiance of the wishes of the minority of the stockholders; and any such act or acts would be clearly the *impairing* of the obligations of the *contract existing* between the stockholder and the corporation within the 10th section of the constitution of the United States, and the 17th section of article 13 of the constitution of the State of Illinois.

> *Clearwater* v. *Meredith*, 1 Wallace 39, 40.
> *Chenango Bridge Co.* v. *Binghampton Bridge
> Co.*, 27 N. Y. 92.
> *Dartmouth Coll.* v. *Woodward*, 4 Wheat. 518,
> and numerous other cases.

XXXIII.   Finally, in every aspect in which this transaction can be viewed, and upon the *well settled principles of law in this country and in England*, the pretended " consolidation" of the G. & C. U. R. R. Co. with the C. & N. W. R. Co. was, and is, *nudum pactum*, illegal and void, and should, as an act of right and justice, be set aside, and the complainant and all those similarly situated with him be re-instated in all of their original rights and privileges, and protected in their exercise and enjoyment. The " consolidation" originally was effected by a *coup d' etat,* and as the stock which the stockholders exchanged for the consolidated certificates is, by the defendants' own showing, now in the hands of William B. Ogden and Samuel J. Tilden, of New York, the proper restoration can be made as speedily as the wrong was committed.

Printed in Dunstable, United Kingdom